Shades of

BLUE

Shades of

BLUE

Extraordinary in the Ordinary

**CHARLES & ANNE
GLOGOWSKI**

TATE PUBLISHING & *Enterprises*

Published by Tate Publishing & Enterprises, LLC
127 E. Trade Center Terrace | Mustang, Oklahoma 73064 USA
1.888.361.9473 | www.tatepublishing.com

Tate Publishing is committed to excellence in the publishing industry. The company reflects the philosophy established by the founders, based on Psalms 68:11,
"The Lord gave the word and great was the company of those who published it."

Book design copyright © 2007 by Tate Publishing, LLC. All rights reserved.
Cover design by Lindsay B. Behrens
Interior design by Lynly D. Taylor

Published in the United States of America

ISBN: 978-1-6024727-2-3
1. Christian Living: Spiritual Growth   2. Spiritual Formation: Prayer

07.11.16

We dedicate this book to our parents Michael and Mary Glogowski, and Michael and Sara Hughes. Now with the Lord, their good example and faith in God was left behind for us to receive and share with others. We pass this gift of faith along with this dedication to our immediate family of Thomas, Laurie, Nicholas, Matthew, Jackson and Erica Glogowski. Not to be forgotten in this dedication, are our extended families and friends who have all contributed to the mysteries that lie in each day's inspiration.

Acknowledgements

Foremost, we acknowledge that the author of this book is the Lord. Without the power of the Holy Spirit, flowing through the inspirations shared, there would be no *Shades of Blue*. We give all honor and glory to the Father, Son and Holy Spirit. We carry in our hearts all those who have been a part of our spiritual journey with the Lord. They are the marrow that flows through the center of *Shades of Blue*.

We acknowledge and thank Fr. Anthony Weiler director for the St. Rafka Retreat Center in Shelburne, Vermont, and The Little Sisters of St. Francis, O.S.F. from Danville, New Hampshire, for their hospitality, suggestions, support and spiritual guidance during the years that it has taken to bring this endeavor to completion.

We thank Laurie Glogowski, a busy Mom, for taking the time to edit, support and make suggestions and Sr. Clare Naramore, R.S.M. for her editing, spiritual advice and many special hours she prayed for and carried the manuscript around with her. We thank Monica Szigethy, an English Arts teacher, for proofreading. Finally, yet importantly, we thank Sr. Angelica Gabrielle, T.O.P. (Cecelia Monaco) for her continuous support with Scripture, shared insights, wisdom, and her encouragement to keep on keeping on.

Table of Contents

In the autumn of 1981, I decided to stay up north, in Saratoga Springs, for the winter. This was very unusual for me since, at the first sign of a snowflake, at my insistence my husband and I packed and headed for Hollywood, Florida.

St. Clement's Church had been conducting some sessions of "Life in the Spirit" seminars. They sounded so interesting I decided to attend. Surprisingly, I was asked to facilitate the next seminar and I agreed and completely lost interest in going to Florida.

Charles Glogowski was a part of my ten-member group. From the very first night, there was something so special about him, his depth of spirituality and his unique way of sharing present day life experiences in the light of Scripture. Each week as we all shared the lessons it seems, we could not wait to hear Charles speak.

Anne, Charles' wife, was in another group. When Charles would go home and share his experience, Anne wanted to meet us and they invited us all to their home. We went to this charming home and met Anne. Her welcome was so warm and sincere. As we began to share our experiences in "Life in the Spirit," every word that Anne spoke was profound and meaningful. Every word was spoken from life experiences.

I remember when I was leaving that night, asking her if she did any writing. She said, "A little," and "Charles is a poet," she added. I felt strongly their words needed to go out into the world.

This book *Shades of Blue*, is a book of many experiences. Every word has a life experience, a vision, a prophecy, an answer, an encouragement- all real and all gift.

May you experience true "Life in the Spirit," as you read it.

Sr. Angelica Gabrielle, T.O.P.

Introduction

Shades of Blue, Extraordinary in the Ordinary, is written to bring life and color into the lives and hearts of God's people. Read as daily inspirations, they will stir hearts into listening to the Lord in every moment of life.

We have covered a wide scope of experiences in hopes of holding the interest of each reader. There is a mixture of experiences from within our own beliefs and those shared with others. Our main reason for writing these daily inspirations is to give others the desire to be in a personal and intimate relationship with the Lord.

We pray that others will let their hearts and minds flow in the grace and wisdom of the Lord, as they read the experiences, messages and words received from God. The depth within each is important, not when, where or how the experience occurred.

Some daily inspirations shared will be lengthy and will require a little more quiet time spent with the Lord.

Others will be short with only a thought or word to carry in the pocket of the mind for the day's enlightenment. Each will be just what the Lord has ordered for the day. No matter where a person is with the Lord, the Lord will come to them and use them to reach others. The fruits and gifts of the Holy Spirit are meant for everyone.

The presence of God unfolds in our life under the bounds of faith, hope and love. Using these as guideposts, we (Charles and Anne) share our quest for Holiness and our inner spiritual journey with the Lord. Through the power of the Holy Spirit we joined together in prayer and thoughts, as beautiful poetry, spiritual insights and rich text came together forming *Shades of Blue.*

Touching the deeper levels of the spiritual life, we answer God's call to unity and the mystical (spiritual) life of the church. We open our hearts and minds to the action and power of the Holy Spirit.

Walking through the veils of time and experience, we journey with Jesus Christ to the Father. This journey with the Father, Son and Holy Spirit unfolds each day as part of a master plan. Veils are like curtains over the mysteries of God. When we come close to the Lord, veils lift and we begin to see and understand the mysteries of God. When Jesus died on the cross for our sins, He made it possible for us to enter into this special presence of God the Father.

...Jesus cried out again in a loud voice, and gave up his spirit. And behold, the veil of the sanctuary was torn in two from top to bottom. (Matthew 27:50–51)

Each shade of blue represents a different stage in our spiritual life. We start with the darkest blue, which stands for the first conversions of heart and mind. Here we see our need for change and for God to be the center of our secular and spiritual life. We move through the different stages until we reach the lightest and clearest blue. This blue touches the Eternal Shores and a deeper relationship with the Lord. When we enter the shades of blue, we notice a secluded place, hidden in partial darkness from our mind and awareness. In this secluded place, darkness lies shielded and sheltered in the shadows away from the light. In the depths of this darkness, God reveals His presence and our need for healing.

Purification occurs in the body, mind and spirit, and becomes a time of joy and suffering. Joy, sensed through the gifts and wonder of God, can come from physical or spiritual suffering. God pours His blessings and graces upon us each day. Perseverance, suffering and the presence of God blend forming a rainbow of love.

This love melts into the pot of gold, the gold of purification.

Blue is the color in the rainbow between green and violet. The color green stands for perseverance. The color violet stands for suffering. Blue is the presence of God, which stands between perseverance and suffering.

Shades of Blue, is about the revelation of God in our lives. We are in the College of the Lord and He is our teacher.

Prayer and Message for the Reader

Enter into each day's inspiration. Picture a beautiful blue sky with clouds rolling and tumbling into the scene. Like the clouds, roll over and tumble into what the Lord wants you to receive from *Shades of Blue*.

Let the prayers draw you into your heart of prayer with Jesus.

Let the visions help you to see with a new light into your life with Jesus.

Let the dreams remind you of your own dreams with Jesus.

Let the words from God help you to listen to God's words for you.

Let the poems bring a new rhythm into your steps.

Let the insights give you understanding.

Let the Holy Scriptures strengthen you faith.

Let the Lord bring forth the mystical life that is deep within your own heart.

Your spiritual walk with the Lord is waiting for perception and acceptance. Many of His blessings will come forth. You are special and the Lord has made you for a reason. He has given you all that you will need to come forth in this new season. God gives us nothing to hold as our own. We are to give and share with others what we have received. "In giving is receiving, in receiving is giving. Receive, receive, then give and give. Give and give, then receive and receive."

"I am doing a new thing. There are *Shades of Blue* in each life that I have created. My gifts of unity and discernment are present to everyone. Place all preconceived ideas or judgments in My Holy Spirit and I will bless the time spent in *Shades of Blue*. No matter where a person is coming from, each experiences 365 days in a calendar year. Your journey in life is a second by second, minute by minute, hour by hour, day by day, month by month, and year by year walk with me. *Shades of Blue* is for "now" and I will use it in this part of your journey."

"Don't get caught up in the worries of today or tomorrow. Ride in and out on each new wave of grace that I am sending forth. You are living in troubled times, but I am still in control and walk with you. I will never leave you. We breathe as one in My unity."

Prayer: Lord, help us to live in the "now," of our walk with you. Bless us, O Lord, and the gifts that we are about to receive.

The Bow of the Ship

The Lord had placed the words *Shades of Blue* in my mind and heart. We felt they were a title for a book we were to write.

My husband said that these words reminded him of the different shades of the ocean. A person sees them when coming home from being at sea. While out at sea, the water is deep blue. When the ship comes closer to land, the water becomes different shades of blue. The color goes from a very dark blue to a very light blue-green.

This is when we understood we were to write about our spiritual journey with the Lord. The ship represents our spiritual journey. It is coming home from being at sea. We are the ships, and we have been out to sea; the Lord is now drawing us home to Him.

Our journey with the Lord is the same as a ship. We come into land from the deep blue water to the light blue water. Our spiritual lives go from darkness to light. We go from the deep blue water of the ocean to the light blue water near the shore. This brings us into a closer relationship with the Lord.

The different shades of blue represent the mysteries of God. As we go closer to Him, He reveals more about Himself and us. The depth of the dark blue turns into the brightness of the light blue, as veils lift from our eyes. This is where the lifting of veils become veils of truth.

As we draw closer to the Lord in the pure waters, the light blue shore of Eternal Life comes into view. We will have a very deep desire to worship in the Spirit of wisdom and truth. The central part of our soul, no longer affected by the world, reaches out to God's love, and the waters just flow against the ship.

January 2

A Restful Prayer and Peaceful Thoughts

Picture yourself standing on the bow of the ship. The bow breaks through the water. The rough water flows against the ship, but has no affect on it. The bow, headed in the right direction, is the same as our soul. In deep blue waters, the soul heads towards the shore and light. It heads toward the shallow waters, into the arms of God. Our every breath is with and in God.

The ship, always led by the breath of God, the Spirit, has become sea worthy. Strong winds and high waves have battered the ship at sea and our conflicts with sin in the world. The ship lists in the ocean waters of each life journey. At times, we have bent into the winds and gone with the waves.

Feel the mist against your face and smell the sea air. The bow breaks through the mist, and the veil of many truths and smell of the sea clears your way into enlightened happiness and joy. Taste the salt on your lips as it acts on the flesh, while God acts on the soul. Here is where the Lord gives us a taste for the joys of heaven and a sample of life with Him.

Our ride on the sea of life is through, in and with Jesus Christ. The journey is between living in this world on our own will and living our life, where we strive to do the will of God. It is here that we experience the Eternal Shores with God the Father. The Lord is now drawing us home to Himself.

We asked Jesus to ride the rough and calm seas with us in our journey to God the Father.

Prayer: Dear Jesus, as our ship goes towards the shore, we know You are there with forgiveness, love and hope. You are the strength in our highest waves as they pound against the rocks of life. As we ride the rough sea, we know You are with us. We ask that our faith be as strong as the waves that pound against the rocks. We ask to go forward, like the waves, to rest upon the sandy shores of "Eternal Life." Amen.

January 3

God's Call to Write Shades of Blue

For at the moment the sound of your greeting reached my ears, the infant in my womb leaped for joy. (Luke 1:44)

The first writing that I (Anne) did was a healing prayer called, "Painting a Masterpiece." I enjoyed this writing, for my heart and mind were full of the revelation of God. His presence to me came out in the writing. My complete joy is in the revelation of God. This was clear by the time I finished this prayer. My heart skips a beat when He is near.

When I finished "Painting a Masterpiece" I began to hear the words, *Shades of Blue*. Deep within my heart, I knew that the Lord wanted us to write about His presence in our everyday life. *Shades of Blue* is about the breadth, length, height and depth of the power and love of God in our life.

Reflecting on past years, my husband and I could see that the Father, Son and Holy Spirit had always been active and present in our lives. Many blessings and graces received often went unnoticed. It was after we asked Jesus to enter our hearts and minds that we noticed His presence. Freely accepting the action and presence of the Father, Son and Holy Spirit has brought about healing. It has made it possible for us to love where we could not love before.

It has taken us more than twenty-five years to write about the revelation of God in our lives. Experiences with the Lord and growth in our spiritual life had to be present before we could write. God quietly, but firmly is drawing us to Himself. He has left His precious love and grace in areas that needed His love and grace.

The Holy Spirit touched us deeply. He quickened our spirit and made us aware of His presence and action in our lives. Our senses have become attentive to His action on our heart and soul.

(You)...may have strength to comprehend with all the holy ones what is the breadth and length and height and depth, and to know the love of Christ that surpasses knowledge, so that you may be filled with all the fullness of God. (Ephesians 3:18–19)

Through prayer, revelation and time, this Scripture spoke to us about the mystical life of the Church. We felt God calling and asking us to encourage others to seek Him in the mystical life.

…and to bring to light (for all) what is the plan of the mystery hidden from ages past in God who created all things. (Ephesians 3:9)

Special graces, infinite riches and treasures of Christ written in the above Scripture speak of the mystical life.

They bring new meaning to the shared experiences of life. We see where our life stories cross in mutual color. When we are not open to the mystical life of God, we miss the deeper revelations of God. The mystical life brings a new commitment to the presence of God in our lives and others. This life with God lies concealed and hidden. Through healing and the desire for holiness in our life, God brings about awareness and honesty, revealing His presence in and with us.

January 4

Abridgement

For us who have undertaken the drudgery of this abridgement, this has been no easy task but a matter of sweat and midnight oil, comparable to the exacting task of a man organizing a banquet, (2 Maccabees 2:26–27, Jerusalem).

The lessons and experiences we were having with the Lord would become an abridgement between others and God. The above Scripture confirmed the call for us to become this abridgement through our writing. It spoke about the drudgery involved in trying to answer this call; it would not be easy and would take many hours to accomplish this task.

It was a long time before we began to understand and listen to God's call to write. Experiences and Scripture kept leading us in that direction. The above Scripture revealed and confirmed God's call.

Spiritual experiences are difficult to explain in the natural realm. At times, it was difficult, but now we see the full value of every struggle. It became a time of learning, and the Lord was teaching us as we went along. We know that the Lord teaches us through our experiences with Him. Through these experiences, it is the lessons, messages and the time spent with the Lord that counts.

January 5
Dreams, Symbols and Scriptures

Your sons and daughters shall prophesy, your old men shall dream dreams, your young men shall see visions; even upon the servants and the handmaids, in those days, I will pour out my spirit. (Joel 3:1–2)

Since the beginning of time, the Lord used dreams to speak to His people. Dreams inspired and blessed God's People, both in the Old and New Testament. We often have dreams that we will never understand, and we know they need discernment. Caution should be used when interpreting dreams. At the same time, we should not get concerned about the meaning. In addition, we should not ignore or put them aside when there is a definite lesson and teaching coming from the Lord.

In this daily inspirational, we will share dreams, symbols and Scriptures that led to our spiritual experiences.

The experiences, understanding and insights received will help others in their relationship with God. Each person's relationship with God is special and unique.

We often do not listen to the Lord when He speaks. Reading about another's experiences will inspire the reader to listen.

The light in the natural senses is dim. We ask the Lord, through the guiding light of the Holy Spirit, to place His insight into our hearts, minds and spirits. We pray that we will always be aware of His wonderful presence.

January 6

Parables and Symbols

Jesus often spoke to the people in parables and used symbols and signs. He used the signs and symbols of their everyday surroundings.

The misuse of words today has caused us to lose the true meaning of words, and in many cases given them meanings beyond there original definitions. The word love has given many the approvals to live a life with very little moral concepts. There are many words of earthly wisdom all around us. Everywhere we turn we have words that tell us what our dreams should be, and what we should or should not do. The words that should be filling us with the special light, wisdom and knowledge of Christ are becoming harder and harder to hear.

Christ will bring the revelation of God the Father into our every moment, and heal the weakness that our society has placed upon us.

The Revelation of God is in the heart of all our experiences. The presence of God is in the heart of all gifts.

The Christian life is a call to experience the awareness of the presence of God. This call is more than calling our attention to God. It means new decisions, changes and conversion that will have a lasting effect on the way we live our lives.

The Lord uses our senses. The ancient ecclesiastical writers made use of the word sacrament, symbol, mystical signs or sacred signs to speak of the Lord's presence amongst them.

Quotation: "For a sign besides what it presents to the senses, is a medium through which we arrive at the knowledge of something else. From a footstep, for instance which we see traced on the ground, we instantly infer that some one whose trace appears has passed." (1.)

The experiences we have with the Lord grant us understanding.

Quotation: "We are well instructed only by the words that God speaks to us personally. What instructs us is what happens to us from moment to moment. We only know perfectly what experience has taught us through suffering and action. Experience is the school of the Holy Spirit who speaks to the heart words of life, and all that we say to others should come from this source." (2.)

Prayer: Lord Jesus, we pray and ask that others will receive many blessings from the symbols, signs and experiences shared. We pray that they will be encouraged to listen to Your words, and take the mystical walk into Your presence. We know, once on this path, there is no turning back.

January 7

Writing is Prayer for Me

Have no anxiety at all, but in everything, by prayer and petition, with thanksgiving, make your requests known to God. (Philippians 4:6)

I have noticed that writing is prayer for me. Prayer is the revelation of God, which comes through the writing. It is a time when the Lord speaks to my heart, and I listen. I speak to Him, and He speaks to me.

My door of communication with the Lord is through praying, reading Scripture, spiritual books and writing. I have learned from experience not communicating with the Lord adds to my anxiety. Deep in my heart I know I have to write. Part of being anxious, at times, is because I have not been writing.

The Lord uses my writings and experiences to draw me closer to Him. I need to write. This is the gift and way the Lord speaks to me. If I do not write when the Lord is drawing me to write, my spirit actually grieves.

Many things can stand in the way of the Lord speaking to us.

Quotation: "If God gives us the grace to approach Him in prayer, He will also give us the grace to write down what we learn through that prayer. Writing is an expanded way to commune with God. It helps us clarify our thoughts, and bring some order to all of the ideas floating in our heads. Keeping a prayer journal can also help us stay more focused on spiritual matters.

"We become more observant of God's presence all around us. It can provide us with an anchor to steady us through the many changes we may experience in our lives. Taking our joys and burdens to the Lord in prayer is always a precious privilege.

"Writing (journalizing) allows us to go back and review what we have learned. We can begin to identify areas of growth, recognize sinful trends, or just obtain an objective point of reference.

"It takes thoughts that are intangible and nebulous, and makes them more concrete, something we can communicate, both to ourselves and to others. Your journal is for your spiritual growth. It is a major help in discipline. It can encourage you to pray more often or remember certain things more readily. You can see many patterns in your life that needs change. It helps in recalling your prayer or reflection during the day. We can recognize His loving care and guidance more deeply." (3.)

January 8

Raindrops on My Head

And do you, O children of Zion, exult and rejoice in the Lord, your God! He has given you the teacher of justice: he has made the rain come down for you, the early and the late rain as before. (Joel 2:23)

One evening when we were in prayer in our upstairs bedroom, I felt raindrops falling on me. When Charles was praying over me, he had a vision of sheets of paper falling from the sky. We felt that these experiences were more confirmations that we should be writing.

After these experiences, we learned about a rain that is called a former rain. We sensed the sprinkling of rain. The rain that fell upon our heads, penetrating and flooding our whole beings was an outpouring of the Holy Spirit. The former rain was upon the seed church, sown upon the earth on the day of Pentecost. The latter rain is the harvest rain, in preparation for the wedding celebration.

The first promptings of the spirit are a little at a time. Touched, slowly, by the Holy Spirit the blessings and graces will soak into our soul. This rain will not run off like water on a parched land. We need to be ready for the downpour of the latter rain, the fullness of the Holy Spirit. This can only come about through the quest for Holiness and the power of God working in each soul.

Recently, as we were working on the manuscript getting it ready to send to the publisher, Charles received the words, "The empty sheets of paper were pages of a book yet to be born." The Lord filled us with His presence as He gave us the understanding of these words. The sheets of paper being empty pages represented the former rain. The book being born (published) is the latter rain, full of the revelation of God.

January 9

Extraordinary in the Ordinary

This God has revealed to us through the Spirit. For the Spirit scrutinizes everything, even the depths of God. (1 Corinthians 2:10)
"Ordinary things are becoming extraordinary. Leave the mind at rest.
Be aware of the extraordinary things that are happening in your lives.
You may think your imagination is working on you, which is not true.
I am giving you the extra to put in the ordinary.
Be My flower for all to see. Show your colors and be free.
One day to die then to live, forever, in Eternity."

We will know the presence of God the Father, by allowing Jesus to come close to us with inner peace. He will bring forth the spiritual gifts and instincts given to us from the beginning of creation. God will restore the gift of knowing, loving and serving Him.

The Lord uses the ordinary circumstances in our life to teach us.

One of the gifts the Lord is renewing in His people today is the gift of being aware of His presence. Moment by moment, it will be done in the ordinary circumstances around us. The gift returns to His people through the quest for Holiness. A call for deeper faith and commitment will come together under the bounds of faith, hope and love.

January 10

Union of Love

The Lord uses the ordinary circumstances around us to show how much He loves us. Each spiritual experience is through the union each has with the Lord. The experiences are our "union of love" with God.

Growth in this union of love depends on how quickly we will say, yes or may I. The next small or giant step in our spiritual walk helps us to grow. Our human nature can adjust to spiritual experiences if given to us slowly.

The Lord teaches, inspires, and draws us close to himself. The Holy Spirit quickens and excites the spiritual life within us. This quickening intensifies our awareness and perception of His presence. Inspired thoughts, words, prayers, dreams, symbols, Scriptures, other spiritual people and spiritual experiences add to this excitement and joy. While always remaining thankful and accepting, we have to be open and docile to the action of the Holy Spirit.

We ask the Lord to encourage and inspire the reader as the journey with Him continues. The Lord is our Joy. The power of the Holy Spirit working in our lives magnifies this joy. Our personal relationship with Jesus Christ "sets our hearts a dancing."

January 11

Settle Your Hearts and Minds

Lord Jesus, bless us with Your peace

and give us rest in Your presence. Let the insights, lessons and experiences shared help us as we walk towards You seeking the inner mystical life. Lead us to the deep waters and shores of Eternal Life. Draw us deeper into a relationship with the Trinity—Father, Son and Holy Spirit.

Help us to know Your flame of love that burns in the center of our hearts. Holy Spirit, flow and rest upon wounded hearts and minds. Bring healing and love into the wounded areas. Jesus, walk side by side with Your Holy Spirit, walk hand in hand with us. Guide us in the right direction and into the presence of God, the Father.

Shades of Blue, start and finish each new day, filling each heart with love and hope.

O Lord, draw us close to You, and lift veils of truth and grace as we run towards You. Bring us to Your bosom with caresses of love and joy. Cover our life with wisdom, wholeness and truth.

Shades of Blue, in dark and light flow across each new life, touching the heart with soft tones that dance with love forevermore.

Coming into the presence of God is the same as night coming into daybreak. The light of the day comes into the darkness of the night. Jesus is the stillness, the soft light that comes into the darkness. He is the sun (Son) that rises in our hearts.

January 12

Spiritual Light

Spiritual light shine so bright, let me shine in the Father's light.
Spiritual truth, please take root, searching always for the truth.
Days are coming, I know, My Lord, when all will shout in one accord.
God truly sent His only Son, the battle is over, and He has won.
Let us thank Him from the heart; we should
have been doing this from the start.
The trials are over for you and me; it is time for peace in Eternity.

January 13

I Want My Heart to Beat With Yours

My heart belongs to You, Lord, forever and a day
It wants to do Your will, in whatever You have to say.
It wants to feel Your love, compassion and understanding too
Therefore, I may be a devoted child, ever close to You.
I want my heart to beat with Yours, with love as my only goal
To help those in need, maybe save a soul.
Someday this earthly heart of mine will beat no more in me,
Then I will know for sure, I am with You for all Eternity.
Secrets of the heart are revealed only to You,
Showing our life from the start, which all of creation knew.

January 14

Sentimental Solitude

"What eye has not seen, and ear has not heard, and what has not entered the human heart, what God has prepared for those who love him," this God has revealed to us through the Spirit. (1 Corinthians 2:9–10)

Come let us adore Him. His love to us, He brings!

"A shower of love will fall upon you.
Be strong. Be humble.
My Sword of truth will open the hearts of many.
Rapture will fill your hearts.
Begotten shall be begot.
Be not forlorn.
Grace and mercy shall prevail.
Love, Magna cum Pietra … love, with great piety."

"O Wonder of wonders!

In this, you will receive My blessings of love. O How joyous shall it be.
In this, My sentimental solitude of tenderness,

I will bring you into My joyous abode, My heart, My home.
In this, My heavenly aquarium, you can swim
and breathe in My living waters.
In this, My valley of valleys, you will experience the
rich reflecting luster of My glory and splendor."

January 15

Open Your Hands

"Open your hands and I will fill your heart. Like a little child and its blank-ee, you can snuggle up next to Me and I will comfort you.
Touch the corner of the blanket and its softness is touching the corners of My heart and its love for you.
Let the softness of My heart melt into yours."

"The human heart is at its softest time when it holds a newborn baby.
You will always be that newborn baby to me.
A heart undivided is a heart that rests in My heart.
Open your hands and I will fill your hearts."

"My love flows over the mountains and plains, over calm and rough seas.
I bring, united, each hand that joins in My heart and send love through ways you are yet to understand.
Walk with open hands and hearts for I will fill you to the fullest with My love and strength."

Lord, show us Your heart.

January 16

Come Play with Me

"Play in the center of My garden. As you go deeper into the

spiritual life, you will find that My garden of love is full of things that will please you. Accept one another and let Me be the one that knows your need and the needs of others. I have anointed you with the ointment of My suffering and love. Care for one another. Take time for one another and time for Me."

"I have surrounded you with My peace and presence this very evening. You are to go from this place and presence and bring My love to others. Bring it to the ends of the earth. Set aside self-desires. Hold out your hand for those along the way that need to know My love. Learn to accept My graces."

"I hold you ever so close, My little children. Snuggle up to My heart and rest in My love, My little ones. Come play with Me in My garden of love. Come play with Me. Be the light of Christian direction. You are the light of Christian encouragement."

Prayer: With a pure heart, I ask to be led by the Spirit of God. Jesus, help me to love all, regardless of their misgivings. Help me to be a good listener and slow to respond until I have had a chance to discern. Help me to live life in the words of St. Francis of Assisi, "Lord, make me an instrument of Your peace." Let me walk this life beside You and to please You, always. True happiness found only with You, is what I desire.

January 17

My Little Children

"Whoever receives one child such as this in my name, receives me; and whoever receives me, receives not me but the One who sent me." (Mark 9:37)

"I will make a path where there is no path.

I will be the light where before there was only darkness.

I will make a way where there is no way.

I will shine light where there is no light."

"All I ask of you is to remember Me, as loving you.
My little children, I have such fullness to share with you. Be with Me.
Spend time with Me. Seek Me continuously. Do you really want to be My companion?"

"Even though everything may appear dark, there is still life in the darkness and light will pierce through the darkness.
Even with the soft voice not clearly heard, pray in the middle of the noise.
Prayers from a heart held in My love and silence will bring growth to the life hidden in that darkness.
The concentrated child, the converted life is the antidote for the world's problems."

January 18

Gathering a Holy People

They shall be called the holy people, the redeemed of the Lord, and you shall be called "Frequented," a city that is not forsaken. (Isaiah 62:12)

God is calling His people to unite in the Holy Spirit and to pursue the mystical life of the Church. He is gathering people that are in pursuit of Holiness. He will plant the desire to worship in wisdom and truth within their hearts.

His people will build the roadway to Him by helping to clear it of difficulties. They will turn away from the desires of the world and will be a good example for others. With God's help they will raise to a new way of life striving to live with higher moral values. He asks them to lead and teach others to live in His presence.

A second time he sent other servants, saying, 'Tell those invited: "'Behold I have prepared my banquet, my calves and fattened cattle are killed and everything is ready; come to the feast.'" (Matthew 22:4)

He is sending His servants to tell the world, all nations, to come to the Wedding Feast. His feast and celebration, the Kingdom of God here on Earth is ready now. The wedding feast is the life and union we experience in living in the presence of God. God has prepared a united wedding feast for His Son and the Bride is His church.

His church is His holy people. The Lord is calling everyone united in the body of Christ to this united celebration. We are all invited to live in the presence of God.

Lo, I am about to create new heavens and a new earth; the things of the past shall not be remembered or come to mind. (Isaiah 65:17)

January 19

First Promptings of the Holy Spirit

You are the salt of the earth. But if salt loses its taste, with what can it be seasoned? It is no longer good for anything but to be thrown out and trampled underfoot. You are the light of the world. A city set on a mountain cannot be hidden. Nor do they light a lamp and then put it under a bushel basket; it is set on a lamp stand, where it gives light to all in the house. Just so, your light must shine before others, that they may see your good deeds and glorify your heavenly Father. (Matthew 5:13–16)

After the Baptism of the Holy Spirit, we became aware of the presence of God all around us. Accepting Jesus Christ into our hearts brings joy and love into the center of our hearts. As beginners, we were in the darkest shades of blue. The first experience I received from the Lord was the Lord touching the first shades of darkness.

The Lord gives us just a little bit or sample of His presence. He shows His fondness and love for us. He touches us in our senses where we can learn and appreciate His beauty and love for us.

One evening, I experienced the taste of salt and fish. I was drinking orange juice and eating potato chips. The juice tasted like salt and the chips tasted like fish. Salt is the Lord's action on our soul. His union with our soul brings out the buried and hidden things in our life. The fish is the person we have become through our life's journey. The salt acts on the fish. God acts on the Person. The fish at times symbolizes the Savior and at other times the faithful.

January 20

The Best Teacher

"Experience is the Best Teacher." How often have we heard these words and found them to be true? What is experience and why is it the best teacher? *Macmillan's Modern Dictionary* says that experience is a personal participation in, or observation of the realities of life. It is something undergone, enjoyed or suffered. This description states that we participate and see the everyday life around us. We undergo, enjoy and suffer through different situations each day.

We experience not only the situations to be careful of, but we also learn the situations that have pleasant results. Experiences drawn upon as needed, lie stored in our memory bank. What a person will do often depends on past experiences. We are very young when we start to learn through our experiences. A simple example, a young child will learn not to touch something hot, for it will burn. If they touch it, they learn the hard way not to touch it again.

One day my daughter-in-law and I took my grandson for a walk. We stopped to feed the horses some apples. I showed my grandson how to hold his hand flat so the horse could get the apple from his hand. In a split second, the horse took his hand and apple into his mouth. This left small bite marks on the back of his hand. Needless, to say it was a long time before he fed the horse again. This experience was one we would all remember.

We experience life around us through the five senses of seeing, hearing, smelling, tasting and touching. Touching a hot stove and feeding the horse are lessons involving the sense of touch. The Lord uses the fives senses of the exterior life along with the senses in the interior or spiritual life. When we accept Christ as our Savior, we begin to live a life of grace. 33

Little by little, the revelation of God begins to unfold and we notice the action and grace of the Holy Spirit in our life.

Quotation: "We only know perfectly what experience has taught us through suffering and action. Experience is the school of the Holy Spirit who speaks to the heart words of life, and all that we say to others should come from this source. All that is dough; leaven is needed and the salt of experience must season it. When lacking this salt we have only vague ideas, we are like dreamers who know the way to all cities and lose themselves on their road home." (4.)

January 21

Go Deeper Go Deeper

"Go deeper; go deeper into your hearts. I am here waiting for you.
Enter in! Enter in! I love you.
Take My hand and I will lead you into many treasures of My heart.
A pure heart, resting in truth does not have
to prove or disprove anything.
The nails of bondage removed set you free.
I am never far away. I am always close to you. I am deep within."

January 22

Walk Hand in Hand

Young or old holding hands tell a story. The story can be about the newness of a relationship or about years shared. Somehow, the holding of hands is more than the gesture of holding hands. Stored up in each handclasp are life's struggles, trials, happiness and joys. You may be reaching out for the clasp of a new friendship, for reassurance, for trust, or for the clasp of love shared.

"Hold hands with me.

Your story is part of the bigger sea.
Along the many ocean shores of sand,
I will walk with you hand in hand."

January 23

Choose Life

I have set before you life and death, the blessing and the curse. Choose life, then, that you and your descendants may live. (Deuteronomy 30:19)

Each person given a free will should make free choices. Through Baptism, with original sin washed away, every person starts out with a fresh start.

The majority of life's responsibilities lies with the individual person and the choices that person makes. Lies can be mixed in the middle of truths. These lies imply that you are responsible for another person's sin or that another is responsible for yours.

Of course, if you know you have contributed in damaging a person's life or been the cause of a person sinning, then that is different and there is much needed forgiveness. Life's contributions can change the focus on the truth and paint a completely different picture.

In many forms of misuse, the person loses the ability and knowledge of the fact that they can be free. Their freedom lies right within the freedoms of what God has given them. Within their own will they can still make free choices. Our past, present and future is in the freedom the Lord gives to us. Our freedom and Joy is in the Lord.

January 24

We Shall Be as One

"In the evening, we two shall be as one.
I shall listen. You shall listen. We speak as one.
If we are alone, it still will be two,
When we pray together, it will be two by two.

When two or more are together in My name, there I shall be.
In marriage, two become one, united for all eternity.
The joy and peace you bring to others will be of me."

January 25

The Graces I Have

"The Rosary in My hand is in the place it ought to be.
Neither feast nor famine can penetrate the power of My Holy Sea.
Come to Me My beloved one for you can see
the light of My Son through Me.
Have you forgotten all the graces I have?
My home is like a living tree of all to love that this might be.
I am the star that brings you safe from out of this rivalry.
May, you see Me in the stars, with His cross and all its mars,
Mother, Mother, save for me, a place of rest in Your Son's sea of life."

January 26

Draw to My Heart, My Little Sheep

"Arbitrary confusion will not open malicious tunnel.
Draw to My heart My little sheep.
Make time for Me each day,
Whether awake or asleep, your heart is My abode.
With My love it can keep the deep ... the deep ... the deep."

January 27

Deeper Waters and Security Blankets

Out of his infinite glory, may he give
you the power through his Spirit for your
hidden self to grow strong, so that Christ may live in your hearts through

faith, and then, planted in love and built on love, you will with all the saints, have strength to grasp the breadth and the length, the height and the depth; until, knowing the love of Christ, which is beyond all knowledge, you are filled with the utter fullness of God. (Ephesians 3:16–19, Jerusalem)

The Lord used the following dreams to teach us about our security blankets. Our thoughts, ambitions, opinions and desires, stand in the way of a deeper relationship with the Lord.

On September 3, 1986, we both had dreams that had many of the same items. We were in each other's dreams along with many other people. Each dream was about the length away from the water, blankets, stairs and other people in the water. I would not jump into the water in either Charles' dream or my own.

Charles' dream: In my dream, Anne and I were on a large ship with many people on it. One of them was the priest that was in charge of our prison ministry. The ship was sinking and we had to jump off. The priest said that I should have no problem with jumping. I had been in the Navy and had training for this. I tied Anne's life jacket with Navy Square Knots. I used these knots so no one could untie her jacket and quickly take it off her.

Anne was afraid to jump because we were high above the water. While trying to get her up on the side of the ship to jump, the ship had sunk deeper into the water. This cut down on the big drop we would have had before hitting the water. I held onto her hand and we jumped into the water.

I told her to swim as fast as she could to get away from the ship. Not doing this could draw us under with the ship. When we reached the shore, we came to a sea wall of stone with steps going up. When we climbed the steps, people were waiting to help us while greeting us with warm blankets.

My Dream: Many people were walking along a narrow path. Others were ahead of me. My arms were full of the blankets I was carrying. I came up to the wall and looked over. Others were already in the water and I could see Charles there.

I would not jump because the water was too far down. I was thinking if I jumped in maybe the blankets would help me from going too far under the water. Instead of jumping into the water, I found large rocks as stairs that brought me along side of the water.

Someone was collecting the items people lost when they jumped into the water. I had gotten a bright flowered skirt, one old spread and one blue designed blanket back from this person. I had seen these items floating in the water when I was looking over the wall. This was the end of the dream.

From this experience, we felt the Lord calling us to the deeper waters, which meant getting rid of our securities; the blankets stood for our securities and the deep waters stood for a call to a deeper relationship with God.

We have many securities that we lean upon and are afraid to give up. Often, we do not want to give them up.

God wants us to submit our whole being to Him. He wants us to lean completely upon Him, and not to be afraid to jump into the deep waters. Some of us will stand along the shore a long time before we will jump into deeper waters.

Some securities affect our senses, emotions, old traits, faults, habits, and our dependence on others for decisions. One security blanket that we harbor in our hearts is the dependency and protection we have built up around an old scar or wound. Hurt emotions and bad habits, formed from the beginning, end up hiding the old scars and wounds.

It really takes prayer and discipline to change our ways of thinking, acting and responding. Like Paul, I cannot understand my own behavior. I fail to carry out the things I want to do, and I find myself doing the very things I hate. (Romans 7:15–16, Jerusalem)

We often look for a way out. We will not take the risks that call for complete trust and dependency on Christ. If we had a choice to make, would we jump into the deeper waters or walk down the stairs? Some of us would choose to jump while others would be more cautious and go down the stairs. The Lord knows us and He works with us no matter which way we choose.

As we move into a deeper and inner relationship with the Lord, we will move away from worldly desires. We have to ask the Lord to remove the desires that hold us in bondage to the world. Bondage can be like the security blankets we carry or the sandals that are tightly strapped to our feet.

Remove the Sandals from Your Feet

But the Lord said to him, "Remove the sandals from your feet, for the place where you stand is holy ground." (Acts 7:33)

Some of us will not let go of our securities as easily as others will. We fear the insecurity or the empty arm feeling when dependency leaves or is taken away. The Lord can wean us off any security blanket that does not give us the full benefit of His love and grace. He can detach us from the bad habits, thoughts and faults that stand in the way of His love. He will lead us in the direction of deep healing and a deeper relationship with him.

Many of us are afraid of the distance we feel between the spiritual and natural life. They are one and the same, but our natural understanding does not let us see this revelation. For the same reason, we will not jump into the water. To jump into the mystical waters, we have to trust, completely, in the Lord, Jesus Christ. We have to ask Him to give us a gentle push.

Prayer: O Lord, send us Your Holy Spirit. Carry us through the height, breadth, length, and depth of the natural and spiritual realms of healing and understanding. Help us to go the distance, from the high sea wall or ship to Your Holy shores. Heal our fears and help us to jump into the mystical waters that are full of Your love and grace. Remove the sandals from our feet. Help us to stand on Holy Ground in Your presence, amongst us now and in eternity. Amen.

January 29

Jump in Trust

"Jump, no buts, you can't take it with you.
Jump in trust, leaving behind all kinds of securities and possessions.
Your whole foundation is being tested.
Only a solid faith will be left to stand and it will be as solid as concrete.
Purified faith has complete trust in only Me
and it depends on nothing else.
Molded, shaped and formed you will be the way I want you to be."

"A little sadness you feel in your heart because you have to let go
of things of old along with things you know and understand.
It is okay. I will fill the emptiness with trust and My love.
Submission is a total letting go, even of things
that appear to be good and useful.
I hold you in the palm of My hand and I will not
set you down in any danger. I love you.
Give all away for something greater. See My Children, how I lead you?
I lead you like a Mother that would never lead her little ones astray."

January 30

Confirmed in Grace

Confirmed in grace is not having to understand everything.
Faith is trust and confidence in God.
I feel the confident assurance building in my Heart, O Lord.
Your word is part of me even if I do not know it verbally.
Satan's lie is that his darkness can have a hold on light. That is His lie.
Darkness cannot have a hold on or contain the light of Christ that is
within each one of us.

"You are a part of me.
I would not let anything happen to you that I would not want for myself.
My motherly love for you is a bond that will last for all Eternity."

Just Be Open for My Graces

"I will place a banner of virtues around you.
They will adjust and fit just right,
Be peaceful. I will do it.
Just, be open for My graces.
Be like a sponge and just absorb."

February 1

Cinderella

One Sunday afternoon while visiting my sister and her family, my three-year-old niece came up to me and leaned over my lap. Looking up, she called me Cinderella. Through this experience, the Lord reminded us of the simplicity in the heart and mind of a child.

The Lord used the childhood story of Cinderella to teach us about the simplicity of a child. He showed us the love Jesus has for us in this simplicity.

Jesus is saying to each of us, "I am reminding you of a childhood story called *Cinderella*. Do you remember that story? Cinderella was the little maiden who worked in the dirty kitchen. She wore dirty clothes but became a beautiful princess. Just like Cinderella, I am going to transform your heart and mind into beautiful jewels and present them to God our Father."

Jesus tells us that He loves us very much.

"First, you have to know how special you are to Me.
I have chosen you to be the princess of My heart.
I love everything about you. I love the way you look.
I love the way you walk and talk. I love the color of your hair and eyes.
I love every part of you. I love you when your
clothes may be dirty or tattered.
I love you when your clothes are clean and beautiful.

I hold you when you tremble and are fearful.
I caress you and am sad when you are lonely.
I am happy when you are happy."

"Cinderella lost her slipper at the ball and the Prince found her and placed the slipper on her foot. There is a special slipper just for you. One fitting perfectly and helping you to walk into the open arms of God, our Father. The things I may ask of you are for your conversion. All are for the honor and Glory of God, our Father."

We must become like little children. A childhood story like *Cinderella* can help awaken our hearts to the simplicity of a child. Jesus will come in and transform our hearts into precious jewels.

Cinderella became a beautiful princess before she went to live in the King's Castle. After we are transformed, we will be carried off to live in the King's Castle. Christ will bring us, into the inner castle of our hearts. This is where we will experience the presence of God the Father.

February 2

Jesus, As We Walk this Life with You

This is the first prayer we put together after our experience of opening our hearts to a personal relationship with Jesus.

Jesus, as we walk this life with you, help us to pray to the Father for all that are sick and in need of prayer and comfort. Lord, You have said, "Ask and you shall receive." We now ask through Your Son, Jesus and the Holy Spirit to look down with love and mercy on all those we pray for (name of person needing prayer).

You know their needs more than we do. Give them strength and the faith they need at this time. Hold their hand and let Your love and peace shine upon them. May they feel Your presence and joy and be free from all pain and suffering.

Let the light from Your glorious face shine upon them, and may they always walk in Your footsteps. Help us too, O Jesus, to accept the times brought back into the valley knowing that through times of testing, our faith in You becomes stronger. Help us to grow in our new life with You and to share with others the glory of Your word.

This we ask in Your name, Lord Jesus Christ. Amen

February 3
Fruits Will Soon Be Harvested

"My words will be understood by all.
Fruits will soon be harvested.
Candles will be lit one after another.
Let all that is within thee remain."

February 4
The Fold of His Garment

When the soldiers had crucified Jesus, they took his clothes and divided them into four shares, a share for each soldier. They also took his tunic, but the tunic was seamless, woven in one piece from the top down. (John 19:23)

Jesus' garment woven in one piece had no seams. His woven tunic of heavenly materials of His love and mercy are for each one of us. There was no sin in Him. All fulfilled the Scriptures in His life, death and resurrection.

Jesus' time with us is never ending. It always was and will always be. He is the beginning and the end, woven through and through with the thread of eternal life. He tucks us in the fold of His garment.

Visualize yourself going up to the Lord. Place all of your concerns in the fold of His garment. Place them in the pocket of His heart. This is a special and safe place. It is the same as touching the hem of His garment.

Lord, within my heart, I want to return to that safe place. This is where I felt Your wonder and awesome presence. I felt Your healing love where I could repent. Your arms held me close to Your heart, where I

43

felt strength, love, forgiveness and unity with You. I felt the pulse of the Holy Spirit united with the heartbeat within me.

O Lord, help me to return to that safe place. This is the place where You held me in Your arms of love and peace. It has taken a lifetime to bring me to this place. Some come young, some come old, and some come older. It is all the same. It is a place in the heart where love can dominate the hearts desires.

Lord, hold me in Your arms and embrace me in Your joy and love. Help me to soak up the riches of Your glory-filled presence. When we rest in you, O Lord, we rest in the truth and truth is peace. On that Friday afternoon, we drove up behind a car that had a license plate, which read, "I Pocket." This was confirmation to us for putting all our concerns in the pocket (heart) and fold of the Lord's garment.

February 5

I That Beautiful Sound

As I kneel in prayer each day, closing my eyes to all around,
I listen and I hear Him say, "It is I you hear, I that beautiful sound."
I feel Him gently touch my brow. Soon I am all aglow.
His Spirit is within me now, of this I surely know.
He tells me not to worry or fret, that He is always at my side.
I put my trust in Him and let, His love in me abide.
I feel so safe and good with Him, all through the night and day.
Before He came, my life was dim. I was lost along the way.
So, praise to You My Lord and God, for helping me to see.
My life was just an empty pod, without my love of Thee.

February 6

Snow White and Pure

"Three sitting with hands, white and bright
I am pleased with the sacrifice.

The valley of tears you will know.
You will see My cross.
Sweetness you will hear.
As snow white and pure
Like puddles full of tears
A nail will pierce the flesh.
The shadow of the cross will come over you.
Pain will leave, but the mark will remain."

February 7

The Bitter with the Sweet

Charles had to go to Burlington, Vermont, for a heart Catheterization and Angioplasty. While he was in the hospital, I stayed at the Sisters of Mercy convent across the street.

I went to Mass the morning I picked Charles up to take him home. During Mass, when I took the Precious Blood from the Chalice, it tasted very bitter. After helping Charles settle in at home for the evening, I went to Mass again. It was the vigil Mass for the next day. When I drank the Precious Blood from the Chalice this time, it was sweet.

We eventually began to understand the meaning of this experience. There would be a little bitter along with the sweet. Charles and I both were having physical problems. We were sure we would have to cancel our trip overseas. When things unfolded, two days before the trip, we were able to place our physical problems aside and go on our trip as planned ... a little bitter with the sweet.

The (bitter) sacrifice of pain and suffering, we placed before the Lord. We went on the trip receiving the (sweet) blessings and graces.

We are drinking pure water and will no longer be happy with chemicals in our water. Spiritually we are drinking the pure water of God and will no longer be happy with sinful, corrupt, or polluted water.

February 8

Our Eyes Met

You have ravished my heart, my sister, my bride; you have ravished my heart with one glance of your eyes. (Song of Songs 4:9)

In a dream about an onion, (shared later) my eyes met with those of the prince or king. He then said, "You were special to Me the first time our eyes met." These words reminded Charles and me of another experience.

Charles and I received the gift of faith from the Lord and our parents. Our parents' faith was a good example for us. From what we have learned and the gifts received, we believe in the real presence of Jesus in Holy Communion.

One day before Mass, we asked Jesus to reveal His presence to us. We were yearning to experience Him deeply within our heart and soul. Not knowing at the time, we were asking for the lifting of the veil of the Sacrament. We now understand a little of what this means. The natural senses do not understand the full meaning of the Sacraments and the mystical life attached to them. In the following experience, the Lord had given us a little glimpse of the power of the Sacraments, and taught us about the veil of faith that protects them.

When we went to receive Jesus, we knew we were to look into the eyes of the priest. Each of us did not know what the other had asked for. The priest was a very special priest, both to us and in his devotion to Jesus in the Blessed Sacrament. When I looked into his eyes, time stood still. I saw Christ standing there. The eyes and complete outer frame of the priest became Christ. I was filled with joy.

When I went back to my seat, I could see something had happened to Charles also. After Mass, we shared. Charles looked into the eyes of the priest and he saw the eyes of Christ.

Therefore, brothers, since through the blood of Jesus we have confidence of entrance into the sanctuary by the new and living way he opened for us through the veil, that is, his flesh. (Hebrews 10:19–20)

During this experience of seeing and receiving Him in Holy Communion, we both felt that we had to hurry away. His presence was so clear to us that we felt uneasy. We were not sure why we felt this way. Maybe it was because His pure eyes could see right through to our soul. If this was the reason for our uneasiness, it was a good example of how sin cannot be in the presence of purity. The pure light of Christ shows up sin. Yet, in the dream of the onion the prince or king (Christ) had said, "We were special to each other the first time our eyes met." The Lord was telling us that He looked upon us with love.

The holy Spirit also testifies to us, for after saying: "This is the covenant I will establish with them after those days, says the Lord: 'I will put my laws in their hearts, and I will write them upon their minds,'" he also says: "Their sins and their evildoing I will remember no more." (Hebrews 10:15–17)

Christ had answered our prayer. Now, we know because we know.

February 9

Basement of Our Humanness

I shall give you a new heart, and put a new spirit in you; I shall remove the heart of stone from your bodies and give you a heart of flesh instead. (Ezekiel 36:26, Jerusalem)

I felt, for sometime, that something was missing in our writings of *Shades of Blue*. As it turned out, we still had experiences to experience. Our experiences, not hurried, move along in the Spirit of God at His pace and not ours. We were soon to learn that the following experience was an important part of these writings.

My aunt's death was just before the Christmas of 1994. The Lord brought many insights into our hearts through a special star in the winter sky. We experienced the fellowship with Christ. This was a fellowship of faith, hope, and love, suffering, joys and praise. The Lord took the burden of my aunt's death and turned it into a special time for all of our family. We went from this to a very difficult time of worry and concern.

In February of 1995, Charles had to undergo more heart tests. In March, he had another heart procedure. This was very difficult for us because Charles had surgery done just four years ago. They thought this surgery would last for fifteen to twenty years. We went into shock when they told us that the mammary artery had shut down. This artery placed into his heart from the back of the chest was to give him good blood flow. There was a 90% block again in this artery so something had to be done right away. They gave us three different options. At this point, we had to make a choice of which option we would take.

This was very different for us. We could not grasp why we were feeling so much of what was happening. We were in a completely different place with the Lord. It was different from four years before, when Charles had his second heart surgery. We both went into this special place with the Lord. We felt everything strictly from a human level. We felt we were in the basement of our humanness.

According to Webster's dictionary a basement is the lowest story, of a building. It is the foundation, bottom or lowest part, a support, fundamental or essential part of a thing.

February 10

Our Life Line

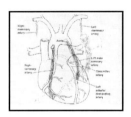

Keeping in mind the definition of basement just given, we had to ask ourselves, what is our support? What is our foundation? Where do we stand in our relationship with Christ? The Lord had brought us to a low point, where we could ask ourselves these questions. We felt every bit of our human nature, rebelling to all that was happening to us. What were we going to do about it? Were we going to remain in shock? Were we going to let the Lord bring us back to spiritual and physical health?

The Lord had brought us to the most essential part of our relationship with Him. This is the place where we joined Him in His suffering, joy, and love for all humanity. With our faith carrying us through, all walls dropped.

We both were very good at not letting others know we were really suffering, but this time we did not try to hide it. One of the walls was a wall of pride. There is a pride connected with suffering. We say to others, not spoken, *Look how well we are doing with this one. Are we not handling and going through this just fine?* All the time, we were suffering.

We wanted to shout it out to anyone that would listen, "We're suffering, scared, and really hurting." This time we did just that.

The Lord reminds us, we do not like things that do not hold up. A quote from a magazine, I was reading, explains it very clearly.

Quotation: "You have no use for things that do not hold up. You're into durability, longevity, extra heavy duty. To put it another way, they're rock solid." (5.)

We do not want to take time, even for illness. The shock is that we do have choices. We did not like the idea that the artery was not durable or rock solid. The longevity was short. After the initial shock is over, what do we do then? We were in touch with the basement of our humanness.

Our support, built only on the deep roots of a relationship with Christ, joined with Christ for all of humanity. Our humanness allowed us to join in Christ's suffering. We felt called to turn to the Lord and to give Him our sufferings, trusting only in Him.

Through difficulties, the Lord had brought our attention back to Him. We, like others, let all our attention go to what is happening to and around us. We have power, peace, joy, comfort and strength in our relationship with Him. He is our Life Line.

Our spiritual experiences in the past gave us a lot of confidence and helped us to handle the trials that came our way. The Lord was saying, "Walk ahead in the positive. Leave behind the negative. I surround you with My love. Rest in My arms and the fruit you bear will not spoil."

February 11

A Christian Life

"To see a Christian life, watch a candle burn.
The silent flickering of the flame is the same as the silent
burning of God's flame of love in your hearts.
Reach out your hands and bring into your
heart the love and presence of God."

February 12

Someday, Someday

A letter to our friends:

We sit in awe and wonder
Where you are today
We made a promise not to slumber
To be reunited in a special way.
We sit in the Chapel on Holy Hill
With thoughts of you in prayer
While snow is falling and all is still
God's peace is everywhere.
Even though miles and miles keep us apart
Our love for you still grows
God's grace renewed in our hearts
Us to you it flows.
We think of the kites flying high
The balloons that you let go
Like little children, why we ask
There is so much to know.
God makes us wait for answers
Sometimes too long we say
Never-the-less, He will respond
Someday—Someday—Someday!

February 13

I Do Will It

Moved with pity, he stretched out his hand, touched him, and said to him, "I do will it. Be made clean." (Mark 1:41)

In his encounter with Jesus, the leper in the Scripture gospel experiences compassion beyond the ordinary. So moved is Jesus at the sight of this outcast that He instinctively reaches out to touch, to heal.

It was determined in 1983 that Charles had Coronary Artery Disease.

His first heart by-pass surgery was in August of that year. Seven years later because of the progression of this disease, he had to have angioplasty surgery. This surgery was done on May 31, 1990, at the University Medical Center in Burlington, Vermont.

He continued to have problems throughout the winter. Further tests showed he needed a second heart-by-pass surgery. After this diagnosis, we found ourselves making a trip to the Cleveland Clinic in Cleveland, Ohio. The specialists Charles needed worked at this clinic.

Charles' operation was on Friday, February 14, 1991. Because it was the second surgery, it was much harder than the first and lasted ten hours. He was in ICU until late Sunday because he was remaining very groggy. The doctors cut down on his pain medicine to help him to become more alert. Monday, he was still very groggy and his coordination, reflexes, etc. were very slow. The left side of his lip was also not moving.

The doctors had determined on Tuesday morning the 19th, that some time during or shortly after surgery, Charles had a slight stroke. That day they had also worked on him from 8:00 a.m. to 4:00 p.m. trying to get a rapid heartbeat down to normal.

On Sunday, Charles asked me if our son Thomas or I had touched him on the cheek. I said no. He had felt someone touch his cheek. That evening in the hotel room I read these words from Living Words for the day, "Moved with pity, Jesus stretched out his hand, touched him and said, "I do will it. Be cured." (Mark 1:41).

We believe that Jesus touched Charles on the cheek and healed him. God was good to us. Charles recovered from the stroke very fast. The doctor said they had never seen anyone recover so fast from a stroke.

February 14

Surrounded By Angels

The experience of Jesus touching Charles was on Sunday. Monday, Charles started to experience a mist of different colors surrounding him in his room. Tuesday, I had brought a cassette tape in to him with music from our trip overseas. The tape had reminded him of our trip. When he listened to it, he started to cry and then remembered something had been happening to him in his hospital room.

Monday, Charles had seen his room fill with a pink mist; Tuesday it filled with a blue mist; Wednesday a gold mist, and a white mist on Thursday. He was recovering these same days from the stroke. Each day the neurologists came into his room to start therapy. They never had to give him therapy. They came in to get him to write and he would be writing. Then they tried to get him to walk and he would be walking. Each day was the same. He would already be doing things ahead of their therapy. Friday of this same week, I talked to my daughter-in-law. She shared a dream that our friend had about Charles. She had the dream on the Friday Charles had the surgery.

This was the dream: she saw Charles surrounded with beautiful angels in pink, blue, gold and white. A voice spoke saying, "Charles, you can come with us now if you want." Charles bowed his head, concerned about his wife Anne. He said, "What about Anne?" He remained quiet for a long time and then said, "Thy will be done, O Lord." Here is where the dream ended.

We believe this dream and the experience of the pink, blue, gold and white mist in Charles' room go together. Charles recovered each day from the stroke while the experience was going on. We believe Jesus touched Charles with His healing hands, and God's healing angels were present in his hospital room. They were bringing God's healing and peace to Charles in the beautiful pink, blue, gold and white mist.

On the day Charles was discharged from the hospital to come home, the paralysis on the left side of his mouth was also healed.

We were far from home during this struggle. However, we realized the distance placed between others and ourselves was a gift from God. The Lord let us see through a life threatening illness what really matters in life. It is not all the fuss and frills of life, but life itself that matters. It very often takes a serious illness or situation to make us see clearly. In the middle of illness, He gave us trust, so why do we not trust in all other situations?

Is it because our eyes again turn towards the world? God alone is all that is important. We should do all we can for earthly matters, and then let go. God is in the very center of our hearts. We must remember to keep the center of our hearts and minds fixed on God. In this way, we can keep going forward in peace and confidence. He gave us a gift to see the separation of earth and heaven. The earth keeps us attached to things of the earth. Heaven is seeing earth for what it really is.

Pain helps us to keep in touch with heaven. We both understood the grace connected with suffering and pain. In just two months time of being free from pain, we could see the worldly concerns knocking at our door, trying to get our attention. We had to fight to keep our whole experience close to our minds and hearts.

Secretly, we did not want the special time of being away with the Lord to end. God had given us many gifts. The most important one was the understanding of loving Him, Him alone and His loving us.

February 15

Be Blessed

"Burning desire for My love can kindle in the
flowing waters from My Heart.
I have a special delight in reverence of Me.
Be blessed in My delights. Reciprocate My tidings."

February 16

My Love Flows

"My love flows over the mountains and
plains, over calm and rough seas.
I bring united each hand that joins in My heart.
I send love through ways you are yet to understand.
Walk with open hands and hearts for I will fill you
to the fullest with My love and strength."

53

February 17

Shadows that Make a Difference

"Be a reflection of the Word of God.
You are but shadows upon the earth, shadows that make a difference.
Be aware of those that are hurting. Look over your shoulder.
Be aware of My love. Look in the shadows of the trees.
Walk in the reflections of the shadow of My love.
Stand within the reflection of the shadows and look
with unconditional love upon My creation."

February 18

Let There Be Light

I was working on my computer, around 9:50 a.m. one morning, when I heard one loud clap of thunder. Right after this, we could hear the wind coming in the distance. It sounded like the rumbling of a train.

Because the wind was so strong, I unplugged my telephone lines to my computer and then unplugged the whole system from the wall. I had an experience in the past where I lost my whole computer system to an electrical storm. I was not going to let this happen again. It was not very long after when we lost all our electric power.

Many, many trees had been torn up by the strong winds, knocking down power lines. We waited out most of the day for the power to come on, but it did not. We were able to start our wood fireplace, so we called our kids to tell them if the power did not come back on, they could come here to stay. As night approached, their place began to get cold, therefore, they came over.

We ended up without power for three days and nights. For many people, this meant no heat of any kind in their homes. In many cases, people could not even get water because of wells and electric pumps to draw the water. The city water lines saved us from that situation. We have three sources of heat in our home: the fireplace, oil furnace and a pellet stove. The fireplace was the only one we could use for heat and cooking. Some heat went to the rest of the house, but not much went beyond the area of the fireplace. There was just enough to keep our water pipes and us from freezing.

Our youngest grandson said that he felt that we were together for a reason. We believed that he was right, and that the Lord uses every situation for our own benefit. As one can see from the above picture, the young ones were unaffected by it. In fact, it was rather enjoyable. I have to admit, I really did not mind it; it was not very bad.

During this time together, thoughts came to all of us about the Katrina victims. We thought of how hard it was and still must be for those that experienced the damages of the hurricane. It became very evident on how much we depend on electric power and the other conveniences that we have all around us at our disposal.

As the weekend progressed, we took the time to share with each other what we thought we could benefit from this time together without the electric power.

I woke up Sunday morning thinking about what my grandson, Jacky, had said about us being together for a reason. I called him into my bedroom and had him hop up on the bed and get under the warm covers. The house was cold by then. I told him about a story I had written for a school project when I was very young, and then we talked about our "no electric power" situation. The Lord had placed it on my heart, that the children of today, with all their electric gadgets, are not developing their own talents. Jacky and I decided that we would get the rest of the family together and share what this time together meant to all of us.

Sunday morning, before the kids went to church, we sat down together and talked about our time together. I asked everyone what he or she wanted to call this time together. Jacky, without hesitation, answered in three words, "Power Outage Prayer."

The summary of what we shared was that we each had to let the Lord develop all the talents that He has given us and not spend so much time on all the "gadgets." This time was beneficial in showing us how important it is to get along with one another. Most important, we thanked the Lord for the many blessings that we receive everyday of our lives.

Sunday night, 10:40 p.m., the lights came on. Were we happy campers? Well, I guess!

February 19

Power Outage Prayer

The wind did arrive on a clap of thunder,
Trees responded, falling asunder.
Heard in the distance, sounded a great rumble,
The wind came with such force, one could only grumble.
Each ones sighs were then unspoken,
As the electric power lines, became only a token.
Conveniences left like a flash of light
Out of mind and out of sight.
The light we held as the night grew dark
Was held in the hands, or in the fireplace spark
Heat was received from every burning ember
Penetrating us with a special time to remember.
Away from all the gadgets, we had been blessed,
A good arms distance, left us only to rest.
Loving one another was what it was all about,
Caring and sharing with every-lasting clout.
Talents need to be brought to the surface,
As we realize we are made for God's purpose.
What did this time mean to us?
A time together without the fuss,
More than that, I would speak and dare,
It is all about our "Power Outage Prayer."

Inspiration

One evening while sitting in a darkened room, I sat watching the snowfall on the ground outside the window. I began to think of how precious it is when we spend time in the presence of the Lord. I especially feel the inspiration and presence of the Lord when I spend time writing about our experiences with Him.

I find that the Lord very often leads me to ask the right questions at the right time. He led me to ask, "Where does inspiration come from and where does it go?" Of course, I know that it comes from Him, but I asked the question anyway. He had something special to say and it had a much deeper meaning.

"Inspiration runs in and out of the crevices of your mind and heart
Touching here, touching there, never to depart
Inspiration hidden, but not far away, rests in the heart
Inspiration in and out, our hearts will take without a doubt"

The Lord continued to speak to me about inspiration coming through the writing.

"A lot of writing done in the dark is glazed with light around the edges.
Light will come from the words written in the shadows of love.
There is power in the words from God.
They are words written in the shadow of love.
All we have to do for inspiration is to enter
the Grand Canyon of our hearts.
Enter the unexplored caverns and crevices of
love and God's glory will guide us."

"Do I need to see the word?" I then asked. The answer I received was, "Not when they are held in the light of Christ, and not when they are held in the light on the snow resting in the darkened night." These words carried the inspiration into further words from the heart.

February 21

Snow Resting in the Darkened Night

Snow resting in the darkened night
Fills the winter evening with bright light
Bouncing off the snow so white
God gives love and mercy in delight.
O light, O light in the darkness bright,
God's glory comes forth, a beautiful sight.
The softness of the Snow upon the bending tree,
Brings to me happiness, hope and refreshing glee.
Pine tree branches heavy with the beauty of the snow,
Form little caverns on the fingertips of the Lord, you know.
Its weight is nothing to bear,
For it holds the springtime, ready to share.
As I sit in the darkness of night,
The light from the snow is resting bright.
The Holy Spirit brought me to this special place,
In the snow held arms of the trees of grace.
Enter in, for Glory's sake,
Your life and love it will surely take.
The snow that is before you and me,
Is only a glimpse of what it is to be.
Carry me! Carry me!
Glory be! Glory be!
O Lord, kiss me with the softness of the
purified white snow of heaven's glory.
Kiss me with Your glory this night.
O Come, O Come Emmanuel!

February 22

Holiness Attracts

Holiness has to spill over and touch others.

Holiness attracts.

Visible joy is evident.

We look up to You in gladness, O Lord.

We cannot contain holiness; it has to burst forward as fire.

It is time to seek Holiness. The more the light of Christ shines into the heart, the more the shadows will show.

Prayer: Dear Lord Jesus, I love You. I ask You to confront, with Your strength and power, any inner darkness that may still be in my heart. Let Your love shine forth to others through me.

Words received: "Step in and out of situations like you would go in and out of a house. Another word for this is flexibility. The desire for holiness is the beginning of happiness."

February 23

Road to Holiness

When you come to the realization of your sinfulness, you are at the beginning of the road to holiness. This road is full of potholes and ruts to stop you. With care and prayer, these obstacles will be overcome.

February 24

The Lord Will Be Passing By

Then the Lord said, "Go outside and stand on the mountain before the Lord; the Lord will be passing by." (1 Kings 19:11)

We went on a retreat to Malvern, Pennsylvania, which was a call to a deeper relationship with the Lord. At one of the conferences, the Spiritual Director said, "During the next conference, some people should remain here with the Lord. If you ask the Lord to reveal Himself, He will." Charles, three other women and I stayed in the Chapel to keep Jesus company, while all of the rest went to the conference.

Prayer: Jesus, we will keep You company while others are at the conference and away.

Jesus, we will keep You company whether it be night or whether it be day. Jesus, we enjoy this peaceful, calm and serene time with You. We know Your angels are here too. How wonderful it would be, if we could see You through our earthly eyes. The glory that surrounds You must be immense. The beauty is something to behold. No wonder we are told only the Angels and Saints can look upon You.

The priest came to the Chapel to bring the Blessed Sacrament up to have Vespers in the conference hall. Anne and I followed Him as he was carrying the Host out of the Chapel.

We walked out of the Chapel. When we walked into the section just outside the Chapel, a heavenly fragrance surrounded us. It was intoxicating. We could not move. We tried to follow the priest, but could not. It looked as if he was flying and his feet did not touch the floor. He got up to the conference hall so fast. We could not believe that we could not keep up with him.

This experience touched the very center of our hearts and souls. We feel Jesus was revealing His presence to us. We received a gift from God for staying with Jesus. The rest of the people went to the conference. As the Spiritual Director had suggested, we asked the Lord to reveal His presence and He did. We felt that the Lord was confirming His "Visitation" to us in this experience. The fragrance of His presence touched us deeply. It will always be a part of our hearts and souls.

In the time of their visitation they shall shine, and shall dart about as sparks through stubble; they shall judge nations and rule over peoples, and the Lord shall be their King forever. Those who trust in him shall understand truth, and the faithful shall abide with him in love: Because grace and mercy are with his Holy ones and his care is with his elect. (Wisdom 3:7–9)

How many times throughout our lives have we had visitations of the Lord? I am sure, there are many, that we cannot begin to know and realize.

For at the moment the sound of your greeting reached my ears, the infant in my womb leaped for joy. (Luke 1:44)

Our hearts leap for joy when the Lord Jesus walked by us with His knowing presence.

The more we realize the closeness of God, the more we are grateful. The awareness of His presence, near or far, can be explained like catching our breath, a quick grasp for air, an "Oh, it's God. He is near." He may touch us in understanding, wisdom and knowledge, as our mind and intellect grasp His presence. This presence may bypass the mind and intellect and be in our heart and soul, alone. "When Jesus walks by with understanding, we will have to catch our breath."

February 25

A Call to the Summit of God

The Lord is calling His people into a deeper relationship with Him. It is a call to climb the very summit of God.

There are different levels of spirituality, where we experience God's presence in our life. We can touch one or the other level for short periods, or we can stay in-between one or the other for long periods.

As we experience God's presence in our life, we will come to new junctions along the path where there are always new choices to make. Will I take the high road or the low road? It will always mean another yes. Sometimes we sit at these junctions for a long time. We go a little higher and closer to the summit of God, but we can spend a lot of time sitting at the junction. We want to have our feet in both camps with one going up and the other going down.

While we were in Ireland, we took a trip to County Mayo heading towards Galway Bay. Everywhere we went we could see the Mountain of Croagh Patrick in the distance. We circled the mountain in our day's journey and then stayed across from it at night. We were so close at one point we could clearly see the path to the very summit of the mountain. We actually came to a junction in the highway, where one road went to the right and the other went to the left. The one to the left would have taken us closer to the mountain. We took the one to the right thinking that we would get closer on the way back. We did not take a picture and we were real close.

We ended up going back a different route and never did get any closer to the mountain. I believe that we left part of our hearts at this junction. We were very sad when we realized how close we were to the summit of Croagh Patrick and did not stop long enough to climb to the very top.

How many times have we been so close to the summit of the Lord and for one reason or another we take the wrong road at the junction?

Two weeks later we went to Bosnia and had a similar experience. While here, the Lord was calling us again to the solitude and deeper relationship with Him. Charles and I both wanted to climb Cross Mountain in the village of Medjugorje, where we stayed. We could only go to the first junction in the climb to the summit. That was as far as we had to go to get our message from the Lord. We sat at this junction and watched those going up and those coming down. The call to a deeper relationship with God is at a new junction, and it means another yes.

February 26

Junction in the Road

The mountaintop straight ahead
Holds not detours that we should dread
The summit of God is what is there
Pouring forth God's love and gentle care.
Its high peaks stand out for all to see,
What a lasting impression it left on me.
No matter what junction you may choose,
In the beauty from this summit, you cannot lose.
The road does come to a junction,
Where In the spirit appears a new function.
To the right or to the left, is the question we do ask,
While straight ahead, the mountain does bask.
This new junction requires another, yes.

Are we ready? On the other hand, do we let it pass?
Even if your direction is in flight,
The summit is never out of sight.
You may say "I will catch that on the way back."
The course can change and that is a fact.
Resting in God's spirit of love and care,
Take your opportunities when they are there.
The Lord does let us take the other road
In His grace a lesson, we will behold.
Remembering the summit of the mountain nearby
The truth we understood with a deep sigh.
Yes, we can behold the mountain's peak.
The meaning of life is what we seek.
The only place found,
Is in the heart of God where we abound.

February 27

Summit of the Heart

We look upon this Mountain View,
As real far off, that is not true.
Placed in the hearts of you and me,
It is as close as can be.
Once drawn in this direction,
The earth's pull loses all affection.
You may start this climb, but in times of
purification, you may want to return.
You will soon realize that there is no turning back.
Your heart will burn deep in God's love.
Like the burning bush, that appeared in Moses' sight,
The summit of the heart radiates God's love and life's light.
The heat from this summit leaves lasting resolve, anew.
The heart no longer belongs to a certain few.
It has reached the most high place.
God's love nourishes the complete human race.

Keep this summit of the heart in full view.
All of God's blessings, graces and mercies will fall on you.
When you do return to earth's temporal place,
You'll bring to others, God's wisdom and grace,
In times of being strong and in times of being weak,
This summit your heart will always seek.
Place your heart in the silence of the summit
Let the fire burn causing earth's dust to plummet.
The center of the heart is what you have come upon.
United love found deep in God's heart, you could rely on.
Earth's attachments are no longer in your sight,
All fences melt away in God's holy light.
You no longer need to linger there,
You have so much to give, so much to share.
Therefore, you can go to and from the summit of the heart,
Because you are free as a bird, free as a lark.

February 28

Always a Higher Peak for Us to Seek

"Fed and led by Me is Ecstasy.
Pure love is My medicine for all success.
Because of Me, you are free.
By being little, you become great.
Dawning days are ending, but hope is on the horizon.
Let My peace be your lullaby.
My colors of inspiration mix and blend in the hues of heaven.
Golden hues I offer you with blessings always anew."

The beauty of God is where we are and in who we are. There is always a Croagh Patrick among the mountains, always a higher peak for us to seek. We will, we shall, and we must persevere in reaching this higher peak.

The Elevated Highway

For I am certain of this: neither death nor life, no angel, no prince, nothing that exists, nothing still to come, nor any power, or height or depth, nor any created thing, can ever come between us and the love of God made visible in Christ Jesus our Lord. (Romans 8:38–39, Jerusalem)

I had a vision of myself walking along an elevated highway. When I walked forward, I noticed people on both sides of the highway. They were not elevated and their eyes were level with the road.

There were many problems amongst the people, but I knew nothing could hurt me. Even death could not harm me. I knew in my heart that as long as I was walking towards the Lord, I had nothing to fear.

I often get the dictionary out to see what the different definitions are for words. Many times these actions work like a springboard. They send me forth into the insight or lesson, where the Lord is teaching or leading me.

The word elevated means to lift; rise; improve; promote or rise in rank or position; cheer the spirits of, sublime, lofty in character, purify that which produces a feeling of awe, reverence, or the like or causes a sense of grandeur, power or magnitude.

From this vision and insights, we knew the Lord was telling us to walk straight ahead. Do not let the problems around us draw us away from the direction He is leading us.

I asked the Lord in prayer, what the elevated highway meant. I felt He was saying it was the highway of faith, hope and love. He wants us to be strong enough in His love to be able to come above the problems of today. He was not saying we were above others, but He was saying He wanted our attention on the spiritual life. Our attention on faith, hope and love can give us the peace and love that we need in today's problems and issues.

They do not belong to the world any more than I belong to the world. (John 17:16, Jerusalem)

The spiritual life is for everyone to see and take part in, if they would only choose this life. This walk with the Lord is for everyone, but not everyone will choose it.

The Lord is encouraging us to go forward in His graces. He wants us to rise above the problems of everyday life. We were on a retreat when the Lord used the large tree behind the cottage to teach us a lesson. The message was to stay close to the trunk (Christ). We cannot climb the tree of life while out on the limb. The limb will give way under your weight, the weight of issues and problems. If we are close to the trunk, we can climb the spiritual tree.

He is going to help us grow in faith, hope and love. Each day we have to battle with the negativity that is around us. The Lord is saying, "Do not lose hope."

This vision is a vision of hope and is the vision the Lord has for us this day. The elevated highway is the highway of faith, hope and love.

March 1

Squirrel

The Lord, using many of the everyday situations around us, teaches us about His love and presence amongst us. He makes us aware of a deeper relationship with Him, where He is the center of our life. He draws us away from the comforts, supports and distractions that lead us away from this deeper relationship.

We are not usually aware of these things unless they are pointed out to us in some way. This is where the squirrel enters into our walk with the Lord. We were without a telephone for a week. During this week, we felt the Lord was telling us to draw back, be quiet and listen to Him. The telephone being out for a week made us very conscious that the Lord was speaking to us.

We watched a squirrel every day. It would run and scamper across our patio. It carried nuts, one at a time, in preparation for the winter months. The Lord was showing us how we were like the squirrel that runs and scampers from this to that. He pointed out the habit and unneeded use of the telephone.

The problems with the telephone lines turned out to be a problem with the squirrels. They had been chewing on the lines, near the city, affecting our lines, three to four miles out from the city. It was a very interesting experience. The lesson from the Lord was about our escaping or scampering from the healing needed in our own lives. The telephone, in this lesson, was a distraction from this healing.

We became conscious of not talking on the telephone. The Lord intended us to be off the telephone much more than we first had in mind. A couple of weeks went by. Then the Lord reminded us again, in a big way, about the over use of the telephone and other distractions.

I looked out a window in the back of the house. I saw a squirrel, coming around the corner of the house with two big nuts in its mouth. It looked like it had swallowed the whole headpiece of the telephone, both the speaker and earphone. It was very funny to see. Was this a lesson? Yes indeed! It was very clear at this point. The Lord wanted us off the telephone and in a quiet place with Him. O Lord, You are funny in getting Your point across. Your message is clear and to the point.

March 2

Forget Not the Keys

I sit in my wheelchair and look out all day.
I hear laughter from voices not far away.
I sit in my wheelchair and look out all day.
For all I want is to walk again some day.
I have books and toys, and many games
Ice skates, roller skates and even toy trains
From all these things I do refrain
All I want is to walk again.
Although I cannot fall on my knees
I pray to God for I know that He sees
I ask Him to forget not the keys
The keys that open the lock on my knees.

March 3

I Hear the Wind Coming

I hear the wind coming, the wind of the Holy Spirit.

"I am going to unite more than ideas, more than what are your wishes
more than your logistics, more than all the plans coming forth
I am going to unite your hearts. I am going to bring down barriers
I am going to do it. I am going to bring about this unity of hearts."

"You will know more about My presence that is within you
My presence within each of you is the unifying factor
The combination of all the graces makes a firm
foundation and a strong support for any project."

"I am touching you in ways that you will never
expect for it is the ways of My heart.
I am going to stir up the areas in your own heart that need healing
in order for My unity to come about from this endeavor."

"Remember I have placed the seed for unity in your hearts.
I will use it to bring about unity in the hearts of all of My people.
You are My people."

March 4

Just Because I Love You

"The light of each new day
returns in the sunrise.
The evening sunset
is in a beautiful array of colors.
The darkness of night covers the land for the night's rest.
The stars shine at night and twinkle bright—
Just because I love you!"

"Winter is cold and leaves a covering of snow that
blankets the earth for spring's nourishment.

The snow capped mountains and evergreen trees
reach up in unspoken expression—
Just because I love you!"

"Spring brings forth new life in nature's view.
The melting snow fills the riverbeds.
The rivers empty into the ocean waters—
Just because I love you!"

"Summer days and summer nights carry the
soft gentle breeze of My love.
Forests rich with green hold up nature's arms.
Oceans shores with sandy beaches are for
your enjoyment and inspiration—
Just because I love you!"

"Autumn leaves glitter with a mixture of color.
Prayer, poems, inspirations and experiences come forth in your heart—
Just because I love you!"

"Love for and by your loved ones is a part of your everyday life.
Wherever you go and whatever you do I am beside you—
Just because I love you!"
"Your physical and spiritual needs are before you in abundance.

Your deepest desires, hopes and dreams fill
My heart, just because I love you!
From the horizons edge come glimpses of My spiritual walk with you—
Just because I love you! Rest in these words
of truth—Just because I love you!"

March 5

Prayers Heard in Heaven

"In this time of confusion I have called you to this ministry.
Things might be a blur until you have sorted
them out. After that, they will be clear.

You will be able to deal with the things thrown at
you, if you remember Me instead of yourself."

"My Beloved children, do not be despondent.
You must be strong in these times.
There will be things that will test you. You must be strong in the word.
You will have to read the Bible and get familiar with
the passages. This does not mean to memorize.
Your prayers, heard in heaven, fill the heavens with joy."

"I love you very much. I am sure you will do well, always.
The gifts I have given you in the past have been minor gifts
compared to what I will be giving you in the future.
You will receive many blessings and yes there is going to be a miracle."

March 6

Shelter of My Heart

"I am the shelter of your hearts. Love is flowing from My shelter.
I am the shelter where all love comes forth. Place
your mind, body and spirit in My shelter.
Shelter your heart in My heart.
Come unto Jesus. Give Him your life today. Let Him have His way.
Each day, place your minds, hearts and body
in the shelter of His heart."

March 7

German Shepherd

If we are unfaithful, he remains faithful, for he
cannot deny himself. (2 Timothy 2:13)

I went to a retreat at the North American Martyr's
Shrine. While there, I took a walk with two friends to the ravine. There
is a beautiful clearing in the center of this ravine. We stood for a long

time in this clearing. When we were standing there, a large German shepherd came out of the bushes from where he was sitting.

After studying us with his hair and ears standing up, he walked toward us. He was cautious and alert to danger. All of a sudden, he cowered down and his ears dropped. My friends were afraid of him, but for some reason I was not. When I encouraged him to come to me, his confidence picked right up. Once I touched him, he became very playful and trusting. He followed us for the rest of the walk, even going back to the retreat house with us.

I felt the Lord was telling us that the German shepherd is a strong dog. Yet, not being sure of the situation, cowered down. We are like that dog in our walk towards the Lord. How long will we sit in the opening or on the sidelines before we decide to go forward?

Although, we cannot see all, we have to change and trust. We have to come out of the doorway or from between the bushes. We have to trust, as we go forward with all senses alert and cautious to the unknown.

We may fear and cower, but we must trust and continue our journey always walking forward like the dog.

When we begin to experience the Lord, through the many blessings and graces He gives us, we become encouraged and continue forward. I had encouraged the dog to come to me. He trusted me and became very happy doing so. We will experience this same joy and happiness when we trust in the Lord. We must trust and listen to the ways that He encourages us to walk forward.

Once, we fully trust in the faithfulness of the Lord, we will become like a little child. We will then respond to a life of love. Jesus will walk with us right into the arms of the Father. Just like the German shepherd, that walked us back to the retreat house.

A German shepherd is a dog known for his protection, strength and power. Jesus is the German shepherd in our lives. He is the strength, protection and power we need in our lives. The prayer of faith is going forward, trusting in the faithfulness of the Lord.

March 8

In His Arms

In the arms of trees, birds gather to nest.
In the arms of God, we too seek our rest.
Like the birds that are happy, and sing out with glee,
So we too one day, will abide in His Unity Tree.
This tree of life will ever be
A source of food for you and me
Never more shall we hunger or thirst
By its fruits, we will be divinely nursed.
He made both, you and me,
To be loved by the Father for all of Eternity.
Thank you Father, Spirit and Son,
Through you, our redemption was won.
We now wait for that glorious day,
When Angels will guide us and show us the way.
To Your kingdom up on high,
Joy awaits us, never to die.

March 9

Do not Miss My Visitation

Beloved, I urge you as aliens and sojourners to keep away from worldly desires that wage war against the soul. Maintain good conduct among the Gentiles, so that if they speak of you as evildoers, they may observe your good works and glorify God on the day of visitation. (1 Peter 2:11–12)

"In Churches, groups of people will be touched.
The cleanup is going to be costly.
They will mirror My presence.
My will be done. Healing will occur.
My people will return to Me.

I am going to turn things upside down and
downside up with My very presence.
I am going to shake My people until they are awake and aware."

"I am no longer going to watch the destruction of humanity.
What I have created was good and it will return to this goodness.
Let no man think that he is more than the creator is.
Heard, seen and felt, I will come, before man can destroy himself."

"Be alert! Be alert! Do not miss My visitation!
I am no longer going to be silent. You will hear Me. You will see Me.
You will feel Me. Keep a listening ear, a clear vision
and an open heart and you will not miss Me.
I will be the one to feed your hunger and
give living waters for your thirst."

"You are Mine. Do you hear Me? You are Mine.
I am touching your heart, mind and very spirit with My Holy Spirit.
This touch will be with fire and the fire will burn
My mark deeper into your very soul.
You are never again, going to desire another person, place or
thing until it passes through My Divine will for you."

"The fire will burn off the residue of where man has
touched sin and where sin has touched man.
Man will become aware of My very presence.
I will be heard. I will be seen and I will be felt. I will! I will!
My presence will overshadow this heart.
My people will walk by causing miracles that are needed to heal.
All was created good. Creation will return to this goodness.
I Am, Who I Am!"

March 10

Praise Jesus

"For this reason they stand before God's throne and worship him
day and night in his temple. The one who sits on the throne will shelter

them. They will not hunger or thirst anymore, nor will the sun or any heat strike them. For the Lamb who is in the center of the throne will shepherd them and lead them to springs of life-giving water, and God will wipe away every tear from their eyes." (Revelations 7:15–17)

'After this I shall return and rebuild the fallen hut of David; from its ruins I shall rebuild it and raise it up again, so that the rest of humanity may seek out the Lord, even all the Gentiles on whom my name is invoked. Thus says the Lord who accomplishes these things, known from of old.'(Acts 15:16–18)

We must give praise where praise is due and that is to praise Jesus Christ.

He is going to restore all our attitudes, traits, our very character and ways of thinking that have been damaged by sin. He is going to heal us. Sin really deserves punishment, but because of Jesus Christ's death on the cross, we can enter into the very heart of God. We receive forgiveness and are adopted sons and daughters. We are to enter into the presence of God in submission.

A great price was paid. We must praise Jesus for He has given us protection and a way to reach the Father.

He has paid the price for our entrance into the holy of holies. All of God's people will turn back to Him. All will flow as little streams toward the larger one. This is in the very presence of God the Father.

March 11

Taking up Residence

Then the Lord will guide you always and give you plenty even on the parched land. He will renew your strength, and you shall be like a watered garden, like a spring whose water never fails. (Isaiah 58:11)

Prophetic words can grow in His presence. This presence of the Lord will keep evil away. Evil will know it quickly and will have to move away. The presence of God within us will spread and grow. He is going to take up residence, not just a visitor at times. His words, with no interference and when not even spoken, can go forth in clarity and understanding.

He places His words in our hearts and minds. There are different methods of understanding His words, but in the end they all mean the same. He wants the keys to His kingdom within us. His words can flow when our thoughts are free. He says, "Make time for Me everyday, I have a lot to say."

Yes Lord, Yes Lord, Yes Lord.

We are gluttons for the Lord and incapable of being satisfied in any other way. He has placed a desire in our hearts for His presence that will be incapable of being satisfied. This will cause us to be living in His presence all the time and to such an extent that it will spill over to others. His kingdom, seen, heard and felt will flow throughout His people. This awareness of His presence is going to happen more and more often and very quickly.

March 12

Doorways to the Heart

"My love brings out love in others. Joy is the cement that binds.
Your eyes are doorways to the heart. You are all growing
like a flower with different shapes, sizes and colors.
Each gift that comes forth in you, blending together with My
glorious colors, will radiate in My garden of beautiful flowers.
The different color or scent each one has is to identify one
from the other. All are very pleasing to My senses."

March 13

Tracks in the Snow

As I look across the beautiful
field of white snow
Tracks of grandchildren go
back and forth in a row
Children, birds, dog, and rabbit alike—
Left their mark of soft delight.
Snowmobile tracks are there to blend

The moments together, the Lord did send.
Tracks will cross from my house to yours
As love and laughter, open doors.
Into our lives, the tracks well placed
We received His love and extending grace
Each track in the snow left a footprint on our heart
Here someone special walked, never to depart.
There is a blessing in this pleasant sight
God has filled each new day with sparkling sunlight
His joy and peace, glistens off the snow for all to see
How great is His love for you and me.

March 14

What Now My Lord?

What now My Lord, I ask of thee,
What path or road will it be?
Please let me know so I may see,
The one to take that pleases thee.
In hills and valleys, mountains too,
I find my peace because of you.
I look for these times to get away,
To be with you, be it just for a day.
You have led me to places I have not known,
Planting within me, seeds to be sown.
Seeds of Love, watered by Your Holy Spirit, come from above,
Coming down gracefully, carried by a Dove.

March 15

Getting Rid of Our Tin Suit

The disciples approached him and said, "Why do you speak to them in parables?"

He said to them in reply, "Because knowledge of the mysteries of the kingdom of

Heaven has been granted to you, but to them it has not been granted." (Matthew 13:10–11)

Words received: "You are going to see clearly! You are going to see clearly!"

But blessed are your eyes because they see, and blest are your ears because they hear. Amen, I say to you, many prophets and righteous people longed to see what you see but did not see it, to hear what you hear but did not hear it. (Matthew 13:16–17)

I pictured a tin man. I kept thinking of a man with pins in all of his joints and in all of his senses, his ears, eyes, touch, smell and taste. The Lord is taking out the pins in all of these things. We are going to be getting rid of our tin suit. The veil that closed around us closed after sin occurred. Nothing in us or around us functioned in union with God when sin occurred. A veil came between God and us. Hence, we received our tin suit, with all of its little pins in the joints and senses. The Lord is removing the veils (pins) placed over our senses. Man will move freely in all of his senses and movements.

March 16

Mechanical Toy

I began to think of a little toy moving in mechanical jerks. Then the little toy began to move freely about. Tied down to earth's heavy desires, we also move about in mechanical jerks. The Lord wants us to be free in Him and move about in that freedom. All our senses are being restricted while we move about in mechanical jerks. The Lord is clearing away all restrictions and we will go beyond the veil and enter into the reign of God.

The Lord says, "You will hear clearly. You will see clearly. You will speak clearly. You will touch clearly. You will smell clearly. You will move clearly in the presence of the Lord."

Before original sin all our senses were in tune with the Lord. Sin put restrictions on every aspect of our life and our senses were no longer free in the Lord to operate. The Lord is bringing everything back to the right order, even our senses.

No more pins in our eyes, our ears, our smell, our touch or our taste. No more pins in our joints. When you enter into the reign of God, you enter into the spiritual realm and our human nature has to stay out. The Lord will use the one to reach the other. He will use the natural to reach the spiritual and the spiritual to touch and heal the natural.

Everything will come together in a right relationship with God. The spiritual senses are the internal senses and the natural senses are the external senses. Sin was the dividing line or veil between the spiritual and natural.

The tin man in the story of *The Wizard of Oz* only wanted a heart. In addition, he needed to have oil to function. Our hearts turned into hearts of flesh instead of stone need the oil of the Holy Spirit in order to function.

March 17

Faith Held High

> "Faith held high is faith, no doubt.
> Hope held high is hope, held out.
> Love held high is love, circled anew.
> Unity of all is sifted through.
> I sprinkle you with the blood and water of
> life that flows from My heart."

March 18

Melodies of Love

"Melodies of love, sincere and true, coming from the heart, are prayer to You."

A Precious Jewel

"Behold, I stand at the door and knock. If anyone hears my voice and opens the door, (then) I will enter his house and dine with him, and he with me." (Revelation 3:20)

The first time we turned to the Lord knocking at the door of our hearts was through a time of suffering. At the time of my Mother's illness and death, our first door opened. We became aware of the healing power and presence of Jesus in our lives. It was the beginning of a new life.

When my Mother was two years old, she inhaled a weed. The weed lodged in the opening of one lung, making her ill all of her life. Medical procedures today can show functions and damage to the lungs. These procedures were not available when she was a child. Therefore, she lost the use of this lung throughout the years. The lung was eventually taken out, but she had to remain under doctor's care.

On December 1, 1980, she went into the hospital. This turned out to be several weeks of suffering for both her and us. Through this suffering, we realized there was another life—a life other than the one lived on the surface with the materialistic world and us as the center.

January 1, 1981, searching for God's help, we went to our first prayer group meeting. The meeting was our introduction to the Charismatic Renewal. We allowed the doors of our hearts to be open to God's healing love and action. Just six weeks later, we received the Baptism in the Holy Spirit. We began to see the presence of Jesus in our lives.

My Mother was home from the hospital with us for a month before she went in again for the last time. Each member of our family spent a precious time of healing with her.

She went home to God the Father on the feast of St. Joseph, March 19, 1981. She had a strong faith and often interceded in prayer for our family to St. Joseph. During her last hours, she said she was going home. She was not referring to the earthly home. Her reference was home to God the Father.

Mother was a precious jewel and had a faith that only grew through her seventy-two years of life. Her life, like our own, was a mixture of suffering and joys. She dealt with the struggles of a chronic illness and the sorrow of losing her husband at an early age. She suffered when her children suffered. Her family was her life and she was joyful when they were healthy and happy. Her love and prayers remain behind her as she still holds her family together in love. Our Mother was a "Precious Jewel!"

We wished we had been open to the Lord and the Holy Spirit earlier in our life. We now can look back and see how He was always present in our lives. Our faith grew and was what we needed at the time. We have to open our hearts and minds to His presence. This will happen when we are ready and the Lord wills it for us. Since these first experiences, many doors have opened and closed in our journey with the Lord.

March 20

Just a Small Speck

While in prayer one morning, I experienced the vastness of God all around and myself being very little. I was only a small part of this vastness. I then thought of a circle with just a small speck in one part of it. I noticed a small speck of paper on the glass top table and understood this vastness more clearly.

We feel lost, small in the vastness of God, and that we are far from God. Because we are small in this vastness, God easily sees us. He breaks through to us. We have our whole being in God. We live and breathe in God.

I realized again, that my joy is in the revelations of God. When God breaks into my humanness and I know His presence, this is the joy of my heart.

March 21

Spirit of Joy

"I breathe upon you joy and peace. I walk amongst
you in the mist, I touch, and I kiss.

You know not when I come, but there I will always be.
Every hope held out, answered so gracefully."

I had a vision of the faces of children. All were different. Some were laughing and some were crying. The faces kept coming and going. I had another vision of a waterfall. I could see through it and Jesus was in the waterfall. Living waters were flowing over the falls. I knew an angel was present and walking about peppering each person with graces.

I then heard the words: "Be one with Me, and you will see what I have meant of thee. I ask so little. Everything, all your happenings, must flow through God. When did I visit you? Belittle not one another, but encourage one another."

March 22

Remember, There is Always Prayer

When all else is said and done and you feel all alone as one,
Remember, there is always prayer.
At times, you may not have all that you would
like and things seem unreachable to you,
Remember, there is always prayer.
You may be sad because of a loss and don't know where to turn,
Remember there is always prayer.
You need a new infilling, of what you ask.
What will give you what you are looking for?
Remember, there is always prayer.
Loneliness takes its toll on a person, who has no one to turn too,
Remember there is always prayer.

March 23

Kaleidoscope of Crutches

A Kaleidoscope is an optical instrument, which exhibits an endless variety of colored figures.

Crutches...a staff with a cross piece used by an injured person that needs support to get around.

Our own will can be a crutch. It stands in the way of doing God's will. We can continue to lean on our own will or we can submit it to the will of the Father. He will bring our will into a time of purification. The fragrances of color and figures will come forth from this purification. You will be in a state of being preternatural. This meaning, experiences will be out of the usual course of nature and considered as abnormal and uncommon.

There can be powerful results from being on crutches and going through purification with the Lord as leader who shakes the Kaleidoscope forming the colors and figures. Like the beautiful forms and colors in the Kaleidoscope, there is beauty in our weakness. Broken, wounded and limping towards the Lord we can join our suffering to the suffering of Jesus.

There is security in your relationship with the Lord when you give your will to Him.

March 24

Refuge in the Arms of God

If anyone thinks he is religious and does not bridle his tongue but deceives his heart, his religion is vain. Religion that is pure and undefiled before God the Father is this: to care for orphans and widows in their affliction and to keep oneself unstained by the world. (James 1:26–27)

The Lord has shaken us up out of a religious stupor, on how things should go.

The depth of the soul flows in the stream of living waters.

The light of Christ shines through the diamond in your heart.

Jesus is the child of your heart.

He abides in you, as He abides in me.

Be aware of His presence with you always.

Listen to Him. Speak Lord for Your servant is listening.

Scripture: "God is our refuge and our strength, an ever-present help in distress." (Psalms 46:2)

March 25

I Was Here Before

When we truly enter into the presence of God we are going
to see that everything is familiar ... I was here before!
We will hear: "Beloved of My beloved! Let no
block come between Me and My children."

March 26

The Glitter of His Love and Gifts

The desert you cross with a pack on your back
will lead you to the Christ Child.
He will take the burdens in this pack and free you
to cross the desert again with new life.
He will deck you out with the glitter of His love and gifts.
Like the watchman on the wall, you will say, "I have
a better view with a better understanding."

March 27

My Rainbow Will Cover All

"The day comes soon.
I shall appear.
Dark will turn to light.
Fire will be upon the earth.
The horseman will ride no more.
Peace and love will flow like endless waters.
My rainbow will cover all."

83

March 28

Vision through the Lens

I had a vision of us holding up a lens. It was very cloudy. I knew that the lens was not clear in fact, it was very dark. I knew we were lifting it up to the Lord.

"Lifting up our blindness to our faults," were words that stood out as I was reading a book. I began to understand the vision of the cloudy lens after reading these words.

We were lifting up our blindness to our faults. We tend to confess the outward and do not confess the subtle things like bad habits, attitudes and deep things within the heart and mind.

March 29

Spiritual Tug of War

"The closer you come the harder it gets. You have entered
into a spiritual tug of war, where evil is against mercy.
Persevere in prayer; the predator's powers soon will be no more.
Once you stop looking at how hard it is, you
can then look at what it really is.
Accept things and seek out what they can really be.
Come, let Me take you inside, let Me take you into My heart."

We have received giving and receiving hands. We keep gifts given to us instead of returning them to the Lord. Our life, children, writings, and ministries are some examples of these gifts. The Lord wants us to return these gifts to Him.

March 30

Listen to the Whispers of the Heart

We need to listen to the whispers of the heart. They carry areas that need healing. The Lord uses the human senses to put us in touch with

His very heart as He draws us close to Him. The Lord says, "Be aware of the mind that muses the wounds of the heart."

March 31

Soaked in the Word

And take the helmet of salvation and the sword of the Spirit, which is the word of God. (Ephesians 6:17)

Keep silence before me, O coastlands; you peoples, wait for my words! (Isaiah 41:1)

The winter of 1993–1994 was a very difficult winter for the whole Northeast. We had unusual amounts of cold, snow and ice to cope with during this winter. Our homes damaged more than usual, added to the burden of bad travel and winter conditions.

We could see large amounts of snow building up on the roof. Doing as much as we could possibly do, we shoveled snow off the roof. When the snow continued to fall, we knew that it was getting to be heavy for the roof. It was too much for us to handle so we called our insurance company. They sent people to shovel the heavy snow off the roof, protecting both our property and us.

The build up of ice became another problem. The cold and large amounts of snow on the roof caused ice to build up along the edge of the roof. When the ice backed up two to three feet, it caused damage inside and outside the house.

We were fortunate that our damage was small. Many others had a lot of damage. We had weather stripping replaced, but only a small roof section needed repairs. Ice had melted along the walls inside the house, but the water stains only blended in with the wood. It would have been a big job to tear down the wood to put new insulation behind the walls, and removing the wood and insulation would have caused more damage than the stains so we decided to let the wood remain with the stains.

One evening, after returning from a prayer meeting, I sat at our kitchen table reading the Bible. I did not have anything to eat or drink, while sitting there. I went to bed after reading the Bible and left it on the table open to Isaiah 41.

Charles went downstairs in the morning and looked at my Bible on the table. It looked like coffee had soaked through many pages of the Bible. He could not understand why I went to bed leaving the Bible soaking wet. When I came down and saw the Bible, I thought Charles had spilled coffee on it.

Both of us, surprised to see the Bible so wet, looked at the ceiling and light above the Bible. The ceiling was dry. The chair and floor had a little water on them. We could not figure out how the ceiling and light remained dry and free from stain.

Brown colored water sprayed the table along side of the Bible. It was in the shape of a sword. We began to understand a very clear message from this experience. The Lord wanted us soaked in the Word of God.

A couple of days later, while sitting at my desk, I could hear water dripping. I looked at the window and saw water dripping in from the ice melting on the roof. I began to wonder if this had anything to do with the Bible getting wet. This room was not over the kitchen. The table and Bible were in the center of the kitchen located under our bedroom.

There were a couple of nights during this bad weather that we heard the house crack from the cold. They were very loud cracks. We concluded that the Bible had gotten soaked from the backup of ice. Somehow, the water had run across the ceiling above the room, down the light chain, soaking the Bible below. There were no marks on the ceiling, or chain, and the Bible took weeks to dry out.

The important message from all of this was the Lord telling us to soak up and absorb the Word of God. He also wants us to be soaked in and absorbed by the wisdom in the Scriptures. He not only wants us to read His written word, but He wants us to wait for His words to us.

The Lord speaks to us in whatever way He can get our attention. In this experience, it was speaking to us through the melting ice on the Holy Bible.

Sitting on the Edge of Heaven

He has his rising on the edge of heaven, the
end of his course is its furthest edge,
And nothing can escape his heat.
(Psalms 19:6, Jerusalem)
I have always been a dreamer
The reason I know not why
I sought for things beyond my reach
Like reaching for the sky
I have been a sinner throughout my life
From this, I cannot hide
I ask God for forgiveness
And within me to reside
If only I can make it
One day I prayed aloud
Just to sit on the edge of heaven
With my feet hanging from a cloud
What heavenly bliss one must feel
To reach that final goal
And to know it is no dream it is for real
Being a pure unblemished soul
And so I dream I too will be
One day with My Lord
I ask a place be saved for me
A spot I can afford
I do not expect the greatest
And all I ask of thee
Is to sit on the edge of heaven
This will be reward enough for me

April 2

X-Rays Tell It All

We are afflicted in every way, but not constrained; perplexed, but not driven to despair; persecuted, but not abandoned; struck down, but not destroyed; always carrying about in the body the dying of Jesus, so that the life of Jesus may also be manifested in our body. (2 Corinthians 4:8–10)

I had X-rays taken of my chest and forgot to take off my cross. When I took the X-rays home, I noticed the cross. It stood out very clearly in the X-rays.

Then I received the following words: "We carry the birth, life, death and resurrection within each one of us."

April 3

Nothing was Really Something

We looked into the living room and became very aware of God in the stillness. We could see nothing in this stillness, but realized that "nothing was really something."

On another occasion when Charles and I hugged each other, we each felt that we almost went right through each other. Responding to this experience and feeling, we became aware of God's presence within us and how He was speaking to us. This was of a supernatural origin.

Time can lessen these experiences if we do not keep them in a safe place. The heart is the safest place to keep them, writing them down helps us to keep them in our minds.

April 4

Stitches in the Air

Unity is very important. True unity within groups of people will help stitch garments together that complement the group and one another.

Where there is unity, a stitching together comes about. If all the stitching is on the one side of a garment, it will not hold together. It is like putting stitches in the air. There is nothing there to keep them together and nothing holds or supports them. Unity will go in and out of the fabric of our whole being if we let the Lord be the thread that sews everything together in His love and grace.

April 5

Broken Jug

But we hold this treasure in earthen vessels that the surpassing power may be of God and not from us. (2 Corinthians 4:7)

But grace was given to each of us according to the measure of Christ's gift. Therefore, it says; "He ascended on high and took prisoners captive; he gave gifts to men." (Ephesians 4:7–8)

Anne had a vision of a dove resting on the top edge of a jug. The Lord helped us to understand that the jug represented us. We are a container made to hold His measure of faith. The Dove on the top edge of the jug was the Holy Spirit.

In the vision there was no handle on the jug. Jesus was saying that He molded the jug without a handle. Man has put a handle on the jug trying to control the measure of the Holy Spirit. We hold the measure given to us in the jug. The Lord controls the amount in the measure. He gives out gifts of the Holy Spirit. The dove is the spout on the jug, pouring forth different gifts meant to draw us up into the higher levels of spirituality.

This vision reminded us of a Revival Service that we went to in Winthrop, Massachusetts. A young man got up to play in the music ministry using a broken jug. It was amazing how he was able to contribute to the music through that empty broken jug.

The Lord says that He is the Potter and we are the clay. We may be broken, but He can still get music out of our broken sinful hearts. He can hear a melodious sound that we cannot hear. We do not have to have everything figured out. All we must do is to remember, unless we are broken, we will not have a contrite heart. With only a small measure of faith, the Lord can still use us. We are the instruments that He uses. He is continuously transforming us into His image. The Holy Spirit guides and transforms this earthen vessel.

April 6

The Solitude of God

You send forth springs into the watercourses that wind among the mountains, And give drink to every beast of the field, till the wild asses quench their thirst. (Psalms 104:10–11)

One day at work I looked up at the calendar on the wall. The picture I saw was of a waterfall. Water was flowing over the mountains into peaceful waters below. There were two deer standing next to the water.

These words came to me: "The living waters of the Lord run from the Mountains down into the valley bringing new life and refreshment." I then knew the Lord was telling us that the soul yearns for God.

April 7

Freshly Dipped in Gold

"You are being freshly dipped in Gold, the gold of a new anointing.
You have been dipped into new life.
Expect an Easter Resurrection to happen to My people."

Freshly dipped into the movement of the Holy Spirit, we received our Easter gift from the Lord. Our Easter Resurrection is to expect to enter into the Glory of God and Eternal Life. The resurrection of Jesus Christ not only meant that He arose from the dead, but He entered into the Glory of the Father and Eternal life. He opened the passageway for us to be able to enter in also.

While in this physical life, we can enter into the spiritual life of the Resurrection. This is for us to experience while here on earth. "Our Father ... Thy Kingdom Come, Thy will be done on earth, as it is in heaven."

Words received: "You are being dipped in the heavenly juices of life and nourishment, which has been given to you through the Resurrection of Jesus Christ."

April 8
Vein of Controversy

We have found if we stay in controversy, it stifles our growth in God and wastes precious time. We used to run into this in our Prison Ministry. While the opposition kept us in controversy our own growth was at a stand still. We will always remember our Spiritual Director in the Prison Ministry saying to the residents, "If you are not part of the solution, you are part of the problem."

We found we could no longer justify staying in controversy. Controversy keeps anger, resentment, comments and judgments about others going. We as human beings can justify just about anything we want to do or not do. We have learned, through the grace of God, that we must do what we can do in any situation to improve that situation. We then must shake the dust from our feet, and go on in our relationship with the Lord.

Controversies keep a person in the vein of judging others. Although very subtle, anger and resentment lie heavily on their backs. We realized we could no longer continue in this vein of sharing our lives. The continuous talk about the controversies in the Church lay heavy on our hearts.

This realization has cost us much, and we hope it has been in getting rid of self. The Lord has shown us very clearly that we cannot judge another. One good reason is their experiences in life may differ from our own. We finally understood the biggest lesson. When we judge, we are actually saying that God is not present to others. God is present to each person. If we do not believe this, then we are saying God does not, will not, and is not working in another person's life. We then can appear to be very unstable ourselves.

We have to remember there is a treasured pearl in the heart. The inner relationship with God is the "Pearl of Great Price."

April 9

Overcome or be Overcome

When we finally listened to the Lord, the Lord gave us the grace to overcome. The words that came to me were overcome or be overcome. We can stay a long time in controversy. We have found that the biggest sins of today are pride and disobedience. That is where controversy keeps us.

We can only share out of our witness and experience that each of us has with the Lord.

A voice cries out: in the desert, prepare a way for the Lord! Make straight in the wasteland a highway for our God! (Isaiah 40:3)

For he is our peace, he who made both one and broke down the dividing wall of enmity, through his flesh. (Ephesians 2:14)

Words received: "Truth does not have to be defended. Truth defends itself."

Our relationship with the Lord does not depend on our opinion about issues. It is all about our relationship with Jesus Christ. We have had many opportunities to stand for what we believe on issues. Arguing accomplishes nothing. Lately, instead of noticing where we differ on issues, we have found ourselves letting go. Sometimes to say nothing is better than saying anything at all.

And to man he said: Behold, the fear of the Lord is wisdom; and avoiding evil is understanding. (Job 28:28)

For me they listened and waited; they were silent for my counsel. (Job 29:21)

Come Out of the Maze

According to the dictionary, a maze is a place with intricate windings. It is difficult to find one's way in or out.

The maze in this example is the darkness of self-will, opinions, concepts, expectations, judgment, goals and the list goes on. We pulled back from controversies, judging and the battles of today. We then realized the Lord is the one in full control.

If we stay in the maze of self-proof, we will be hitting our head against a brick wall. Locked in this maze keeps us locked in the negative arenas of life. Spend only the time the Lord has allotted for this maze then move on to a much higher place. We have felt the Lord calling us away from this maze for quite sometime now. Every Christian must do what the Lord is calling one to do. A person must be ready to move out of these arenas and go on in their spiritual life.

We went through the problems existing in the church today and many other areas in our life. We did what we felt the Lord had called us to do at that time. We found the Lord removing us from the active arena of life. As long as we are alive, we will have one foot in the arenas of life. The Lord wants only a foot to be there, not a heart, not a mind. He wants them for himself.

Our life will be safe in the arms of Christ. Christ holds out His arms of unity and the mystical life. The Lord led us to a restful place with Him, where we could grow in our relationship with Him. It has taken us a long time to become restful in this place. The view we see now is from a different perspective. When not engrossed with the arena they are in, one can see differently. Looking in on a problem is much better than being in the center of the problem, all engrossed.

Dictionary: An arena is anyplace of public contest or sphere of action, as in the Roman amphitheater…

The maze (arena) has kept us in darkness. We place our eyes on the problems around us instead of the grace and mercy of God. We then lose sight of the Scriptures. They tell us of the power of God and the fear of

93

God in our hearts. The Scriptures draw us to unity and the mystical life. Where are you in this arena?

Words received: "The Lord has hollowed out the heart and soul, do not fill it again, with untruth."

April 11

Train Robbery

Finally, draw your strength from the Lord and from his mighty power. Put on the Armor of God so that you may be able to stand firm against the tactics of the devil. (Ephesians 6:10–11)

While in the Holy Angels Chapel in Lourdes, France, I heard the words: "What appears hard can turn out to be easy and what appears easy can turn out to be hard." These words had very profound meanings as things unfolded on this trip.

March 1988 dream: Charles and I were sitting at a counter in a room. It looked like a dining car on a train. We were waiting for a train or something. I saw people coming in through a door at the far end of the room. I knew evil was also entering. I hid my diamond ring under papers that were under the counter.

One person came up to me and her presence was strong. She had a drawing feeling, but I still had very strong feelings that there was evil present. Although she appeared good, I claimed the protection of the armor of God. Another person came up to me and asked how I managed to stay away from this person. I said that I had claimed the armor of God for protection.

A month later, we went on a sixteen-day Marian Year pilgrimage. During this pilgrimage, we stopped at the Shrine of Our Lady of Lourdes in Lourdes, France. We had gone there after Fatima, Portugal. From Lourdes, we would go to Rome, Italy.

While we were in Portugal we found out there was going to be problems with the train. A woman in our group began to make a fuss about the long train ride we would have from Lourdes, France, to Rome, Italy. This same woman made many complaints during our trip. She had a noticeable anger. Off and on, we would have to struggle with this anger and complaining.

The long train ride that we had to make from Lourdes to Rome was going to be all day and all night. We would be on the train for ten hours during the day, stopping for only two hours, and we would then be on the train again overnight. Six people and their entire luggage would be in one small sleeping compartment. The night before this trip, we began to get concerned about the long train ride.

Another woman, a new friend of the complainer, came around suggesting we get a plane to Paris. She said, "We could then get a train to Rome." I was seriously thinking of making the change. Charles said, "Do not let the lady influence you."

We were walking to the St. Michael's Chapel in Lourdes, when I passed our Spiritual Director. He said he thought everything was going to work out. There would be adjustments made on the train for anyone that wanted to switch from a sleeper car to seats, if that was what we wanted.

As soon as I walked into the St. Michael Chapel, I saw that all of this was a temptation. It would not have been good to break away from the group and make last minute changes. These words came to me, "What looks like something easy could be hard. What looks hard is actually easy." Spiritually, the better way to go is the hard way, the way of the cross. Praise God!

The two women sat beside one another in the Chapel. The one was the complainer and the other had strong influence. Together they had tried to get others to transfer to a plane from Lourdes instead of a train.

I began to look at the two different personalities. With nothing hidden, the one person was very outspoken. One could see her as she was. The other was quiet, but tempting. The second could be much more dangerous. Satan comes as an angel of light. I finally concluded it would have been bad to separate from the group. Praise God for the protection of His angels and His quiet voice often spoken through others.

These same two women separated from the rest of the group at nighttime. They stayed in the seats while the rest of the group moved to sleeping cars. Six people and their entire luggage packed into one sleeping compartment. Even if they wanted to, no one else could get into the car. This turned out to be a much safer condition.

We felt this train experience was the unfolding of the above dream. The temptation was to change from the train to a plane. Separating from the main group would have been dangerous. It was much better staying with the group in the sleeper compartment.

We had the window in our car open to give us a little air, and one of the women in our car stopped a robber from coming in through our compartment window.

Falling asleep and riding all night in the seats became a difficult experience for the two women. The two women spent the next day in Rome in the Police station reporting the stolen money and passports. When the trains move along the French Riviera at night, the robbers get off and on the trains between stops.

By the end of our trip, we realized that the Lord had also blessed us by placing the two women with us. As time unfolded, the one became our interpreter in many difficult situations on trains, bus and planes.

We know that all things work for the good for those who love God, who are called according to his purpose. (Romans 8:28)

April 12

The Embrace of Love

"The embrace of love we receive in our life is only a preparation
for the divine embrace of God's love at our death.
The joy we have in sharing God's love with one another is only a
foretaste of the joy we will have in sharing the joy of the Lord forever.
Formed by the Word of God, we were made and
created from the dust of the earth."

April 13

Power of God

Pray in the spirit and secrets will be revealed.
Why have we forgotten about the power of God?
In the darkness, we have forgotten the power of God.

April 14

See How I Love You

"See how I love you, through one another.
I love you, I love you, and I love you.
When you touch one another, you touch Me.
When you hug one another, you hug Me.
When you love one another, you love Me."

April 15

In Quietness, I Am Heard

"In quietness I am heard; in love I am felt; in faith I
am seen. True sorrow is strength for the soul."

Do not get hung up on where you are with the Lord.
Rather ask the question, "Where should I be with the Lord?"

April 16

Aqueduct

Everywhere I turned from April of
1987 through late 1988, the Lord was
drawing my attention towards aqueducts.
This happened before our first trip to Europe in 1988, when we saw
many aqueducts, especially in Rome.

The aqueduct is a conduit built to carry water from one place to another. The materials used for aqueduct construction may be masonry, concrete, cast iron, steel, or wood. Aqueducts built of stone, brick or a mixture of limestone and volcanic dust filled the countryside in ancient times.

There are modern aqueducts still in use all over the world. The Catskill Aqueduct, for New York City, extends 120 miles. The Colorado Aqueduct, in southern California, carries water through 29 tunnels across the desert from the Colorado River. There is a 685 mile Aqueduct in California, and major aqueducts in Winnipeg, Canada, and Rio de Janeiro, Brazil.

When or where the first aqueduct originated is still a mystery. In ancient times, Jerusalem used a leaky aqueduct made of a series of limestone blocks. The Greeks built masonry conduits to bring water to their cities. Rome had many aqueducts and was the only ancient city reasonably supplied with water.

Romans were proud of the excellent water supply of the imperial city. Some of these aqueducts arched over with hewn stone were so large that in some parts hay wagons could drive straight through them. Nine aqueducts brought about 85 million gallons of water a day from mountain springs. Later, five additional aqueducts were built. About 200 cities in the Roman colonies had aqueducts. One famous Roman aqueduct, the Pont du Gard, still stands across a river near Nimes, France.

To this day water flows into Rome through aqueducts of one kind or another. By gravity alone and without the aid of pumping engines, copious streams conducted long distances despite the obstacles presented by mountains, valleys, or low-lying level plains.

Most of the good water near Rome leaves a calcareous deposit. Therefore, it is much easier to clean out large channels than an underground piping system. (Notes taken from A Day in Old Rome, page 302 and the Encyclopedia, page 580).

A very special friend told us what he remembered about aqueducts and water faucets in Rome. There can be as many as eight faucets in a residence to draw water. Depending on the kind of water one wants to use, these faucets have either very bad water or clear and very good water.

The messages and lessons we received from the Lord through aqueducts were powerful. What faucets were we drawing from, from the faucet of the Holy Spirit or from the faucets containing bad water?

Chemicals build up on the walls of the aqueduct, just like sin that builds up in our hearts. The Lord has been hallowing out our hearts taking out the stain from the chemical of sin. For many years, we have mixed non-truths into our lives. This is as bad as chemicals being added to pure water and as tightly as thread woven into fabric.

Words: "Some again, are filling their hearts with non-truths."

April 17

Little, O Little Me

We have to be humble in the eyes of the Lord, otherwise we see only ourselves in goodness or failure. Very often when we have to defend ourselves against hurts the self-will and self-love gains strength and sees the need to protect.

The Lord wants to heal the little child within. He says, "Sit down next to your little self-will and self-love. Tell yourself how much you love that little child that has had to defend itself with self-will and self-love. I love you, O little child, I love you. A house is not a house unless it is full of love. A heart is not a heart unless it is full of love."

April 18

Close to Your Heart

"My people keep My gifts close to your heart.
Let My mother be the window to your life with Me.
Let My saints by your guide to new life.
Protect and keep My truths close to your hearts."

April 19

Travel Light

"Let go of criticism. Let go of judging.
Do not take on other opinions. Do not judge in thought, word or deed.
Travel light headed. Travel light hearted. Travel light handed.
Keep your hand, head and hearts clean."

On the shuttle bus from the airport, I found myself caught in a group of people carrying big tuba instruments. It was overwhelming. The thoughts I received from this experience were:

We would not have irritations if we were evenly yoked with the Lord. We are walking uneven. We are trying to walk without Him. We are uneven in our thoughts, words and deeds because of our sinful nature.

We need healing in all areas of our senses, thoughts, words and deeds. We need healing in our body, mind and spirit and in our head, hearts, and hands. We look in a mirror and all we see is me, me and me. We do not see the true me with all imperfections, faults etc.

"You better measure up." Does that sound familiar? No matter who we are, a strong part of us has this ingrained in us. In our American culture, "we better measure up."

April 20

Cultivate the Heart

A recipe to "Cultivate the heart:"
The Ten Commandments are blueprints to live by.
The prayer of the heart will be to do God's will.
Love of the Trinity is truly learning to love.
The Lamb and the wolf will lie down together.
Humility is faith and faith is humility.
Humility is the door to understanding.
Understanding is seeing and living in the goodness of the Lord.
Be conscious of wrong, bad doing, not condemning.

Beautiful Path to the Resurrection

To walk down the path or road to Calvary is the same as the beautiful path to the resurrection. To walk the path of the passion is to see the risen Christ.

If we were to look at two paths side by side, one to Calvary and the other with trees and sunny, we would probably choose the sunny path with the beautiful trees. The Lord is saying we cannot go down the sunny path without walking at the same time on the path to Calvary. They are one in the same and run together.

At times this path will be rocky and dangerous, and at others it will be sunny and pleasant. No matter what the experiences are along this path, they will all come together in God's love. Both of these paths start and finish in the heart of God. Knowing this, you cannot lose no matter which path you choose for they both will come together in the end.

April 22

Reward is the Final Touch

"Tranquility is like a blanket keeping out the cold and unwanted.
Peace is the twin of love that lasts over all.
Freedom is like the bird of the air with nothing in its way to stop it.
It rides on the paths and air currents formed and controlled by God.
Destiny is the path each one of us chooses during his or her lifetime.
Reward is the final touch by Our Savior for a job well done."

April 23

You Can See the Stillness

Prayer: Lord let us see into Eternity. Let us hear with Your understanding and love with Your wisdom.

"You can see the stillness and the people on their way spiritually.
Do not neglect the word I may give to you one day.
Reflect on it and pray to understand what I have to say.
I want you both together now and through all Eternity."

April 24

The Soul Yearns for God

As a doe longs for running streams, so longs my
soul for you, my God. My soul thirsts for God, the
God of life; when shall I go to see the face of God?
(Psalms 42:1–2, Jerusalem)

Charles and I went to my cousin's home in the Pocono Mountains in
Pennsylvania. We went from there to a retreat at St. Joseph-in-the Hills
in Malvern, Pennsylvania.

I lay awake, most of Sunday night, listening to the deer walk through
the woods. They were going to the lake for water. I could not see them it
was so dark, but I could hear them. There was a constant rustling noise
through the trees all night. I had hopes of seeing them at daybreak, but
I could not. The noise stopped just before daybreak. I felt very strongly
that the Lord was speaking to us through this experience.

We left my cousin's on Monday morning for our retreat in Malvern.
This day was very hot. The grounds and retreat house were beautiful.

Early in the retreat, the Spiritual Director confirmed the Lord
was speaking to us the Sunday night before. She spoke these words on
Tuesday morning, "Hunger and thirst after the Lord, as the Hind thirsts
after running water. Panting after Him, get refreshed, get closer to Him,
and spend more time with Him."

These words reminded us of how I had heard the deer walking
through the darkness all night. They were thirsting for the lake waters.
Like the Hind or female deer, we must walk through the darkness to the
living waters. Trust that God is leading us closer and closer to Him.

April 25

I am Always With You

"You are all here because of Me, to be filled with My spirituality.
Reap the words that fall on you, sow a harvest true.
May you be love, may you be free, and may My
spiritual dove shine on all of thee.
So be open to My spirit, let no one turn you away.
The more you ask of Me in spirit, the stronger
you will be. I am with you always."

April 26

Full of Thoughts

The presence of God, heard in the stillness and solitude, is in and around us. Our minds are full of thoughts most all the time. We do not listen to the Lord or others when we have our minds full of thoughts. Our own concerns, problems, opinions, etc. keep us locked up in self-love that coaxes us along this path.

Busy as a beaver, the mind can be, full of hopes and dreams yet to see.

It is the stillness and solitude we seek, the presence of the Lord will keep us meek.

April 27

He Sits Alone

He sits alone, not on a majestic throne, but on one made of stone.
His head is bent, His eyes are sad, as if He
lost the best friend He has ever had.
Is that friend you or I? I pray Lord, let it not be.
I knowingly would never cause Him pain,
For with Him I have nothing to lose, but much to gain.

I try to move closer to Him seated on that boulder,
In hopes, He will put His arm around my shoulder.
He knows my thoughts and my desires; my
faults are always before Him,
Still He waits and never tires of my asking His forgiveness for my sins.

April 28

Abide in My Light

"Peace! Be still and know I am God.
I am the light in this world. Abide in My light.
I come into the world in rays of white for
purity and rays of red for forgiveness.
You must send My light into the hearts that have need of it.
Many have not given themselves to Me.
Be forgiving of them, as I am.
God's rays of glory are shining forth to cover all."

"You can overcome evil only with the grace that I give you.
Focus on Me always, not on others or
anything else. Remain in the light.
You will not be at loss for anything.
We can easily turn away from the light, towards the darkness.
It is like switching channels on TV."

"God closed the eyes of St. Rafka. She could only see the light of God.
God wants our eyes turned toward Him.
All walk through darkness at times.
One at a time, God lights candles to lighten our way."

April 29

In Anticipation

I sit in anticipation and wait, for someone to open that special gate

Revealing to me the road to follow, the grounds
of love are sacred and hollow.
One can rest assured, in this place—he is cured.
Of physical sickness and spiritual too, God's love
and anointing flows powerfully true.
All are welcome to come and see what God planned for you and me.
Joy and peace never to end, will guide you to angels He will send.
So praise His name night and day, to all you meet, fear not to say,
"Our God is calling you and me, to receive His gifts, they are all free."
These gifts come from a pure heart that has loved us all from the start.
They are straight from a heart that does not bend,
leading us to a life that does not end.

April 30

Baby Elephant

"Everyone who listens to these words of mine and acts on them will be like a wise man who built his house on rock. The rain fell, the floods came and the winds blew and buffeted the house. But it did not collapse; it had been set solidly on rock." (Matthew 7:24–25)

As you read the following dream, think of the elephant as the spirit of control. I had a dream of a baby elephant. The baby elephant followed Charles and me. We tried to get away from it, for we knew it would not be long before the mother elephant would come in pursuit of her baby.

We ran from the baby elephant knowing the mother would be close. No matter how we tried to get away from it, it kept following us. We saw a trailer and buildings a ways from us. The trailer was the closest, so we went into the trailer. After getting into the trailer, we noticed that the trailer was all glass and that there was a door at the other end.

We knew that we had to get out of the trailer. The mother elephant could easily tip the trailer over, and not only that, if she saw her image in the glass windows she would still go after the trailer. She would think she had to protect her baby from another elephant as well.

The baby elephant represented the slight and subtle touches of control. It is so cute, like any little baby animal would be, it would cause one to forget the mother elephant that would be close behind. The elephant's trunk represented the outreaching arm of control, whether with the baby or the mother.

The elephant being a very large animal stands for the power that is connected with control. Like a bull in a china shop, it can wreck anything in its way and will trample anything that tries to stop it.

We have had a couple of experiences in the past when we have seen evil run to protect evil. Therefore, the mother elephant is going to protect her baby; in this case, the big monster of control is going to protect all of the little monsters of control.

The glass trailer represented a false safety. A glass house built out of control, false truths, motives, or intentions will crumble to the ground under pressure. A friend attended a class on dreams and said that a trailer represented a place that was moveable and one may not be staying there for very long. It might be a short-term visit. A strong building with a firm foundation is the only safe and secure place found only with Jesus Christ as the center of our lives and hearts.

Through sharing this dream with our Spiritual Director, we were led away from a situation that could have brought our freedom in the Holy Spirit under the control of others. Even though it was a very enticing proposition presented to us, it was only another subtle means of control being presented. The shinning glitter of the baby elephant of control gave way to the truth found in the freedom of the Holy Spirit.

May 1

Trinity Tree

We went on a retreat to St. Rafka Retreat Center in Shelburne, Vermont. We were not familiar with the heating system in the house. Therefore, the first night we sat in front of the kitchen stove to keep warm. While sitting there we received words from the Lord.

"Fallen are they who sin, but I can help them to win.
Center, center I am in the center.
Because of me because of me,
My spirit will settle on you, all three."

While on this retreat, three of us sat in the rain under a tree by the lake. The trunk of the tree was divided into three huge trees. We called this our Trinity Tree. The Lord blessed us three-fold. We sat in the rain and watched the raindrops bounce off the lake, and our hearts began to fill with the presence of the Lord as He gave us words to remember.

"Trinity Tree is where you are, in the woods at
the lake in the house or at the gate.
My presence is in your heart. Let Me out!
Do not keep Me locked up.
Your mind blocks the free flow of this gift.
Doors will open, doors will close, but you
will know the one I have chosen.
The sadness you experience and the cry you
make to Me is the confinement
I experience in a suppressed love within your heart.
What you have experienced in the area of suppressing this
love is okay because you have been learning prudence."

"My spirit flows, My spirit glows, be ready to follow wherever it goes.
You may think you have been away from Me, but you
have been going through a period of purification.
Be still and know that I am God. I am with you always. Be not afraid.
Though darkness surrounds you, I am the light.
Keep your eyes on me."

"It takes pockets of time together to listen to My spirit.
You cannot stay away from these times and
expect to be full of My spirit.
My inspiration flows through the hearts of My people.
That is why I have given you each other.

As Mary spoke to Elizabeth, the child leapt in her
womb. Let My presence leap in you heart."

"Let nothing disturb you, all things are passing.
My grace is support for you. Keep open to Me.
Cast your cares on Me for I have care of you.
Peace, be to you."

"It takes only one light to start a stream of
light flowing into the hearts of many.
All lights lifted up, through one Easter candle,
through one light. Be My little light.
Do you see? Do you understand? How My light will never go out?
The darkness will not comprehend it. Darkness cannot see the light."

Do we walk in heavy shoes? Do we walk with heavy hearts and heavy
minds?

Let us slip into the comfortable shoes of the light of Christ. While
being led in the simplicity and guidance of the Holy Spirit, let us not be
tied down to the burdens of the heart and mind.

Our call today, is the simple way. Simplicity will break through
the darkness because of its reflection of Christ. Learned men did not
recognize Christ, the simple people recognized him. The same is true
today. He speaks when we are quiet and His light will shine through any
darkness.

Into Your hands, Lord, I commit my spirit.

May 2

Anna in the Summer of the Lord

Anna is in the summer of the Lord.
The Lord has brought His Special Servant, Anna
into the full summer of New Life.
This is where the flowers are blooming,
The grass is forever green and has no need for grooming.
The morning brings the birds to the trees,
Where they sing their love song to please.

The chirping sound of the crickets fills the evening.
This secret place is where there is no more pain, suffering or grieving.
The butterflies spread glory with their wings.
Anna touches the creator of all new things.
Rivers are filled and flowing with waters ever so clear,
As she drinks of these waters she hears, "My dear, my dear!"
Without any restrictions they do flow.
The presence of God fills her heart and
brings new life, A-glow, A-glow!
The golden hues, all wrapped around this Season,
In this place, there is no need for a reason.
God's love is here to love Anna,
His Servant, drawn into the Heavenly Manna.
We love you Anna, Oh Servant of God!
Rest in this summer place,
Remember us, as the Lord fills you with His Love and Grace.

May 3

Lift Up Your Hands

"Lift up your hands.
Lift up your voices.
Lift up your mind and hearts.
I will shower you with riches of heavenly origin.
Blessings and graces of this I partake lay before me."

May 4

I Walk Amongst You

"I walk amongst you in a gentle, caring and loving spirit.
I reach My arms around you and brush away each burden and care.
I hold tears, burdens and cares close to My heart.
Let Me melt away the burdens and cares of each new day.
Open your hearts and your minds and receive My spiritual food,

That is rich in the depth of My love. I say…I love you…Jesus"

May 5

Dew Drops Refresh the Roses

I will shake all the nations, and the treasures of all the nations will come in, And I will fill this house with glory, says the Lord of hosts. Mine is the silver and mine the gold, says the Lord of hosts. Greater will be the future glory of this house than the former, says the Lord of hosts; and in this place I will give peace, says the Lord of hosts! (Haggai 2:7–9)

I bought a bouquet of flowers for our spring 1998 home retreat. These flowers, like the one in the picture, were red roses and had dewdrops on them. I knew that we were to use the roses to represent each person at the retreat. The dewdrop on the rose was the Lord pouring His Holy Spirit upon us.

I did not have any words to go with the roses, and I did not know what I was going to use until we went to Burlington to pick up our friend, Sr. Clare.

As we were walking down the hall in the convent, we saw a picture on the wall of one single rose. The rose had dewdrops on it, which fell down forming a dove. Right away, we felt we received confirmation of the roses I had bought for the retreat.

We knew we were to use the words written at the bottom of this picture, "As Dew Drops refresh the Roses each day, the Holy Spirit renews our faith daily to go on."

May 6

Lord, I Believe, Help My Unbelief

Not believing or not knowing where you are in your spiritual walk with the Lord blocks your spiritual growth.

Very often, knowing can have the reverse effect of pride on your walk with the Lord. Not knowing or believing where you are in your relationship with the Lord, can stop the powerful use the Lord has for your life as a worker amongst His people.

Fear and doubt contribute to this unbelief. We have to be a believing people if we are to believe in the revelation of God in our life. Believe where you are in your relationship with the Lord. The block is more of our unbelief than our belief. The Lord loves our why. Ask and you will receive.

Prayer: Lord, I believe, help my unbelief.

May 7
The Walls of the Flesh

"My blessing will go over the wall of the flesh.
Even the sea will not hold back the blessings and graces.
I will break through the dike of the flesh.
I will go above, under, around and through.
Nothing will hold back My blessings for you.
As I keep soaking you with the living water, it
will eventually break up the flesh.
Pulled out into the deepest part of My Ocean of love, you
will soak in My presence and fragrance of love."

Pound, O pound, O Lord.
Break up the crust around my heart.
Let the rough waters pound.
Pound, O Lord.
There are results. I can feel and hear the undertow.
The stones pulled out, returned and hit against the shoreline.
The stones were washed and soaked repeatedly, until purified.
Purify my heart, O Lord.
The air I breathe is full of Your presence, O Lord
My every breath inhales Your presence, Your beautiful fragrance.
Let each breath of Your fragrance bring me
into Your manifest presence.

Let this beautiful fragrance, seep through the walls
of flesh and weaken the power of self.
Weaken the walls of self-indulgence and replace them with self-
discipline and Your will over my will. Become truly true and real to me.
The Lord will bless us, one way or another. He
will get the graces and blessings to us.
He will go over the dikes, the walls of the flesh.
He will hammer away at them one way or another.
The grace and blessings will overflow.

May 8

Taste and See the Goodness of the Lord

The rough waters are pounding upon the rocks.
The rocks represent our hearts and the parts not
given to the Lord. Some waves will be unexpected and will give you an
extra dose of the Holy Spirit. You will get all wet and may even lose your
balance.

Picture these rocks with many cracks and crevices. Watch the
waves come in and hit the rocks with a mighty force. Water splashes
everywhere.

Watch Out! You may even get your feet wet. There is a lot of force
and power in moving water. Especially, in the living waters God is pounding against our flesh with His living waters. These waters will eventually
break through the dikes of flesh.

Being in the presence of the Lord will have the same effect as the
rough water of the sea. This time alone with the Lord will break through
the rock of the flesh. One works as well as the other. Both are forces of
water, one of the strong waves against the rocks and the other the living
waters welling up in our hearts and rushing forth from the presence of
God.

As strong as the ocean waves are, they do not have the power, grace
and love that comes forth from the Lord and the living waters present in
our hearts. Ask the Lord to hit you hard with His Holy Spirit and break

through the walls that are blocking you from receiving His fullness of gifts in His manifest presence.

Breathe in the fragrance of the salt air, the ocean or the river of His glory.

Breathe in me, O Lord! O Breath of God, breathe in me!

If you come into these waters, you are going to get wet and because it is the Lord drawing you to Him, there will be no turning back. Come to these waters often. Taste the salt! Taste and see how good the Lord is.

May 9
Come Forth Into My Kingdom

"Come forth into My kingdom.
Do not be afraid.
Your heart has been made new for Me.
Your eyes are the truth I can come through."

May 10
Listen

"Listen! Listen to the waters as they run by.
Walk! Walk with your hearts open for Me.
Talk! Talk with My words on your tongues."

May 11
A Very Deep Truth

A very deep truth, understanding and knowledge come from deep within a heart full of the presence of God. This understanding and knowledge leads this heart. A heart given to God will leave no room for the likes of Satan's pride, which caused original sin. "Your road is your will." You can choose which road to take. Will we choose God's will that takes us into the deep truths in the heart or will we choose our own will as our same old guide?

If we reverse the direction we are going in and bring our will into submission to God's will, we will travel down the road towards new life, where wisdom and knowledge is deep within the heart.

May 12

When You Seek Truth

Jesus then said to those Jews who believed in him, "If you remain in my word, you will truly be my disciples, and you will know the truth, and the truth will set you free." (John 8:31–32)

When we seek the truth that is present within our hearts, our faith becomes stronger and stronger. With our faults and weaknesses overcome, we can grow in faith. In our weakness is the strength of God. Every situation overcome with the help of God's grace draws us deeper and deeper into the heart of God within our hearts.

May 13

When in Unity, There is No Conflict

There was no conflict in the heart of the Mother of God. Every part of her heart was united to the heart of God through the power of the Holy Spirit. Our hearts touched by everyday situations may be in conflict and not in unity with Jesus. Purification must take place, where our body, mind and heart unite in Christ. Conflicts will be set aside.

Words received: "When in Unity there is no conflict. Conflicts can be contained when the heart is united to Christ."

O Mother of God, teach us how to carry Jesus in our hearts. Teach us how to clothe Him, how to feed Him, and how to love Him. Teach us how to care for Him, as you cared for Him in your heart. Teach us how to clothe, feed, love and care for Him in our hearts.

Come Into the Clearing

Very often through the previously mentioned retreat the words, "Come into the clearing," would come to mind. I heard them again, when we walked up to the Pieta, in the center of a beautiful clearing.

Charles and I prayed in front of this Statue. A little Sister peeked around the corner of the Statue and scared us. She was looking at the details of the Pieta. She was an artist and had taught at the different levels.

We talked with her about the statue of David. She told us how Michelangelo shouted at the statue to speak. She said, "Everyone has their own way of expression and the Lord will use it. Attached to their works of art, an artist, author and composer can find it hard to let go of their works of art." This message was just what we needed to hear. The Lord was talking to us again, bringing our attention to previous writings and experiences.

He is drawing us, like the deer, to live near the still waters. He is placing a thirst in our hearts for a deeper relationship with him. This is where we can grow in the simplicity and solitude of His love and graces. When we come into the "clearing in our hearts," the Lord can speak to us, teach us, and refresh us.

We left the retreat house at 3:00 a.m.and saw a deer standing at the edge of the parking lot. We knew the Lord was reminding us of His call to Holiness and to a life of living in His solitude.

Prayer: O Lord, Let us see clearly what is important. Help us let go of what is unimportant. We open our hearts to you. Fill every corner of our hearts with you. Let us take pictures with our hearts and souls. Let the fragrance of Your love fill our hearts. Let the satisfaction and purification of Your presence purify and cleanse our hearts. We love you, Jesus.

115

May 15

Words for the Workers

All her idols shall be broken to pieces, all her wages shall be burned in the fire, and her statues I will destroy. (Micah 1:7)

"Hold onto your hats because My blessings are coming forth.
Your work has not been in vein.
You have stirred up the waters.
The undertow will just have to settle back into
rhythm with My mighty waters."

"The heavens above heard your plea.
I will not let it go unanswered.
The old walls of Jericho even felt the rumblings."

"Enter into the summer time with me.
Let the excitement of each new day carry you through the summer.
The summer time is a time for the bees to buzz, the flowers to bloom,
The green grass to grow, the frogs to croak and the birds to sing."

"Soak up the sun (Son) and all of its riches.
Beach towels spread upon the sands of My time.
Kites fly up high for freedom they seek.
The "natural," they will not meet.
The clouds from My Glory, they will greet."

May 16

You are My Child

"Peace, My child! You are My child and I
will use you. The spirit is willing.
I Love you. My words, use them wisely, they will guide you.
In My name, guided you shall be. Love will conquer all.
I am with you always."

"Build for Me. Hope for all the nations. I love thee. See
Me in thy eyes. The fruit is there. God is for you.

The sand washes away from around the stone, but the stone remains.
What is to remain in your heart has been firmly planted there,
what is to be washed away will be purified in the sands of time.
Peace is yours. If you love Me, follow Me. I am the
hand of time. My will for salvation, will be filled.
My people rejoice in My coming, Father, Son, and Holy Spirit."

"Anna, Anna, Sapphire. My love is there, just ask.
The cross is heavy, but I shall help you bear it.
My love is with you. My mother, love her, she has answers and power.
If only you ask of her. She will be there in
glory, in the glory she deserves."

May 17

Hang on His Every Word

...but they could find no way to accomplish their purpose because all the people were hanging on his words. (Luke 19:48)

From reading the above Scripture, I realized for the first time how much I look for God wherever I can.

I hang on Jesus' every word and His ways of speaking to me. I ask the Lord Jesus to free me from whatever it is that stands in the way of my close relationship with Him and the Father. We make our hearts for a den of thieves. This being all the junk that stands in the way of our close relationship with God.

Prayer: O Lord, let the rejection of others, not bother me. Heal me of the need. Birthing of Jesus in my heart, come forth. Lord, do not let me lose those precious pearls to the world.

May 18

Supernatural Inspiration

Because it is the Lord speaking to the heart, supernatural inspiration is what should be coming out of our spiritual experiences. If this is not happening then we are probably not listening to the Lord.

A life lived in the Holy Spirit requires times spent in listening to the Holy Spirit. The Holy Spirit will refresh the body, mind and spirit.

Inspiration expressed in many different ways of loving and caring about others requires listening to the Lord from the heart instead of the mind and intellect.

May 19

Go Forth in Love

"Go forth in My love.
Blessed are the poor in spirit.
Come to the living waters.
You need My heart, My mind, My will, My understanding.
You are the hope for My people."

May 20

Porthole of the Heart

Anne had a vision of looking out of a porthole on a ship. She could see a beautiful sailboat sailing on the beautiful blue water.

The Lord was showing us what it is to look out of the porthole of the heart. When a person looks out of the porthole on the side of a ship, they can only see what is right in front of them. It is a limited view, and not as big as it would be if they were standing on the deck of the ship. We have to stand on the deck of God's love and look out of the porthole of His heart.

Seeing the limited beauty before you makes you realize the need for the inner beauty—the "bigger" view. The Lord seemed to be saying, "As you are looking out of a porthole on a ship, you may come to realize that your view is obstructed. This is also true of the mind and heart that still has sin and corruption present. The beauty has to be on the inside, as well as on the outside."

If you look through the porthole from the outside into the ship, you might be where you can see the mechanisms of the ship and what makes it run. Does it run on steam water, or does it run on gas? Maybe you can see the cylinders of the engine going up and down. A porthole is a channel; through this channel, one can see the working fluid of steam water, gas, etc., as it flows in and out the cylinder of an engine.

The eyes are the window to the soul or heart. The porthole is the channel for the light of Christ to shine into the troubled areas of the heart. This light will expose sin, faults and corruption that may be present. Are calm waters present where the soul is peaceful? Are there rough waters where the soul is troubled?

The eyes tell the truth when you look deeply into them. They tell a story. Do you see happiness and joy? Do you see sadness and pain? The eyes are a masterpiece of God's Glory and goodness. Do we close the eyes to our hearts and shut out the good that is there to see? Our will is freely given to us. It is up to us whether we will close or open the window to our heart and soul. The light of Christ flows in and out of the porthole of our heart. Are we reflections of the light of Christ? Does the light of Christ shine through our eyes? What do you see? I see that "His eyes are upon me."

May 21

Momentarily Monopoly

Words received: "Some come to Me reverently.
Some come to Me maliciously with malice in their hearts.
Momentarily monopoly..."this control will only last for a moment, a short time."

May 22

I Love You, O Little Ones

"As all nature reaches and leans towards the sun.
You My loved ones turn towards and lean on Me.
I love you, O Little ones. I caress and stroke your heart with My graces.
I lift the burdens of each day and sing to you, a
new song, Maranatha, O Maranatha.
Each new day, each new meeting is an encounter with the heavens
above, the Father, Son and Holy Spirit and Their Love."

May 23

Heavenly Spirit of Love

Very often when the gifts of the Holy Spirit are functioning within a community, the ministers have to take a step backwards and settle back into the realization that the manifestations of the Lord's presence is only because of the power of the Holy Spirit that is present. Sometimes through the excitement of being in this presence, self starts to get in the way. This is especially true in the healing and music ministries.

One evening, after becoming aware that a problem might be present in a situation, I received the following words: "You do not have to have everything planned ahead of time. Let the Holy Spirit lead in the music not the music lead the Holy Spirit." The Lord was saying that His People were going to be filled with songs from the Heart of the Father. His healing and music will come through the Holy Spirit.

God is sending the "Heavenly Spirit of Love" to us. It is a melody of love carried to us right from the Heart of the Father. A direct line of communication through the Holy Spirit brings us in touch with new songs. New songs with new words and rhythms are yet to come together. The Holy Spirit is the "Heavenly Spirit of Love" that is being sent to fill us with a "New Song."

Orange Blossoms

" ... The bread and the summer fruits are for your servants to eat, and the wine for those to drink who are weary in the desert." (2 Samuel 16:2)

"All the things over and done with have their fulfillment in me. Seek not to hold onto them. They can only flow towards me. As the river of grace flows, it carries the rich elements of My master plan. Your hopes and desires are flowing in this rich river. It is rushing towards you, away from you and within you all at the same time. For My River of love is all around and within My creation."

"I created all elements. Right from the element of surprise to the elements contained in all that exists. Made up in love are all the basic elements. Hold onto only love. Everything else will only dissolve in time. Love does not pass away with time. Love only grows with time and eternity."

"Orange blossoms are beautiful in color and fragrance. They carry the "element" of a delicate beauty that yields to a delicious fruit rich in the citrus sun (Son). There is a garden; a special place, rich with the fruits not yet tasted either physically or spiritually. When the individual heart reaches this special place, it will bask in the fresh juices of eternal love. My glory rests upon the heart open to these blessings while still upon this earth."

"I will fill the hearts of those that desire Me, as I desire them here and now. They will be the citrus trees planted near the heart of My son. They will share the fruit of the tree with others that want to know My son. This citrus fruit will not leave a strong acid to burn the lining of the heart. It will only leave the velvet touch of My presence to soothe the heart that desires only Me."

May 25

Velvet Touch

Come, Oh gentle Potter, and make my heart smooth as velvet in Your hands.

The hand of the Potter touches and forms a place to take up residence in our hearts.

All need His velvet touch.

Everything is rich when placed in the Potter's hands. The Potter does not mind the dryness that comes from the clay or the heart. He has the elements needed to turn that dryness into a masterpiece in His hands.

The heart is what the Potter molds and shapes into a heart that can contain His love and presence. The heart becomes a "container" that holds His love and presence. When called upon by the Lord, this heart is picked up and poured out over many. The spout, like the spout on the "Broken Jug," is the Holy Spirit and is always ready to draw in and give out the grace held within.

God's river of light and life fills the container and is always present to the heart. The heart becomes the container with rich fruits poured out. This is the heart awake to the presence of God and His Velvet touch within.

May 26

The Onion

"Should there be a prophet among you, in visions will I reveal myself to him, in dreams will I speak to him." (Numbers 12:6)

I woke up one morning at quarter to six from a very important dream. I did not want to wake up. I tried to remain asleep, but did not have any success. In the first part of the dream, I was telling two woman friends about a very special man. I said He would be an interesting person, for them to know. I told them this as if it were a message for them, but not for me.

Then this special man came into the dream. Our eyes met. He said, "We were special to each other the first time our eyes met." I felt this to be true. Words cannot express the way I felt when our eyes met. It was something I knew in my heart. He chose me and I became very important around His kingdom. He was a prince or king.

In the next part of the dream, I could not see Him. He had a way of seeing exactly what I was doing in His palace. I was having a good time, going to the different rooms, telling the people about Jesus. I then found myself on a bus, telling the poor and handicapped people about Him. After this, I was walking down a hill, singing and praising God. There were many people following me. I returned to the palace and went in and out of the rooms again. In one room, there were people worshipping the cross upside down. I remembered using the authority of the name of Jesus to correct them. I then showed them the correct way to hang a cross on the wall.

I kept waiting and watching for this prince to come back. I was special to Him and He had an interest in me. When He came back into the dream, I became ecstatic and was silent in His presence. He then came to me with an onion in His hand. He wanted me to take it and eat it. With no words spoken, this knowledge was present. I knew I would eat the onion, but at this point, I woke up. I tried so hard to go back to sleep to be in His presence.

May 27

Reminders of His Presence

Moses then told Aaron, "Take an urn and put an omer of manna in it. Then place it before the Lord for safekeeping for your descendants." So Aaron placed it in front of the commandments for safekeeping, as the Lord had commanded Moses. (Exodus 16:33–34)

Pictures can be reminders of the presence of the Lord amongst His people. They help to preserve the spiritual experiences in our hearts and memories. The above picture is a reminder of God's presence that remains with us.

We showed an original picture in yesterday's reading that was taken of an onion. Jesus, in this picture is handing me an onion, as He did in the dream about the onion. He is asking me to take the inner journey of healing that leads to life. He held the onion in His hand and then gave it to me to eat. The layers of the onion or wounds of sin surround the heart and soul.

The above picture for today's inspiration is a transposed picture of the original. It transposed when we copied it from the scanner to the computer. Two days later, I put the original picture back into the computer and it came out normal. We believe the transposed picture shows us how the Lord purifies our soul. The sweetness of His presence is at the center.

The Lord certainly had our attention through this experience. Surprised by joy, a closer look at the picture confirmed out understanding of what the Lord was saying.

The first picture asks us if we will take the inner journey. The second shows the soul in purification. We live our lives between the natural and spiritual realms. We will return and touch the ordinary, but must remember that our direction is heaven bound and we will on occasion experience the extraordinary. It is the will of the Father for us to take this journey. Through these pictures, dream and words the Lord was letting us know how special we are to Him.

May 28

Skin of Self-Love

"I may ask you to eat an onion, will you eat the onion?" With layers of the onion peeled away, you will eventually get to a very sweet center. Will you work through the different layers or wounds of sin that surround your heart and soul? Will you take a journey towards the center of your life with Me?"

"It is difficult to take this path. It often hurts to the very core, of your being. The layers of flesh and self-love run deep. These layers peal off a little at a time, starting with the skin of self-love. You try to hang onto this skin, for you know not the difference."

Onions easily grown from seed are adaptable to different temperatures. Planting can take place year-round as long as the soil is rich and moist. Onions ripen in the field. It is believed that they came from Egypt. They have a strong smell and taste. They have many layers and are both bitter and sweet. When we peel these layers away, tears will come to the eyes.

Our life in the inner journey with the Lord is like the onion. The journey can be slow, painful, and full of obstacles. It is difficult to let go of familiar things. Pride, fear and self will all struggle to stay in control—nothing is normal or easy. We have to come to terms with many difficulties and suffering.

The onion offered to us is the spiritual onion of prosperity and healing. When we eat this onion, wounds of sin are healed. Eating the onion represents our saying Yes to Jesus. We allow Him to enter our heart and mind where His love heals areas that need His healing touch. Jesus will hold us in the palm of His hand as we go through this desert of healing. He will peel the onion in gentleness and love. The old layers of sin will fall away. Blessings and graces soak the tough skin with the sweet core of His love.

May 29

Flesh Pots of Egypt

In the Scriptures of Numbers 11:5–6, the people of God began to complain.

"We remember the fish we used to eat without cost in Egypt, and the cucumbers, the melons, the leeks, the onions, and the garlic, But now we are famished; we see nothing before us but this manna." (Numbers 11:5–6)

The Israelites wanted to return to the fleshpots of Egypt and the onion fields of old ways and sin. The Lord is telling us not to return to the onion fields of Egypt. He wants us to remain in the rich and fertile fields in the desert of healing where we will grow and prosper.

At times, it will be bitter and at others, sweet, but joy is always experienced during this time with Jesus.

There is sweetness in the center of our soul, which lies under the wounds of sin. God's presence is in the sweetness that works in our heart and soul to remove the layers of bitterness. Through His love and grace He draws us toward the center of the soul. He wants us to experience the sweetness of His love. With layers of sin peeled away, the soul yearns for the fullness of God and wants to be in His presence.

Taste and see how good the Lord is; happy the man who takes refuge in him. (Psalm 34:9)

The heart and soul will grow and thrive when fed the bread of life. The hand of God the Father held out to each of us is feeding us bread from heaven; His Son, Jesus Christ.

So Jesus said to them "Amen, amen, I say to you, it was not Moses who gave the bread from heaven; my Father gives you the true bread from heaven. "For the bread of God is that which comes down from heaven and gives life to the world." "Sir, give us this bread always." Jesus said to them, "I am the bread of life; whoever believes in me will never thirst." (John 6:32–35)

May 30

A Moment of Grace

"You have received a moment of grace.
As the rains have soaked the earth with rains of refreshment,
I have soaked you in My word.
The rains of My words have fallen upon you this night.
I have soaked you with rains of the Holy Spirit."

"Be soaked in the word! Absorb every word
and grace that I shower upon you.
Graces fallen upon you will never be washed away.

Just being in the presence of My words, you are in My presence.
I have been in every one that has been read and
will be in everyone read in the future."

May 31
I Will Not Let Anyone Misuse You

"I will not let anyone misuse you. You have opened the door to
the north, the south, the east and the west for revival to enter.
Being centered in the spiritual depths of God's love and gifts
is different from being centered on the carnal surface.
The depth of the gifts is present in you. Therefore,
it is harder to be harmed or misused."

June 1
The Clouds

"The clouds! The clouds!
Look to the clouds.
My glory is seen in them and on them.
All eyes of the world shall see.
My Mother loves all.
She constantly prays to Me for you.
She does not get the reverence she deserves.
Love, her, as I, her Son, Jesus loves her."

June 2
My Peace Can Only Be Enjoyed

"Mystical meanings come from devout devotions.
Faithful service results in knowing the Father's will.
Our faith is our peace and our peace is our faith.
My peace is like no other. It cannot be described, only enjoyed."

St. John was a favorite of Jesus. He had trust in Jesus and was in faithful service to Him. He understood the mystical meanings behind what he experienced in the presence of Jesus. He had united his will with the will of the Father through Jesus. We will have tremendous peace and faith in Jesus if we remain devout, trusting and in faithful service to Him.

June 3

The Waters Continue to Flow

"The waters continue to flow with strength and grace.
Shades of purple flow through the stages of sin.
Life with the Father is never ending. I promise that it is there."

June 4

I Am a Jealous God

"There are times I want you all to Myself. Times when I can speak to your heart and there is no interference. These times will have a special quietness and great intimacy, when we are one in mind and Spirit."

"These are special times, and should be cherished and not forgotten. Like a first love, it goes beyond human description. All of these times are a foretaste of the Heavenly rewards I have in store for those who walk with Me in this Spiritual realm. This is offered to all for the asking."

"I have led you to special pastures, where we can come together away from all worldly distractions. These special places of simplicity are for those of the same spirituality. Enjoy and make use of these gifts for as long as they last. One never knows when the road will end and the Highway to Heaven begins."

June 5

Mind So Young, Body So Old

"Mind so young, Body so old. Rely on the young mind to keep the aging body in motion. Youth is love and love never dies. Without love, the body decays and becomes dormant. My world is full of love beyond your understanding. Joy and happiness fill the air, and one cannot help, but breathe in the intoxicating gift I give to all who trust in Me."

"Every time you sit before Me in My Presence I open the doors of heaven for you. I cannot contain myself and must release My love to you. I want you to feel the heat of My love as it surrounds you. Feel My arms around you, knowing that you are safe. Do not fear the things that are happening in the world, they must be. Did I not promise a New Heaven and Earth? They are already in the process."

"Dark clouds, followed by a glorious newness the world has yet to behold, seem to be on the horizon. Pray for those who do not believe, there is much power in the one who does believe. Pray for unbelievers to be open to My words. The truth will set them free."

June 6

He Kissed Me

Charles had the following dream: I was at a retreat. There was a lot of people and confusion. Everyone wanted to get near the retreat master, the main speaker. I just wanted peace and ducked into a room to get away from the crowd. After my eyes got use to the dark room, I saw that it was a chapel. I was praying all alone, when the door opened and someone came into the room. When I looked at the person, I saw that it was Jesus with the long robe and long hair. Something told me to go over to Him and I knelt down along side of Him.

I said, "Bless me Father for I have sinned." He said to me, "Speak to Me, as to My Father." What did I want of Him? I asked Him to free me from my mind with all of its sinful thoughts and desires. He placed His hands on my head near the temples and pulled my head towards Him. Kissing my forehead, He began to pray for me. All I heard Him say was, "Father," and He continued to pray. I did not hear anything after that. Surprised, I felt His breath upon me, and it was pleasant. It was not like someone with bad breath. In fact, I could not inhale it fast enough, as it was so pleasant. Then my dream ended.

Three years later, September 3, 1993, I went on a retreat. While on this retreat the priest, Spiritual Director, for the weekend held confessions one morning. We all went up to the priest while he stood at the end of the room.

When my turn came, I felt as though I was standing in front of Jesus. The priest was tall and had on a long, white robe. He put his arms around me and pulled me close to Himself and said, "Tell me what you want God to free you from." I proceeded to tell him that again I wanted to be free from my sinful mind and thoughts. He gave me absolution. Then he took me by the head and pulled me to him. He kissed me on the forehead and gave me his blessing. I then went back to my seat.

Overcome by the Holy Spirit, I could hardly walk. I could not tell Anne what happened. I was so emotional and ready to cry. After I sat a while, I remembered the dream I had. When I got home, I looked though my journals and found the dream that I shared above. Again, I was overcome by the Holy Spirit and God's love.

June 7

Waves Splash Upon the Shore

"The waves splash upon the shore,
Clearly bringing God's graces, more and more.
The hidden secrets seen,
Under the light of the Holy Spirit they beam."

"You cannot drink from the top of the well.
You have to go deep into the ocean to draw out the riches.
Allow the waves to carry the blessings that splash upon you.
It is a time for the Lord to bring His inspirations to you.
You cannot guard against them.
Let them splash upon you."

"Believe that it will happen. The Lord will carry them to
you in many ways, from a bus, a plane or even a train.
Hear the whistle in the distance and know the train
chugs towards you full of God's wishes for you."

"God has brought His inspiration to you in many ways in
the past and will bring them in new and surprising ways.
Be open to His inspirations. New forms of inspirations are
coming forth. The arts are full of God's inspirations."

"Up until now, you have only been drinkers from the top of the
well. I am going to bring you into the depths of the ocean.
From these depths, you will draw others to the
shores of intimacy and life eternal."

"Every wave that comes forth from My Ocean of love
will splash upon the heart of the new believer.
One can only get wet. My Son will be there to hold the
towel of comfort and wisdom. For wisdom is a towel.
It will leave knowledge, as it dries the tears of the past."

June 8

Burn Away Impurities

I had a vision of a piece of paper on fire. It was burning in the upper
right hand corner.

Words received: "Being in the presence of the Lord burns
away impurities, at a pace, only the Lord understands. On
occasion we may smell the smoke (incense)."

If we, in our physical condition, sensed a fuller presence of the Lord, we would not be able to move. We would fall flat on our faces. Thank God for His hidden blessings. He does on occasion lift the veil so that we do sense His presence. If we experienced it like it really is, nothing in our physical lives would matter. We would not be able to or want to move from this presence.

A time will come when people will experience His presence in this way. We can receive this presence if we would only let Him give it to us.

June 9

Activity Can Distract

"Lord, it is good that we are here." (Matthew 17:4)

Questions: O Lord, Where are You leading Charles and me? Why do I desire to be with others who are seemingly active in the Holy Spirit?

"The others are looking for Me in the activity present.
You are to seek Me in the solitude of My presence.
There is nothing wrong with either. I can speak to you
much more deeply in the silence of My presence.
Activity can distract. Your most powerful experiences
with Me transcended the activity.
I am heard in the still small voice and quiet
movement of My Holy Spirit."

June 10

Little Sailboat

He woke up, rebuked the wind, and said to the sea, "Quiet! Be still!" The wind ceased and there was great calm. (Mark 4:39)

Stormy seas of squalls and strife,
It is not yours to control my heart and life.
Like a little sailboat am I upon this sea,
Your control is not upon me.
The sea is unpredictable and the boat tossed about,
Rough waters and high waves come on it with great clout.
Trust and faith in the master will keep the boat upright.
Giving Him charge lessens the storm's controlling might.
Lord Jesus, I do not want to ride the stormy sea.
I just want to ride in the boat with Thee.
I do not want to steer the boat, with strife,
Balancing, rowing with my life.
I want You to steer, balance and row,
Rebuking the wind, as we go
I want to watch You calm the sea
Resting quietly at Your side, I will be.
I have tried to steer, balance and row
Trying to control, while brought low
When storms and squalls begin to advance
I rely on Your protection and on Your lance.
O Lord, I trust only in You,
To lead me forward and bring me through
Keep Your hand on me; guide me in the right direction
Fill me with Your Holy Spirit and Your everlasting affection.
Your glorious rainbow of light splashes across my sail
Your Holy Spirit guides my Little Sailboat with a calm and lasting gale
With You at the helm, my part I will do
Thy will be done in me O Lord, let everything be new.

June 11

A Breath of the Holy Spirit

"By paths, you walk towards My heart.
By leaps, you grow in My love.
By hands, you join each other around My eternal ring.

By voice, you reach the center of creation.
By life, you breathe a breath of oxygen, a breath of the Holy Spirit."

June 12

Be Examples

"My people, be captive of nothing of this world.
Be only captives of My heart.
Be instruments not of this world.
Be instruments of My peace.
Be examples of nothing in this world.
Be examples of My presence in your life.
My love, My heart, My presence is your life."

June 13

A Sponge Soaking Up

Prayer: My God, let my love for You be as Your love is for me.
I want to be like a sponge soaking up all the graces given to
me by Your Holy Spirit. Let Your love spread within me and let
nothing stop Your love from flowing out to others.

June 14

I Walk With and Beside You

"There is no place that you walk
That I have not walked before you.
I walk with and beside you.
You are in the atmosphere of God, and
Where you go, you bring that atmosphere with you.
Can you not see? Trust in the words."

June 15

Walk Out of the Forest

"Walk out of the forest and
rest with Me for a while.
The forest is the world, as you know it.
You can hear and see Me, if you only take the time."

June 16

Forest

He took the blind man by the hand and led him outside the village. Putting spittle on his eyes he laid his hands on him and asked, "Do you see anything?" Looking up he replied, "I see people looking like trees and walking." Then he laid hands on his eyes a second time and he saw clearly; his sight was restored and he could see everything distinctly. (Mark 8:23–25)

I had a dream, and in this dream I was standing at the edge of the forest. A young man with cuts and bruises on his face came out of the forest. I knew he was a sinner. He came up to me and I sat next to him. I cleaned his cuts and loved and cared for him. He got up and went back into the woods. I knew that he went back a changed person. With others annoyed, I took the time to care for this sinner. This was the end of the dream.

The dream was on a Sunday night. The following Tuesday a young man had come to stay with us for two weeks. He was going through a difficult time in his life. One day, when this young man was still with us, I read the above Scripture, and all of a sudden it became very clear. This young man was the person in my dream. The Lord had drawn the young man out of the situation he was experiencing. He was to stay with us for a couple of weeks. In Mark 8:23–25, Jesus drew the blind man out of the town.

In the dream, the person drawn out of the woods had cuts and bruises on his face. He was a sinner in despair. He came up to me and I loved and cared for him. He went back into the woods a changed person. God had placed this person with us to teach all of us. He was getting our attention and drawing each of us out of our old ideas and ways of looking at life. There is a need for a change of heart. Turn away from sin, old habits and doing the things that we used to do. We are sinners and have many cuts and bruises caused by sin.

Jesus gradually restored the man's sight. He will restore our sight, gradually, bringing us away from our failings. He loves and cares for us, as He loved and cared for the blind man.

So He can get our attention, God's presence is often hidden. He is always there in the sufferings and joys. Through helping this young man, we learned about areas in our own lives that need healing. Love is reaching out to others. Giving of ourselves is where we receive. In giving and receiving, one knows who one really is. We received a reward of spiritual value.

June 17

Bona Venture

"Bona Venture!" (Bona: good faith, Venture: chance, risk, stake)
Have faith, take the risk and let Me do the rest.
My oil trickles down into the wounds and heals them.
Soothing as it heals with no scars left to heal.
Drink deeply of My love, drink deeply of Me.
The division is in your spirituality.
Forget what has happened in the material world.
Your spirituality is more important.
Memories Manipulate"

Everyone resents the control and manipulation of others. One has to remember that the resentment of control can also control you. Memories of the past bad experiences can control and manipulate your way of thinking and healing.

The Lord will often use other people in your walk with Him. However, He says, "Let no one rob you of your spirituality. Your spirituality does not depend on other people. Your spirituality depends only on Me."

June 18

Safe Place

I received the special words, "This is a safe place," during an experience in front of the Blessed Sacrament when we were in a church in Wynnewood, Pennsylvania. During a portion of the service, the priest called everyone to come up around the Blessed Sacrament.

After only being there for a few minutes, I became frozen in the spirit, not able to move. After everyone left the church, I remained standing and frozen next to the Blessed Sacrament. I had one hand out towards the church pews and the other pointing to the Blessed Sacrament. I then received the words, "This is a safe place."

I now understand these words. In troubled times, our safety is to spend time with Jesus in the Blessed Sacrament and to receive Him in Holy Communion.

June 19

Let My Goal Be Your Prize

"Let My peace be your truth.
Let My truth be your life.
Let My life be your love.
Let My love be your guide.
Let My guidance be your obedience.
Let My obedience be your goal.
Let My goal be your prize."

June 20

Breaker, Breaker

One morning, around 1:15 a.m., I lay in bed not able to sleep. I was praying and telling the Lord how much I loved Him. The words "Breaker, Breaker," came to me. I argued with the Lord that these words went with a car CB and then pushed them aside. I thought they could not possible be words from God. What could they have to do with anything?

Then, I say then, words and thoughts started to come together. I began to think of the writings on *Shades of Blue* that I had started putting together and had not worked on for more than two years. I said, "I will have to remember these thoughts in the morning," I then felt the Lord wanted me to get up and put them down on paper. At 1:15 a.m., I put down these words:

> "Jesus is bringing us into the clear waters of His love.
> Our destiny is to the shores of Eternal Life.
> Break from controls. Do not want to control anything.
> Rest in the bow of His ship, and watch as it heads for richer shores.
> Rough seas have tossed you about.
> It is now time to rest in the calm waters of the Father's Love."

Prayer: O God, My Father, calm the storm in my heart and soul, mind and spirit. Bring me into the beautiful hues of Your love. Jesus, I want to wade in these waters.

June 21

He Is Persistent

The words, "Breaker, Breaker," were from the Lord and given to us to get our attention. When you use a CB in your car, "Breaker, Breaker," is one of the terms used. Surely, there are times the Lord has to use something loud and different to wake us up. Charles said, "CB could stand for 'Christ broadcasting,' and that He is speaking to us."

This is an example of simplicity, keeping our minds simple and free from the confusion and noise of the world. Jesus wants to place the desire in our heart to live along the shores of Eternal Life. This is where there is peace and the knowledge of God the Father. In this life, nourished through the Sacraments, we can grow. We can accept or refuse.

As we think of the breakers and the ocean, the Lord will use their special qualities to teach us. The deep part of the ocean represents the world and all of its attachments. The different colors blend from dark blues to light green. We cannot always notice that we have gone into another part of our spiritual life. We are now in the waves that splash upon the "Eternal Shores."

We are talking about the Eternal Life. It is in the clear waters of the mystical life. The Lord is calling His people to the "clear waters" of the mystical life. Those living in these waters will grow. Then, they will help others to progress along their journey to a deeper relationship with God the Father.

Charles related these experiences and thoughts to his experience on a ship. When a ship is coming into the shore, it takes extra steps to get through the breakers successfully. There is a certain point that has to be broken through. It could get rough. It is often hard getting through the reef and strong undertow.

June 22

Freedom to Live Above the Earthly Pull

We feel that we have been in the breakers since our trip overseas. The breakers representing the turmoil, earthly pull, and undertow of those things that pulls on our spirituality each day. God wants us out of the turmoil. We may have to take extra steps to remain in His peace and out of the turmoil around us.

We felt that we had been plowing through temptations. The Lord was allowing them to happen to break us from the controls in our lives and surroundings. We have to stop trying to control circumstances around us, thinking everything depends on us. We have to depend on Christ as little children depend on their parents.

Help with different problems, if possible. Always be present to the Father in what He calls us to do in earthly matters. Stay in the Father's will, the clear waters. This way, we can have a relationship with God the Father. He will help us to survive the problems in the Church and world today.

Words received: "This too will pass, you will go on and all else will remain."

One day when I was going up the stairs, I looked down at the furniture in the parlor. It became very clear that material things are stuck in time and are stationary. Children of God have the freedom to live above the "earthly pull," and still be in this world.

We are to be in this world, but not of it. God had given us a different view. We began to look at life threatening situations, illness and trips as times for great blessings from the Lord. We received a glimpse of the shoreline of "Eternal Life." Keeping our eyes on Jesus, we are to live in a relationship, with "God Alone." From the growth in that relationship, we then can reach out to others.

Since you have been brought back to true life with Christ, you must look for the things that are in heaven, where Christ is, sitting at God's right hand. Let your thoughts be on heavenly things, not on the things that are on the earth, because you have died, and the life you now have is hidden with Christ in God. But when Christ is revealed—and he is your life—you too will be revealed in all your glory with him. (Colossians 3:1–4, Jerusalem)

The Cross of Christ goes from shore to shore, beginning to end. It touches the shore from the beginning of time, to the shore, the end of time ... Eternal Life.

Jonah

Those who serve worthless idols forfeit the grace that was theirs. "But I, with a song of praise, will sacrifice to you. The vow I have made, I will fulfill. Salvation comes from Yahweh." Yahweh spoke to the fish, which then vomited Jonah on to the shore. (Jonah 2:9–11, Jerusalem)

The Lord was saying our foundation should be truth. This would mean new convictions, new choices, blessings, graces and temptations. "Are we ready for what the Lord wants to do?"

The Lord was showing us how Jonah was in the belly of the whale, the desert. The whale spit him out upon the shore. We were also in the belly of the whale, the desert. Spit out on the shores of Eternal Life, like Jonah, we draw closer to God the Father.

Jonah, spit out upon the shore, did the Lord's work. When the Lord showed His mercy on Nineveh, Jonah, like a little child, went off and pouted. The Lord is asking us to have mercy upon those we differ with, not going off like Jonah and pouting. Jonah wanted to stay where he was comfortable. We, called to a relationship with God the Father, must remember that Jesus came to bring us to the Father.

We tried to understand what the Lord was saying through this experience with Jonah. We then remembered a previous experience, which we have already shared. The breakers and the words we received then came to mind. I will repeat them here because of the value in understanding this experience.

Jesus is bringing us into the clear waters of His love
Our destiny is to the shores of Eternal Life
Break from controls. Do not want to control anything
Rest in the bow of His ship, as it heads for richer shores.

Words received: "You, tossed about by rough seas, must now rest in the calm waters of the Father's Love."

Coming through the breakers, we have been spit out on the shores closer to God the Father. This is where we must be open to the Father, Son and Holy Spirit. Are we ready for what the Lord wants to do?

June 24

Strings of My Heart

The Lord is our savior: we shall sing to stringed instruments in the house of the Lord all the days of our life. (Isaiah 38:20)

"I sit between the strings of your heart
As your prayers strum a melody of love to Me
No lessons are needed to play this heavenly instrument
The instrument is the heart given to all
Desire only to please Me in simple and childlike ways
The desire of the heart is all that is needed to
compose a melody of love to Me
Remember, in simplicity not in duplicity melodies are composed."

"You touch the strings of My heart when you keep
Me company. Notes of pure love fill the air.
If you could only hear the majestic melodies, that
vibrate from your presence with Me.
Joy to the world is what I came to give. Very few
receive it because they do not believe in Me."

"Microscopic morsels are coming your way
Penetrating everything that stands in their way
Piercing the flesh and painful too
Allowing the bile to flow out of you."

June 25

I See

"I see, I see," the blind man said
After Jesus placed His hands on his head;
What a glorious sight it must have been
Seeing the Lord after a life so dim.
Open our eyes we can cry out too
Seeing for the first time, anew;

Our walk with Jesus must truly be
One of Faith, hope and humility.
Like the blind man, give thanks and follow Him too,
Your heavenly rewards will soon come into view
So, no matter what your walk in life may be
Jesus says, "Come Follow Me!"

June 26

The Dove in the Web

Since 1983, we have been having Home Retreats at our home in the spring and fall of the year. The Lord speaks to us in many ways during these retreats.

At these retreats we usually have an Emmaus Walk. For this walk, people separate into pairs. They usually share how the Lord is speaking to them during the retreat. At one retreat, Charles walked with a woman that saw a web in the tree across the street from the house. Later she shared her experience with us. She said the web reminded her of her. She came to the retreat finding that she was in a web; when the day proceeded to unfold, she came out of the web.

We took the above picture of this web. One can see the dove crouched down. The dove is confined in this small area and is unable to move freely about. Sometimes, we feel as though we are confined and unable to move freely in the Spirit.

After that day, we began to receive many insights about the dove in the web. We went on a retreat in Vermont shortly after this retreat. The dove and web were very much on our minds. We felt that the dove in the web represented us. The web of unbelief pulls us into the weakness that is still in our hearts and minds.

The Israelites that never reached the Promised Land began to murmur and complain in their tents, which led to "unbelief." We understood how the web of unbelief coats over our hearts and minds. The power and action of the Holy Spirit becomes dull in each of us that are the Body of Christ. We are the Church. If we cannot hear or see the action of the

143

Holy Spirit, somewhere or somehow we have become dull to His action and presence.

The Scripture Matthew 25:1 speaks about the five sensible virgins and the five foolish virgins. We can be like the five sensible virgins or the five foolish virgins that did not take any oil, grew drowsy, and fell asleep. We can be drowsy, asleep and foolish in division, murmuring, complaining, etc.

June 27

Free My Little Dove

"Fly little bird, fly to Me. Shake off the dust and you will be free.
Icky, sticky glue. Cry out to the Lord.
Free My little dove for it cannot free itself.
Walk with Me. Talk with Me.
I am the light of the world, walk in the light."

We talked about how birds and other animals can be stuck in oil slicks; they cannot move and eventually die when covered with oil. We then talked about spiders. They form a web when we are asleep. This web is also sticky, like glue, and once something is stuck in this web it is open for attack. The spider is very quick to devour its prey.

There are many dangerous situations in our lives, where we can be stuck in this oil, this sticky glue. We are like a little bird in a snare, but the Lord will set us free. We cannot get free. We cannot get free on our own. We need Jesus and prayer.

Charles had a vision of a beautiful box tied with a beautiful ribbon. He knew it was a gift—the Holy Spirit. It was in a ball of thorns. He knew in his heart that the gentle and tender Holy Spirit could not remain in a nest of thorns. We then talked about the web over the Dove, the Holy Spirit.

We have been asking ourselves, how are we grieving the Holy Spirit? Where are the thorns in our hearts and minds that push the Holy Spirit away? What forms the web around the action of the Holy Spirit in our lives?

The negativity projected toward us from north, south, east and west, became very clear to us. Our society, friends and others, add to the reasons that the web of unbelief stays so tight around our minds and hearts. Negativity feeds unbelief and stops the flow of God's grace and love through the Holy Spirit.

We were only home a few hours when the insights of the retreat came to mind again. A couple of phone calls confirmed the power of negativity. Like the spider that works at night, negativity is very subtle. It works in the darkness that remains in our hearts. This darkness needs healing by the power of the gentle, tender dove and loving hands of our Lord, Jesus Christ.

June 28

Winnowing Winds

Lord, stir up the Sea of Galilee in our hearts. Splash the living waters upon us.

The wind is strong, yet so gentle, soft, blowing us around.

"Like the raging of the Sea, I will come over thee.
You are reeds in the wind.
I am calming your hearts to be trouble free,
like the little child you ought to be.
Hear the sounds of the sea.
I mix the air with the wind causing turbulence to begin.
Rocks and Shoals move about.
Rains (reign) of the Holy Spirit are upon you
Winnowing winds welcome you!"

June 29

Renovation

Speak, Lord, Your servant listens.

"The call to renovation is the renovation of the heart.
Winnowing winds will not waste away, as they blow away the chaff.
These winds bring freshness, peace and love.
In the voice of nature, now I speak.
In the voice of the wind, I speak.
In the voice of the water, I speak.
In the waters above the heavens, I speak.
The desire of the heart is all I seek, be it
ever so humble and ever so meek.
This is a memory you will never forget.
Praising and glorifying the Lord will be for all eternity."

June 30

Wisdom in the Wind

"Look beyond the bread you eat: See Your Savior and Your Lord."
(Song based on John 6)

"Clouds of gray will not spoil the day.
Chronic catastrophes will come in merciful measures.
Discernment, discussion and dialogue go together.
Comatose with me, fall into a deep sleep with me"

"When you are up close to the mountain you lose
track of the beauty you see at a distance.
As I draw you deeper and closer to me, do not lose
sight of the beauty you see at a distance.
Many obstacles can stand in the way of this close view.
Look beyond the small portion you now see
and remember the bigger view."

Little Seed in My Heart

Then he carried off a seedling vine, and planted it in fertile soil; by the side of a wide stream, as a border he set it. The seedling grew, and turned into a vine, not tall but well spread out; its branches grew up toward the eagle, its roots grew down. It turned into a vine; it sent out stems and put out sprays. (Ezekiel 17: 5–6, Jerusalem)

I felt something special going on in my heart. It felt like a seed planted itself there. I kept thinking of a little bear cub snuggling in for the winter. It felt as though the little bear cub was snuggling into a comfortable spot. It also felt as though a flower was growing along with the seed. The next day I received these words:

"Little seed in my heart...you snuggle in never to depart. Like a little bear cub you cuddle up, for the winter you prepare. In the spring, you awake and bring forth, love, joy and an outreach of care. You settle for a long winter's nap to die and come forth anew. The flower blooms now and will be ever so true."

Through the course of the next few days, I began to realize what was going on in my heart. The Lord had planted the seed of desire in my heart. The desire was to worship in wisdom and truth. The above Scripture confirmed the Lord planting the little seed in my heart—the fertile soil. The seed will eventually grow into a vine that will spread out. Our growth in this relationship with the Lord will encourage others to worship in wisdom and truth. Firmly planted and rooted in Jesus Christ, the heart reaches towards the Lord, the eagle.

When a person truly feels this desire, one can no longer mix truth with non-truth. If they become uneasy, Christians will know there is non-truth present in disguise. Their desire is to worship in wisdom and truth and share this desire with others.

We are to be faithful to the teachings of Jesus. In these days, it will be hard. Ask the Lord to give you the gift to worship in wisdom and truth.

July 2

Worship in a Spirit of Wisdom and Truth

Through the previous experience, just shared, we heard the message to worship in a Spirit of wisdom and truth. The Lord began to teach us what this should mean to each of us. Even if our actions and intentions are good, our environment can still affect us. Evil is all around us. We need constant refreshment of the blessings and graces that can only come from God.

We once mixed evil with good. Unknowingly, evil was woven like a tapestry in our hearts and minds. God has been weaning us from this mixture. We must desire to fill this tabernacle with only His truths. This weaning makes the evil around us more noticeable. This is because God has been making us stronger and stronger.

We are not to let the evil back in. We must ask God to place the watchman of the Holy Spirit, at the entrance to our hearts and minds. The Holy Spirit is pure love, and pure love is pure truth. The clear message was, "Beware of those that can kill both the body and soul."

We began to ask what the Lord was calling each of us to do. Are we listening to God's call? Are His people listening? Do we trust in His love? Are we faint-hearted and are we losing our wonderment?

"He is our all in all, our loving Father.
What more must I do to show you?
Turn My flicker into flame."

Prayer: O Lord, give us the grace to trust in You.

Let us put on "God Gear" ... God's gear of humility.
He chose us ... do we trust and have the courage to be His chosen?

Words received: "Don't you realize that you are God's temple and that the Spirit of God is living in and among you?"

Somehow, we still do not have the full realization of this truth. Instead of drawing from the riches, we have become like the barren tree that stands in the middle of the plush forest and sighs, "Oh look at me, so poor. How dry I've become."

"I am not far from you.
Absorb yourself in My love, absorption, by absorption, and by prayer.
Teach, listen, love, and feel…My people are in need.
Offer hope to the hopeless and love to the loveless.
Open your heart…offering Me simple sincerity.
Some do not know simple sincerity and truths as true love.
Free the captives from themselves. Set them free to Me.
You have been shown the good and bad sides of the senses.
You have experienced both and must choose.
Be ever on guard. Be an example, but not by words.
Love is silence, silence is solitude and solitude is prayer."

July 3

Keeping Everything in Our Hearts

"Keep everything in your hearts
For it is for its own time, only
Not in your time or in your way
But in God's time and in God's way."

July 4

Looking Through the Window

There is always more depth to the person, more than what is presented to the world. This depth is only seen through God's love.

As I was looking at the American Flag this morning, I thought of a window being in the flag. Oh, what a story goes behind that material flag flowing in the spring breeze. If it could speak, what would it say?

"I carry the lives and hearts of many in every star and stripe.
I carry the joys as well as the sorrows, the untold stories of might.
I carry the dreams and desires left behind,

For lives given up to a harder time.
I carry the hopes of a future rich with love,
Red, white and blue flown from above."
"I carry each delicate heart to a place of rest.
Without a doubt, it will be the best.
I carry God's blessing and grace,
To a High standard of glory for each race.
I carry my colors of red, white and blue
Just for you! Just for you!"

July 5

The Delicate Heart

Each person is like the flag. Handled in a delicate and honorable way, each heart carries a story untold. Only God knows the heart of an individual. He knows the life that each has had to endure. He knows where the person has walked. He has been there along side of them. He knows where others have failed or injured them. He knows where they have experienced sorrow or joy. He knows why they did or did not do something. He knows why they took different paths than those He would have chosen.

God is the only one that truly knows a person's heart. We must be aware of the delicate heart, a delicate rose, planted in the garden of the Lord. Each one of us has a delicate heart. Some are delicate and damaged more in life than others are. We must always walk forward in God's love and compassion.

Anytime we have prayed for others, we have experienced the gentleness of Jesus. His gentleness has always been present in any areas of healing that we have gone through. If we always remember the delicate heart, we will flow in the grace and compassion of the Lord.

In the times ahead, we are going to need the love and compassion of the Lord. It must be evident and a part of our lives. Many are going to be searching for the Lord and only His love and compassion will be able to help them overcome the evils of the world. We have all tried our thing, we now have to really step into the love and compassion of the Lord.

This will in many cases mean letting go of our ways of doing things and just let our spirits flow along with the Holy Spirit in completely new directions. The power of His love and compassion will override all evils present in the person or world.

Oh Jesus, please help us to bring out what is deep inside of us that should be expressed about Your love for others and us. So much has tried to block the wonderful experience and knowledge that You have planted in our hearts. We can sometimes be our own worst enemy. Things both within and around us block the gifts You have given to us.

Lord, place us where You would have us. Place us where Your gifts are of most value. Take us where You would have us go. Help us to be open so that Your gifts can flow freely. Protect us and take us out of situations that block Your gifts. Lift the areas of control that are still on our lives.

July 6

Glorious Arc

See the rainbow and praise its maker, so superbly beautiful in its splendor. Across the sky it forms a glorious arc drawn by the hands of the Most High. (Ecclesiasticus 43:11–13, Jerusalem)

Charles, our son, daughter-in-law, two grandchildren and I went to the nearby state of Pennsylvania. We stayed in a home in the mountains on the very edge of an animal preserve.

We had trouble getting this vacation together. It took from May 1 until the third week of July to straighten reservations. Problems occurred right up to the week before we were to start our vacation.

We believe the Lord wanted us to have the right place to spend our vacation. It took three tries and three different houses before we were able to find a home to rent for the week. We know there were other forces trying to prevent us from taking this vacation. We felt the spiritual struggle. It took trust to go forward and not say, "Let's not go."

The Tuesday night before we went we were still questioning the

Lord about this trip, we wanted it to be His Will and not ours. We spent some time in quiet prayer asking if we should be making this trip. Did He want us to cancel or did He want us to go?

That very same night I had this dream: My sister went around the corner of our house to check on the children. I went around the other corner. I looked up at the sky as I came around the corner of the house and I saw clouds shaped like a rainbow. This was for a short time. The bow of the rainbow took the shape of an arrow. It pointed straight up and was the colors of a rainbow. I told my sister the Lord was telling us to be peaceful. After this, I woke up.

Like the sun shining upon the Temple of the Most High, like the rainbow gleaming against brilliant clouds, (Ecclesiasticus 50:7, Jerusalem).

We did go on vacation and on the second day received confirmation of our decision. We were right where we were supposed to be. While sitting along side of a built-in swimming pool, I noticed the pool was in the shape of an arrow. This reminded me of the arrow in the dream that I had on Tuesday night. The lake, Arrowhead Lake, is where we stayed. We knew the name of the place where we were going, but it never meant anything until that very moment.

July 7

Return to Solitude

This vacation turned out to be a blessing from the Lord. The solitude was just what we needed to get back in touch with the Lord. We became aware of His presence all around us. We are the ones that go away from His presence. He is always present to us. The chores of every day living, place a distance between us.

This distance clouds our awareness of God's presence with and around us.

The very first day of vacation, we began to get confirmations from the Lord. We were right where He wanted us. He brought three special things to our attention. Charles turned on the TV and came upon a religious show. The speaker was a priest in whom we have confidence. The next show was a Polka show, where we heard music special to us. The third confirmation was the deer we saw when we went for a walk—the deer are very special to us in our relationship with the Lord.

God's beautiful nature surrounded us all week. We saw anywhere from two to two dozen deer each day. We saw a big black bear one evening, and enjoyed many other things around us. The most outstanding thing that touched our heart was the solitude, the quietness of the surroundings. The noise level was down to zero. In our journey with the Lord, we have had experiences full of the presence of the Lord. The solitude and quietness of the surroundings brought back some of these special experiences.

It became clear by the end of this week that the Lord was showing us how problems in the world affect us. We let them steal His joy and peace away from us. We have to *let go* and *let God* be the one to carry these problems. We have to be open to when and where He wants to use us. Most especially, we have to trust in Him.

The Lord had impressed upon us that we have to take time away from our regular routine. When there is silence and solitude in our hearts, the Lord can speak to us of His joy, love and peace. Called to return to the solitude of God, we turned again in that direction.

> "In silence wisdom is found, if only one listens
> to the Lord with an open heart.
> Love is silence, silence is solitude and solitude is prayer."

July 8

I Remember

...I remember, and my soul melts within me: I am on my way to the wonderful Tent, to the house of God, among cries of joy and praise and an exultant throng. (Psalms 42:4, Jerusalem)

Prayer: O Lord, we ask to be attentive to Your presence as the deer is to the sounds of nature around it. We see the deer standing near the running water, alert and aware of

Your presence. We ask to be alert and aware of Your presence around, in and with us.

Bring us to the living waters, often. Let us drink of these waters. Let us walk in Your steps, as we walk through the woods of our inner being. Open our inner vision, our inner eye. You walk upon our hearts like the deer that walks in the woods. You are there, with a sound not heard and motion not felt, touching us ever so deeply.

This was more than a vacation. It was a drawing, ever so deeply, back to you. It has been so deep; the arrow of time has not penetrated the senses with meaning. The arrow of Your love has penetrated the soul with Your majesty, love and mystery. My soul aches in a new way as I experience a sorrow and happiness, ever so deep. Only Your love and embrace will satisfy it.

Lord Jesus, I love You with a love beyond the expression of words that go through my simple mind. Only the touch of Your embrace is my desire. Every time You touch my heart with a new experience of love, my heart reaches heavenward embracing You repeatedly.

I have left a part of me in the silence of Your love and in the solitude of the Pennsylvania Mountains. Hold my heart in Your hands, Jesus, stroke it with the honey of Your love. Bring this deepness deeper. Touch every corner of my heart, mind and soul with Your healing love and embrace. I love You, O Lord.

July 9

Special Block of Time

In his great might he banks up the clouds, and shivers them into fragments of hail. At sight of him the mountains rock, at the roar of his thunder the earth writhes in labor. At his will the south wind blows or the storm from the north and the whirlwind. (Ecclesiasticus 43:15–18, Jerusalem)

We realized the Scripture we read before our trip spoke about storms. Our home state and area were undergoing very bad thunderstorms the whole week we were away. There was a lot of damage with as many as 1500 trees down. Our son and daughter-in-law lost a good portion of their vegetable garden.

After we were home, we had confirmation of the weather we had all week. There was sunshine mixed with rain off and on. We had Rainbow weather. First, you would see the sun, next there is rain.

The Lord had taken us out of our own surroundings and placed us in a "special place," a "special block" of time. We were safe and secure in His love and Peace.

July 10

A Call to an Early Christian Solitude

We went on a retreat for five days in November of 1991. We went with a few people from our home area along with a Spiritual Director from Massachusetts. This retreat was at a cabin in the New Hampshire Mountains. It was a wonderful place to spend a week with the Lord and each other. The weather was warm and the sun was shinning. Everything just worked together towards a wonderful week.

The first talk on the retreat reminded us of how we felt the presence of the early Christians when we were in Rome. This was especially true when we were leaving Rome for the countryside. Sensing their presence so strong in Rome made us wonder what it would be like in Jerusalem.

The early Christians would go into the countryside to pray and enjoy the solitude. They saw how they had to get away from every day struggles to grow in the solitude. They had to learn to listen to God and discern how He was speaking to each of them.

The Lord was teaching us to overcome difficulties instead of being overcome by them. To do this we have to be like the early Christians and go into the solitude. If we do this, we will become stronger and can help others in return. We could see that we were in the same situation as the Early Christians. We have to leave the Rome of self-desires, opinions and the like, so we can listen to the Lord. Going away to be quiet in the presence of the Lord, will help us to return to our homes and others in better physical and spiritual health. We have to love from the heart and not from the systems that we have built up around our heart and mind.

After the morning reflection, I saw the glistening waters upon the lake. I then received the following words:

"I speak in the desert of your heart.
It is the only place that the "self" can see its need and thirst for God.
"Glistening Waters!" Upon these waters, I glisten and I sparkle.
I give a new home that does not depend on the
world or on what you can or cannot do.
I give a new richness that is pure love and feeds
all of creation for all of eternity.
When troubled waters come, do not let life speed past you.
Take time to listen and let the waters of My
richness fill your heart and soul.
Let peace and silence go so deep that nothing
can disturb its grace and blessing.
The sun glistens on the waters, shining for all to see.
My love for you is there. It could be upon the lake, the river or the sea."

"The world does not know this place. This place is where the Father holds and caresses the heart. It is where the Son shines His light of redemption over your soul. It is where the Holy Spirit nurtures, feeds and strokes your heart and soul. It is where there is the fire and love for unity in the Trinity. The Mother of God is there to give you a Mother's unconditional love and encouragement."

"Walk this walk with Me. Hold My hand and let Me take out what needs to be taken from your system. Where your system has failed you, I will use My system of love to fill your heart and soul. The human condition cannot satisfy a heart given to God in solitude. The knowledge received and the truths engrained will not let you ever again be happy with what the world offers."

"Your heart and soul sealed with My covenant of love wears the ring of promise around it. Let the calm waters of My love come upon the shores of your heart and soul. Let the little splashes of water break upon the corruption that the world has flooded upon your heart and soul.

Let Me renew your system with the moisture of My heart, the blood and water completely emptied from My life for all of mankind upon the cross."

Our Spiritual Director said, "You will be happy with the gift of the world to you from God."

Prayer: Lord Jesus, bring me to the cross of my emptying out. Let the blood and water of Your death on the cross heal my wounded heart, mind and soul.

I then saw a light over the water—the sun glistened and sparkled. It sparkled so much that it looked like a dove fluttering over the water. All I could think of was the fluttering of the Holy Spirit. It only lasted for a few seconds and then vanished. I know it was from the Lord because of the way it came and left, not to be seen again. This confirmed the image we saw on our window at home. When I showed this image to the Spiritual Director, he said it looked like the Holy Spirit.

"Stay off the shores of corruption. Enter only by the ways I give you.
I will rise up the waters of safety around you.
Do not trust the waters of deception; much
is hidden under these waters.
The sun glistens on the waters, shining for all to see.
My love for you is there. It could be upon the lake the river or the sea."

Prayer: Lord Jesus, bring Your light and heat into my heart. Break up the congestion.

I then experienced an emptying out. I began to think of the congestion that is present in my heart. It was like a cold that we experience in our lungs or head.

July 11

Digging the Deep, Deep, Deep Wells

There are deep wells within the heart that have to be uncovered. The heart works as the pump that unplugs these deep wells. Revival is an individual relationship with the Lord, and in this relationship the Lord brings forth living waters from these deep wells.

What wells stop up the free flow of living waters within the individual heart? Where is the hidden pressure within these wells? Wells tapped into or broken open release the pressure.

Going to revival meetings, conferences, etc., is the prime needed to get these wells flowing again. Negativity that comes over us is like the Philistines stopping up the wells. Negativity is the distraction to stop the flow of the well.

You can give from your well, but instead of them using it positively, they use it negatively. An example of this: when getting ready for a Christian service, people call with negative news. The Philistines represents the evil and negativity that stop the wells within the heart.

Our first well was a shallow well and ran dirty and very low. Finally, we had to have a deep well dug. It sits now capped for future use. Are there any wells capped within our hearts? We now have city water, where we have a constant supply.

"The old wells still have to be unplugged.
There is a risk in opening these wells.
The love that can flow is worth the risk,
There are also fears there to stop the flow.
Fear is the root of every sin.
If you saw sin, you would not sin.
The love in the ending is worth the risk in the beginning.
I Thirst!"

July 12

The Raven

My friend, Donnie, and I were talking about "The Raven," a poem written by Edgar Allen Poe the month before she died. I had gotten the book from the library for her to read after we had been talking about it. I knew the Lord was going to talk to me through this book. I did not know what he was trying to tell me, until a year after Donnie had died.

We had a Mass said at our Church for Donnie. It was just a year from her death. On the day of the Mass, I kept hearing a Raven (crow) in the back yard. It was noisy and kept it up all day. Later in the afternoon, Charles went to see why the bird was making so much noise.

It turned out he had thrown away some stale homemade bread. The bird was making the entire racket over the bread. On Holy Saturday, a year ago, I had given Donnie a loaf of homemade bread for Easter. She was in the bathroom when I brought it to her. I left it on the couch for her to find. It turned out that I never got a chance to share with her again. She went into the hospital right after Easter and went into a deep sleep. We felt bad that we had not gotten a chance to talk with her again.

The noise we heard in our back yard from the Raven happened on the day of Donnie's Mass. We knew the Lord was blessing us for our friendship with Donnie. He was telling us through the raven and home-made bread that Donnie was with Him. He wanted us to be at peace.

July 13

Raven, Never More

The next part of the Raven experience unfolded, when we were on a trip to Burlington, Vermont. Charles had to go to a Hospital in Burlington for heart tests and possibly surgery.

We had gone through many struggles before we finally went to Burlington. The doctors had wanted us to go to Albany or Boston, but not Burlington. We felt all along that we wanted to go to Burlington.

After we checked out the doctors from Burlington our local doctors decided to let us go there.

The first three nights, Charles and I stayed at the motel. The fourth and fifth nights, while Charles was in the hospital, I stayed at Mt. St. Mary's Convent across the street from the hospital.

The first evening I stayed at the convent was the night of Charles' surgery. I went into the Chapel to thank the Lord that everything went along okay and I prayed Charles would have a good night. When I was going to the back of the Chapel, I saw a little Nun looking through the bookshelves. I went up to her and we became immediate friends. Her name was Sr. Clare. We had a lot to share. We sat up until 11:00 p.m. and talked about our mutual experiences. The Lord just led us from one subject to the next. Sr. Clare said that we were "kindred in Spirit."

During our sharing, I told Sr. Clare about my experience with the "Raven" and my friend, Donnie. She then told me how a newborn Child in her family was given the name of Raven. Her last name was Naramore. She said, "Can you imagine, Raven Naramore?"

I did not realize until later how much she looked like my friend, Donnie. The Lord placed the Raven experience before me again. I knew, from this experience with Sr. Clare, the Lord was confirming we were to be at Burlington. He was telling us He was with us.

Notice the ravens: they do not sow or reap; they have neither store-house nor barn, yet God feeds them. How much more important are you than birds! Can any of you by worrying add a moment to your lifespan? If even the smallest things are beyond your control, why are you anxious about the rest? Notice how the flowers grow. They do not toil or spin. But I tell you, not even Solomon in his splendor was dressed like one of them. (Luke 12:24–27)

This Scripture helped us to understand our experience with the raven and Sr. Clare. The Lord was telling us not to worry. The words "Never More" appear quite frequently in "The Raven." Can you imagine how we felt, when we connected Sr. Clare's name of Naramore, to the Raven? Raven Naramore was the name given to the new child in her family.

July 14

The Wadi Cherith

The Lord then said to Elijah: "Leave here, go east and hide in the Wadi Cherith, east of the Jordan. You shall drink of the stream, and I have commanded ravens to feed you there." So he left and did as the Lord had commanded. He went and remained by the Wadi Cherith, east of the Jordan. Ravens brought him bread and meat in the evening, and he drank from the stream. (1 Kings 17:2–6)

We went on a trip to Yugoslavia in 1990. While on this trip, twelve of us went to a Church in former Yugoslavia. Most of us were still in the Church when Charles came up to me and said, "You are not going to believe what I have just seen outside."

I followed him to the Chapel behind the church. I did not see it at first. Charles had to point it out to me. There in the Chapel was a large statue of Elijah. On the wall, behind the statue was a painting to depict the Scripture 1 Kings 17: 2–6. I shared this same Scripture with my friend before we had gone on this trip.

The statue was of Elijah holding a scone in his hand and a large black Raven on his right shoulder. The picture showed him in the mountains with two Ravens standing on the rocks and an angel hovering overhead in the clouds. "Oh, My God, My God," was all we could say.

July 15

A Deeper Thirst

As the hind longs for the running waters, so my soul longs for you, O God. (Psalms 42:1)

When we were overseas, Charles, a friend and I went to an outside Chapel. While praying, I became very aware of the people walking over the stones. It reminded me of the experience that I shared about the deer. The people sounded like the deer in the forest. The deer walked to the lake for a drink of cool, clear lake water. We believe the Lord was drawing us to Himself and creating a deeper thirst for a deeper relationship with Him.

July 16

O Mother, Sweet Mother

O Mother Sweet Mother, such tenderness You give.
Lift our hearts up to Your Son, there help us to live.
O Mother, sweet Mother, with a gentle touch You reach out.
Help us to seek the spiritual life with no doubt, no doubt, no doubt.
O Mother, sweet Mother, from You the graces flow.
We shout Father, Son and Holy Spirit, we will grow and we will grow.

The Mother of God was the first to hold the Body of Christ in her womb, her heart and her hands. She presents the Body of Christ to each one of us. We are the Body of Christ, and she holds us close to her heart as she looks in our direction in tenderness. Through her gentle touch and tenderness, many graces flow to us. Her deep spirituality can help us grow in a relationship with Her Son, Jesus, God the Father and the Holy Spirit.

July 17

Be Still and Listen to God

I see the cross before me, upon the distant hill
Listening to the sounds around me, it seems so still.
No breeze seems to be blowing, yet the trees do sway
It seems like God is saying, "Yes, they pray in their own special way."
The villagers are busy with their daily tasks
Pilgrims scurry about while in this village they bask.
Oh, the beauty that surrounds one in this heavenly place
Only proves God's love for all as He showers us with His grace.
He puts His mark upon us each and everyone

We know that in this village our heavenly walk has begun.
So take home with you the messages given from above,
God's Heavenly Mother will surround you with her love.
Shall not My Mother comfort you? Just call upon her name.
The love she has and wants to impart to all, every sinner the same.

July 18

Ireland so Green

I can see why the Mother of God has chosen this place,
To make herself known and be seen face to face.
The people are simple and lovable too,
They go out of their way, just to please you.
She has showered this place with roses and green,
No matter where you go it can be seen.
These people are grateful, and in their own way
Say thank you with Grottos you see every day.
They honor her with this show of love,
Blessed are they from heaven above.
I love what I have seen in Ireland, so green
Above all; the love, the calm and the serene.
Taking home memories ever so grand,
I will cherish these days I have spent in this land.
I go home very inspired,
Although I admit, a little bit tired.
I say "Thank You" to Jesus and His Mother too,
For making this trip special, through and through.

July 19

Chapel

In the Chapel on "Holy Hill,"
I sit all alone with Him,
I pray for guidance and the will,

Never to hurt Him again by sin.
I hear the hum of music
In spite of hammer and nails,
No matter how one views it,
Inside God's love, prevails.
I sit in awe and contemplate
Redemption, I could now see
Never too soon, never too late
His love for you and me.

July 20

Crying Out

If only the outer could become the inner,
My soul cried out one day.
I would do the things God wants me to
In a special and blessed way.
I would love the way God wants me to,
Not how I want it to be.
It would be unconditional and Agape,
The love meant for you and me.

July 21

Do not Play Games

His power and His presence are in our lives.
His presence is beyond silence and thought.
Take a moment to feel His presence in your heart.
Let the Lord carry your mind beyond the thoughts collected.
Let Him carry your heart beyond the silence of understanding.
Soaking in His power and presence in your heart will repair not only
Your mind, heart and soul, but will draw others to His presence.
These are serious times. Do not play games.

I Wish

I wish I could see my Angel,
Looking down on me.
I wish I could see him over there,
Sitting on that tree.
What would he say to me?
Would he say anything at all?
Would we just look at each other?
Would it be like staring at a wall?
What if his message was sad?
How would I respond?
Would I still welcome him?
To whom I am eternally bound?
Would I listen to what he had to say?
He is my spiritual brother.
I know his message comes from God,
Certainly not the other.
Wisdom and grace needs to be here,
I pray for both of them.
When one is in the presence of truth,
You cannot run away.
And so my guardian Angel,
I ask of you this day,
Push and shove me if you must.
Just keep me heading the right way.

July 23

The Lord is Watching

The Lord is watching and is pleased.

"I saw and I was pleased.
Joy, Love, Hope, Faith, Obedience.

Obedience is such a wonderful virtue.
Like the Eagle that rides on the wind,
Ride on the wings of the Holy Spirit.
The Holy Spirit moves swiftly in the wind."

July 24

The Tree Alone

As we look not to what is seen but to what is unseen; for what is seen is transitory, but what is unseen is eternal. (2 Corinthians 4:18)

While walking through the woods one day, the Lord brought our attention to a beautiful pine tree. This tree was standing by itself, spreading its limbs up and out in many directions. It could grow this way, for it had space and sunlight. The Lord used this tree to tell us that we have to come out of the woods or the world many times. We have to stand out and away from the rest, so we can grow in His peace, strength, freedom and wisdom.

He was asking us to come out of the woods and away from old habits, traits, and faults. Here is where we have to ask Him to heal deeply rooted scars that have wounded our hearts and minds. We can be separate in mind and heart from sin.

"Draw back and away for a while. Listen to Me
and grow in a closer walk with Me.
Do you know that from the smallest seed the tallest tree can
grow? You can grow just like that tree. See how tall it is.
See how its branches grow in every direction. Of course, it
means taking chances, being confident and trusting in me.
Will you take these chances?"

"Notice how the pine tree is out and away from the others.
It is growing in all directions because of no
confinement or crowding by others.
You may have to pull back and away from many activities so
you can listen to Me and grow in wisdom and virtues."

The Lord has planted a seed for a beautiful flower to grow in the heart of each of us. That flower is His Divine love. Like the tree, separate and growing in all directions, we too can grow if we have room to grow.

July 25

Thickest Part of the Woods

We will come to a time in our spiritual walk with the Lord, where only Jesus and you or I can walk together. It means going on alone with Him. We cannot bring others along this part of our journey. We cannot force them along with us, their will and limitations may be different. How God has called us may be different from how God is calling them.

We believe a large part of our struggle is that we really are afraid to make this journey alone. Therefore, we try to pull others along with us. We are all moving along the same path, but with the help and grace of God, each of us will go it alone. The Lord uses us to help one another to grow. At one time or another, in our walk with Christ, He will ask each of us to be ready to go it alone. Our walk will be with just Him as our guide and teacher.

As we walked out of the clearing, where the pine tree was, we noticed there were many trees. Going deeper into these trees, we walk into the thickest part of the woods. There were more dead trees in this part because of being overcrowded and not getting enough sunlight. Here one could lose sight of a clear path to follow. There were more snakes to contend with on this path.

The thickest part of the woods in this case represents the deeper parts in our hearts and minds. Overcoming self-love takes place here. The snakes represent the faults, sin and self-love that need forgiveness, healing and love. There are many snakes to protect and hide the many faces of self-love. It is very advisable now in our spiritual journey to have a Spiritual Director. A good director will help us stay on the clear path while we walk through the thickest part of the woods.

Our death to self, experienced alone with Christ, is a struggle. A Spiritual Director and others placed in our spiritual journey can only walk so far with us. Done alone with God is the deep struggle of letting go of the old self of the flesh. The deep healing that we speak about in this book is the walk into your own heart and soul where you are alone with the Father, Son and Holy Spirit. This means picking up your cross and carrying it to a place where all suffering becomes joy.

The change to the inside of our hearts and minds is what affects the outside and those around us—unseen changes. We perceive God outwardly, but we have to bring this perception inward, knowing that He is deep within us. Everything that is good within us is from Jesus present within us. He brings light into the darkness. Everything that is not from Jesus, He will separate from our hearts and minds.

The presence of God will fill every corner of our minds and hearts. We have made our hearts a den of thieves. There is junk standing in the way of our close relationship with God. This means change and letting the little seed grow.

Jesus is everything to every person. We must ask for the birthing of Jesus in our minds and hearts. We must look for God everywhere. Hang onto Jesus' every word and His ways of speaking to us.

Lord Jesus, let us be like the pine tree that is free to grow and spread Your Divine Love in many directions. Help us to grow tall and strong in Faith, Hope and Love

July 26

A Basket

> "I give to each of you a basket, full of love.
> I give to each of you a basket, full of understanding.
> I give to each of you a basket, full of sunshine and flowers.
> I give to each of you a basket, to sustain you
> on your journey home to Me."

> "Do not be intimidated by others, speak My words freely.
> There are those eager to hear and learn.
> A revival of love burns away the thorns of mistrust."

Holly Tree

"The Holly in the trees is the Holly of My love.
Come by the water and spend some time with me.
The Holly tree, meant to be a plant
of peace, will give you peace.
Come, come, and sit
with Me under the Holly Tree."

"Holly, holly, peace there will be under the Holly Tree.
Sun will shine; moon will be bright under the Holly Tree.
Hopes and happiness, meant for you and me, rest under the Holly tree.
Holly, Holly, Holly Tree!"

The Lord is calling His people to be Holy people, like the Holly Tree. In this lesson from the Lord—the Holly represents the Holy and the tree represents the Christian. The Holy Christian set apart for the service of God is the essential part, the heart and core of God's plan. The Holy Christian will be keen in Spirit or action and have quick perception. They will give support, strength and courage to others. They will move through God's people, little by little and spread the Word of God.

"Christ is going to come in power and wisdom, through
dedicated people. He is raising up those who can follow Him.
Christianity will be the city on the mountain that all
the nations will stream to and say, "Teach us.""

Grace Is

Grace is strength, comfort, counsel and help.
… is stronger than enemies, wiser than the wisest of this world.
… is the mistress of truth.
… is the teacher of discipline
… is the light of the heart.

…is the comfort in trouble.

…is the banishment in all desolation.

…is the nourishment in all devotion.

Grace is…

July 29

Be Separate in Mind and Heart

The Lord has planted a seed in each one of us.

The inside of the cup has to change.

It will affect the outside of the cup.

Thoughts can bring us into actions of sin in our life.

The Lord wants to heal the way we think.

The Lord has planted the desire for healing deep within our hearts and minds. The inside of the heart needs to change in order for it to have a lasting effect on others or ourselves. Bad or negative thoughts can draw us into actions of sin in our life. The Lord wants to heal our sinful attitudes and ways of thinking.

We can perceive God outwardly through our surroundings and others around us. He is asking us to perceive Him inwardly, knowing that He is deeply within us and waiting for us to respond to His presence.

"The tree by itself can grow in all directions. It has room to grow. Come out away from old things you do and have done. Be separate, in mind and heart. You can be separate and alone with God in your mind and heart if they are separate from sin. It means change and letting the little seed grow. God is everything to everyone."

Our Prayer: Lord, place the Holy Spirit at the entrance to our hearts and minds. May all thoughts go through the screening of this presence. Help us to be separate in mind and heart, as we stay aware of Your presence within.

July 30

Indestructible Seed

You have been born anew, not from perishable but from imperishable seed, through the living and abiding word of God. (1 Peter 1:23)

I had a vision of tree roots hanging on very tightly to the earth. The lesson we learned through this vision was, that the tree represents ourselves and how we should be hanging on to Our Savior Jesus Christ, staying firmly grounded in Him.

This taught us how we are nothing in ourselves, but are everything in Jesus Christ. We need to be completely dependent on Jesus, confirmed and affirmed in Him.

A tree that is to grow strong must have its roots firmly planted, as it holds onto Earth's rich soil. This is the same for Christians. A Christian must be firmly planted in Jesus Christ and grow in the image and likeness of God the Father, Son and Holy Spirit. The rich soil is the indestructible seed of Jesus Christ.

July 31

Carry Me

The more we enter into the spiritual realm, the more we let go of the natural realm. The way we respond to the prompting of the Lord has a lot to do with how we lived in the past.

O Lord, only Your love can carry the hurt. Carry me! Carry me!

I am too weak and afraid to walk on my own, as I journey beside You and follow You home.

Carry me! Carry me! I will follow You home.

"I have heard you, My child."

August 1

Seeking Only God

Love virtue, you who are judges on earth, let honesty prompt your thinking about the Lord, seek him in simplicity of heart; since he is to be found by those who do not put him to the test, he shows himself to those who do not distrust him. (Wisdom 1:1, Jerusalem)

The three words, seeking single simplicity, kept coming to me at different times. Through these words, the Lord brought our attention to the simplicity of a child and the single vision that is theirs. Our hearts can be open to God's will in a life of simplicity.

We try different ways to reach the Lord. We realize a person must have the single vision and simplicity of a child. We must be sincere about the fact that it is God alone we are seeking. He alone will fill our hearts and minds with His love. We cannot have one eye on the Lord and the other on ourselves.

Trust is the healthy soil for the seed of simplicity to grow. A child trusts when it receives all its needs. Nourished with food, kept warm and loved by their parents, children grow in healthy relationships. Trusting in God, we grow in a deeper relationship with Him and others around us.

The rams (pictured above) along the road in Tipperary, Ireland, look for the shepherd. They know that he will be faithful to them for their care and needs. They respond to him in simplicity and trust.

When we trust in the faithfulness of the Lord, we will become like a little child. With this trust, we will respond to a life of love. How do we trust in the faithfulness of the Lord? In our journey in life, we strive to do just that. We give each day and each situation to the Lord. We trust in His strength, power and most of all His love.

But the virtuous live forever, their recompense lies with the Lord, the Most High takes care of them. So they shall receive the royal crown of splendor, the diadem of beauty from the hand of the Lord; for he will shelter them with his right hand and shield them with his arm. (Wisdom 5:15, Jerusalem)

August 2

The Creator's Silent Presence

He created ... the pink color and soft petals of the flowers.
  ... the green color and freshness of the meadow grass.
  ... the glittering sprays and motion of the waterfalls.
  ... the hard and smooth rocks along the brook.
  ... the rough and smooth waters of the ocean waves.
  ... the mixture of blues and greens.
  ... the multicolor of our lives.
  ... the past, where each life has started.
  ... the present, where each life is right now.
  ... the future, where each life will go from here.
He created ... our past, our present and our future ...
He created ...

August 3

Angels Scamper

Angels scamper to see the risen Christ come over the horizon.
Around the table of the Lord we share the joy of the angels.
Even the horizons bow to the majesty of our Lord, Jesus Christ.
Let our horizons begin and end in Jesus Christ.
Jesus walks all horizons with us.

August 4

Simplicity and Peace is the Answer

Wisdom to confront the evil of today will come through the simplicity and peace in a one-on-one relationship with God. Simplicity and peace is needed to know how to deal with the problems of today.

Locking horns with others in disagreement is not the answer. We have to avoid bad teachings. Do what we can when necessary, always following where the Lord is leading. Our example of simplicity and peace in God is the answer. It will be the example we give that defeats evil.

We can go here and we can go there to be fed spiritually, but will not find many places with the true Christian teachings. We will have only Jesus to be fed by and turn to. He will bring His Little Children all back to Himself.

We always have to remember God's mercy. Some may be farther away, but through God's mercy, they will come back to Him. In fact, they could be first. Since Scripture states: "The last will be first and the first shall be last." All will be brought back to the basic teachings and a life in simplicity and peace.

August 5

Surface Shields

Reach into the Glory of God. God is drawing His church and His people to Himself in both life and death. He is saying to come close to Him. Come into an intimacy with Him. It is more than the surface, more than studies.

As you enter into His presence in intimacy, the "surface shields" will fall away. It is like a rocket ship returning to the earth after an expedition into space. The surface shields burn away as it enters back into the earth's atmosphere.

The Lord wants to burn away our surface shields to bring us close to Himself. He wants us to enter into His atmosphere, His glory, His presence. We must go into His space and return to share with others the gifts He gives to those that love Him.

Surface shields are those things that prevent us from entering into God's space, God's atmosphere. These must be burnt off. What are the surface shields that keep us on the surface in our relationship with God? Are they our need for knowledge or control? Are they our worries and fears? Are they the daily news and circumstances around us? Are they the good works we are doing? Are they our busyness?

Surface shields have their place in our walk with God, but a time comes when these have to be burnt and left behind. It is time for God's people to take up the sword of truth and put on the "shield of faith."

Words received: "Faith is the heart of the matter!"

Many "surface" studies have been done on our faith. Now is the time to jump into our "space suits" and let the Lord take us to places that enter deep into what our faith really is and what it can be for each one of us.

We live in troubled times where only our faith can shield us from the elements of surprise that greets the arrival of each new day. What is faith to me? It is a knowing that there is more to our relationship with God than what can be seen on the surface.

Prayer: O Lord, help us to lift our hearts up to You and to surrender our surface shields. Burn away whatever prevents us from drawing near to you.

August 6

Chances for Future Growth

When did we see you ill or in prison, and visit you? And the king will say to them in reply, 'Amen, I say to you, whatever you did for one of these least brothers of mine, you did for me.' (Matthew 25:39–40)

We were leaders of a Prison Ministry and went to a prison near our home every Sunday for seven years. There were many lessons and blessings received during these years. We shared Scripture and spoke about the presence of God in our lives. With love tested on many occasions, chances for future growth lie before us.

Our experiences at the prison helped us see another side of life. It had been good for us and was a time of growth. The Lord was teaching us to live the Beatitudes. Since we are very structured and strong willed people, we are accustomed to being "free and independent people." We make all of our own decisions and choices in life.

Many situations happened at the facility to break our strong will. We found we had to be very vulnerable and ready to adjust to unforeseen changes. We had to be ready to respond to these changes with God's love and wisdom. If not, a well-needed lesson was nearby. We would run into different situations with the residents, staff and rules of the facility, and we had to be open for correction and vulnerable to change at unexpected times.

We had to adjust to the rules of the prison. Plans made for our visit would not go as planned. They changed by lack of time, entry regulations or some other circumstances over which we had no control.

The Holy Spirit had something entirely different planned and used whatever changes the facility made. He could adjust to anything, where we as humans had to learn to go with the flow of the Spirit. We are still trying to be vulnerable and aware of the actions of the Holy Spirit. Through this new ministry, we soon learned we too were held in bondage. In many ways, we were prisoners. We were not in prison ourselves, but we did learn about the ways we were in bondage.

Lives full of wants and self will often miss the love of Christ. We asked the Lord to make us always aware of those around us that were hurting. His love is deep in the lives of those hurting and suffering. He is in the prisons, on the streets, in the hospitals and in other areas of need.

August 7

Precious Jewels Placed in our Hands

By wisdom is a house built, by understanding is it made firm; and by knowledge are its rooms filled with every precious and pleasing possession. (Proverbs 24:3–4)

Jesus had revealed to our prison ministry, how precious the residents of the prison were to Him. Each of them was a precious jewel placed in our hands. These jewels needed care with protection, love and truthfulness. A jewel has many characteristics. Each jewel is different when placed in the same vase. One can break easily, while another is stronger in consistency. One shines brighter and one affects others around it. We have to remember that each person is unique and precious to the Lord.

We shared the truths of our faith in the wisdom and truth of Christ. We did not bring in false doctrine or ideologies. These things would bring confusion into the special hearts and jewels of the Lord. We had to remember that we represented the Lord, Jesus Christ. We gave them the gifts and love He had given us.

We shared with people from all cultures in life. Each person's story was his or her own, that carried his or her own burdens and problems. The sin in the world has contaminated us all. With God's grace, we will survive this contamination. It is by saying *yes* to His call that we will know Him.

The Lord would not let us count numbers. Sometimes there would be twenty-five or thirty men to share with, sometimes one, two, or maybe none. It was important to share our lives and faith with the people that the Lord sent to us. The number present did not matter.

The Lord had blessed our ministry with many graces and a love for the men. We were free from placing any judgment on the men, as we shared with them. No one is ever free from the temptation of judging. We found, at least, while we were with the men we were not curious why they were in prison. We were all running the same race. Praise God!

August 8

Giving is Receiving

It is more blessed to give than to receive. (Acts 20:35)

Because of a controlled environment, the residents' material needs were few. They live in surroundings that have brought them in touch with the simplicity of life. The simplicity of life is where the soul can grow rich in God's love.

One Christmas we had gotten hats, socks and gloves for the residents, but soon found out there was a rule against this. We wanted to give from our material possessions. The Lord wanted us to give only out of His love. His love is all anyone can really rely on and has the most value.

With a good deal of discernment and prayer needed, we shared our lives with others. We have found this is true whether in a prison ministry or in our everyday surroundings. A positive way of sharing with others is to become like little children. Share from the heart of our lives and experiences in our faith. In the center of simplicity, we will find the center of our whole being. Here, we receive the love of God the Father, Son and Spirit.

Charles felt the prison ministry had set him free from self in so many ways. He could see his faults. He was more open. He recognized his sinfulness and his need for the mercy of God. He realized more and more how special the men were in the eyes of God. Jesus said He came to free the sinner. Charles said, "This must be the freedom I feel. I feel this every time I go to the prison. I receive much more than I can possibly give."

The resident's prayer time with the Lord was an example for us. When the men went to the altar at communion time, they knelt around the altar. Their lives touched the center of humility. Humbly, they prayed to the Lord with just themselves to offer. Nothing of this world blocked their time with the Lord. Their prayer would actually draw all those present in the Chapel, into the heart of Christ. We shared in a very special moment with the residents and Christ.

One important revelation of our whole Prison Ministry was when we received blessings from them. They needed to know this. We never went away from the prison with an empty heart. We were always full of the love we received from them. The blessings and grace of the Lord, Jesus Christ was there for us all to receive. They give so much to us. Christ's words in the Scripture of Acts 20: 35 explain this revelation much better than we could possibly do. "There is more happiness in giving than in receiving." We brought love and hope into their lives. Our lives crossed in life's journey. With the grace and blessings of God, we pray and hope we have made a difference.

Charles received the following revelation after returning from a visit at the prison: "Sharing God's love with the residents is the joyful union with God the Father, Son and Spirit. God's love is the same love and joy experienced when the soul leaves the body. This is love and joy in completion and the return of God's little ones to Himself."

August 9

Float in the Presence of God

We lost many gifts and natural instincts because of original sin. We lost these gifts because we separated from God. One of these was knowing God's will for us ... clearly. Another, we knew symbols and the meanings of these symbols. Freely given to us was seeing God's presence in everything. We could see His presence in nature and in every situation.

We have to float in the presence of God in and around us. If we come close to Jesus in inner peace, we will again know the presence of God the Father. He will bring forth the natural instincts and intuitions given to us in the beginning of creation that were lost because of original sin.

Natural instincts and intuitions are like the oars on a boat; they guide, direct and open our eyes to the Holy Spirit. This is seeing the truths of God through a new vision, seeing things that are sheltered in the shadows.

August 10

What Door Do I Open?

Strive to enter through the narrow gate, for many, I tell you, will attempt to enter but will not be strong enough. (Luke 13:24)

During the night, Charles heard me say, "What door do I open?" The following night I kept getting the number 72. The Lord then reminded us of the Auriesville Shrine that has a coliseum with 72 doors. No matter what door you enter into the coliseum, they all enter into the presence of the Lord.

"The Lord will open the door.
All we will have to do is go through.

To open the doors, *yes* is all that has to be said.

Jesus holds open the doors.

The light of Christ will always shine on the door that He opens."

In a vision, I saw hands holding open doors, same as an open book. One side of the book was full of light, telling me it was the door that Jesus will open. The light opens the narrow door into the revelation of God. His light will shine on our understanding and truth will unfold.

August 11

Seventy-Two Doors

After this, the Lord appointed seventy-two others whom he sent ahead in pairs to every town and place he intended to visit. He said to them; "The harvest is abundant but the laborers are few; so ask the master of the harvest to send out laborers for his harvest." (Luke 10:1–2)

The National Shrine of the North American Martyrs in Auriesville, New York, is 35 miles from our home. We often go there to spend quiet time in prayer with the Lord. The Mohawk Indians martyred St. Rene Goupil, St. Isaac Joques and St. John LaLande on these grounds. These three men were America's first and only canonized Martyrs. The blood of Martyrs was the seed of Christians in North America.

The shrine has a circular coliseum with 72 doors that go all around the coliseum. We kept thinking how the 72 doors represent ourselves. We were like the 72 in Luke 10:1–5, "We are the laborers that the Lord has sent out ahead of Him, sent out in pairs."

With these thoughts in mind, I called the shrine and asked them to send me some literature on the Coliseum. When this literature came, it confirmed the above Scripture. The 72 doors of the circular church recall the 72 disciples sent forth by our Lord on their mission of preaching.

Our struggles and joys unfold, somewhere, in the center of the above Scripture. The seventy-two doors represent our lives as we go in and out of new lessons and experiences with the Lord. Each of us enters into the

Sanctuary of God's heart to go out into the world again. Many doors have opened and closed in our journey with the Lord. The Lord is taking us through these 72 doors. When one door closes, another will open.

We have been through the doors of the Cursillo Movement, Charismatic Renewal and Revival Groups, Padre Pio Prayer Groups, Faith sharing groups, and Prison and healing Ministries. We have taken trips to Portugal, France, Italy and Yugoslavia. These movements, groups, ministries and trips helped to increase our faith.

August 12

You are to be My Arms and Legs

Now you are Christ's body, and individually parts of it. Some people God has designated in the church to be, first, apostles; second, prophets; third, teachers; then, mighty deeds; then gifts of healing, assistance, administration, and varieties of tongues. (1 Corinthians 12:27–28)

When we go in or out of another new lesson or experience, we often think of the 72 doors. Each door we go through, people have left their footprints upon our hearts. Lessons and experiences with these people left lasting blessings and graces.

The Lord reminds us, often in so many ways, what it is He asks of us. One Sunday I looked up at the Crucifix along side of the altar. It looked like the body of Christ had no legs from the knees down. I thought the Crucifix had been broken and was going to mention it to someone after the service, but before the service was over, I could see the missing parts.

The Lord reminded me of a crucifix that we had seen in a Monastery at Betalha, Portugal. The crucifix was in the section dedicated to unknown soldiers. The corpse on the cross had no arms or legs. A wounded soldier saw the cross beside him. He heard the words, "You are to be My arms and legs." The Lord calls each one of us "to be His arms and legs."

August 13

Whispers

Whispers are heard, but are not seen
Like winds in the night, at times could be mean
Some can be soft, like clouds up above
Setting in motion, a ministry of Love
Others like storm clouds that darken the day
Bring with them destruction, sometimes to stay
Whisper in Love, it is the right way
There will be no fear of the night or the day
Whispers of God come through to the heart
With love and compassion, for you to impart
Whisper to God, daily in prayer
Knowing He loves you and gives you His care.

August 14

Heavy with Fruit

The trees are heavy with fruit.
Carry your basket into the orchards.
Harvest the fruit before it spoils.
Fill your basket to the brim.
Place it on the table in My great banquet hall.
Open wide the door to Christ.
Open it wide to the God who lives in you and around you.
If you let the Lord have free will in you,
You would no longer worry, be sad, hopeless or lonely.

August 15

Gift of Discernment

And I am giving counsel in this matter, for it is appropriate for you who began not only to act but act willingly last year: complete it now, so that your eager willingness may be matched by your completion of it out of what you have. For if the eagerness is there, it is acceptable according to what one has, not according to what one does not have; not that others should have relief while you are burdened, but that as a matter of equality your surplus at the present time should supply their needs, so that their surplus may also supply your needs, that there may be equality. As it is written: "Whoever had much did not have more, and whoever had little did not have less." (2 Corinthians 8:10–15)

"You have gifts of the Spirit of discernment.
You must know that you will have all of the necessary
elements that will be beneficial to your community.
This will not be all you will have to do in the future.
I love you and know that you will do My will.
Please see the love I have for all of My
Children and make known My will."

"Please put Me first.
You will know I am to be first always.
You have the qualities to do much of My work.
You will know in time what I want of you."

"Love your fellow brothers and work with them
Know that I am with you.
Look around you always for those in need.
I hold you in My arms, and can know you will please Me.
You are to Me a fountain of peace, a book of grace and a letter of joy."

"Hope … that we will always be one.
We must please the Father almighty.
Together we can achieve all of these things.
Go in peace My Child and know I am always with you.
Hosanna!"

August 16

With All Your Hopes and Dreams

"With all your hopes and dreams you can come to Me.
I am with you at every breath. I am your breath. I am your life.
When you hold Me in your heart and mind,
The world around cannot touch you.
All the heartaches of the world, I have in My sight.
I want them in your prayers.
Remember My mother and pray often.
You can use her graces in your work for me.
My Mother is the Mother of the nation.
Hold her for the whole world to see."

August 17

Life of the Lily

Taste and See the Goodness of the Lord.

The first experience we had with the lily was when a nephew had passed away. We brought home a lily from the flower arrangement that was on his casket. We placed the lily on the kitchen table and a fragrance and liquid dripped from the lily for over a week. During this time, we knew that the Lord was saying this nephew was with Him.

Our second experience with the lily was the day after we had gone to the wake for my cousin that had passed away. We were in the chapel at the Little Sisters in New Hampshire, where Charles sat down next to a beautiful large white lily on the stand. All of sudden the lily gave off a beautiful fragrance and then a drop of a thick liquid fell on the stand.

I then got the words "even though the lily has been broken from the main stem, it can still give off a liquid and fragrance." All of us that were present felt and smelled the liquid that had fallen on the stand. The fragrance and liquid comes from the life that is still present and carried from the main center of the lily to the extended parts. I then thought of the Scripture read the day before. "Taste and See the goodness of the Lord."

God's creation carries extended values. Jesus' life, death and resurrection carry a future into the brokenness of humanity. This shows that God will bring all good back to Himself.

The two experiences we had with the lily's fragrance and dripping of liquid had to do with two deaths in our families. We felt the Lord had given us an example of how life continues after death—it may stop here in the physical but not the spiritual.

Our life, like the life of the lily, cut from the main plant, the physical, still carries the nutrients of the spiritual life within. If a person is not able to communicate physically in thought, word or deed, they still have a spiritual life within them.

When the physical gives out through age, illness or other circumstances beyond the person's control, both the physical and spiritual life held within should be treasured in value and dignity. They are part of God's creation extending values out to all generations with the morals and values of the Divine nature of God.

August 18

Christ is the Center of All

While spending time in prayer and going through my notes that I had written about the lily, I noticed that I had put them on a page with the above drawings. These two drawings are of tree trunks. The first drawing represents the diagram that I had seen in a secular book in the library. It told where Christianity started. This diagram reminded me of a tree, where I thought of Christ as the center with His many branches. All branches, connected to the main tree, are reaching up towards heaven.

Through the second drawing, the Lord was showing us where the strength of the tree is and how it stands straight and tall. The main trunk goes down into the ground where the roots support the tree that is above ground. Some of these branches extend out pretty far from the main trunk.

A tree surgeon would tell you that the branches and roots extending out beyond the trunk stay equal with one another to balance the tree. A tree that has fifteen-foot branches above ground will have fifteen foot roots extended out under ground. The above ground tree is only as good as the below ground roots.

In our Christian walk with the Lord we will only be as strong as what is deeply rooted in a personal relationship with Jesus Christ. The two drawings show us how we have to be centered and rooted in that deep relationship.

What a lesson for our spiritual life! A deep spiritual life extends below the surface. Our spiritual life, fed from the deep depths of the presence of the Lord, lies within our very hearts. We will only be as strong as the depth that is within.

There is a picture of Christ known as *The Coat of Many Colors*. This is Jesus with all the nations' flags as His cloak. The most important thing about the above drawings and *The Coat of Many Colors*, is the Lord showing us how He is the center of all life and love. He wants our arms stretched out like the branches of the trees, accepting Him into the center of our hearts.

August 19

The Dry Areas of the Heart

"The dry areas of the heart are being flooded with the
fountains of living waters, waters that are overflowing.
We cannot help but be filled with His presence as we
notice and become aware of His presence."

"Strong praise begets strong gifts, which beget strong communities.
There are two forms of grace: regular grace, which is
on us now and active grace, which is all the time.
Praise opens the heavens and brings forth both forms of grace."

I Hear You Call

I hear You call. I hear You call
Although I cannot see
I hear Your voice. I hear Your voice
Are You really calling me?
I am not worthy. I am not worthy
Is what I feel inside
To be called by Thee, to be called by Thee
To walk with Thee beside.
I fear to take the first step
It seems too good to be true
That I should be allowed to talk
And walk along with You.
I must be dreaming. I must be dreaming
Is all I have to say
Things like this just do not happen
To sinners like me I say.
When God wills things
Do not stand in His way
For you will miss His Glory
Coming to you this day.

August 21

Listening

Listening requires the heart to be open to the movement of the Holy Spirit, where the spiritual senses awaken. A new sensitivity towards the things of God becomes alive and active in Him. The ears become eyes and the eyes become ears. Listening and hearing becomes seeing. Seeing becomes listening.

Touching lightly and skimming over the surface of the natural listening, a listening person will be a teachable person and will have a listening heart. One will know how important it is to listen to others or how harmful it could be if not. Listening may require a reaction or a response of encouragement, or direction in one's own growth or that of others. Little ones around them may only need a listening ear and a small hug, while the maturing individual may need a listening ear and a great big hug. A listening heart will have the ears and eyes of God and will see the giftedness of others and in God's creation.

Listening is where the grace of what is unspoken meets the eyes of what is unseen. The listening person hears and sees what is not seen or heard. This is a spiritual truth even if it sounds contradictory.

When entering into the spiritual ears and eyes of the heart of God, the eyes are part of the hearing as the ears are part of the seeing. One might say, how is this a part of listening? The stillness becomes a sound and the sound becomes stillness, seen with the spiritual ears and eyes of the heart.

Through the listening ears and eyes the messages, insights, words and more from God come together like melting snow running towards the over-flowing rivers in spring. This is nourishment needed for each person's summer time with the Lord.

August 22

Volcano

One day, while in deep prayer, my heart experienced a deep purging and my thoughts turned to thoughts of a volcano.

A volcano has openings in the earth's surface through which lava, hot gases, and rock fragments erupt. Powerful forces within the earth cause them. Lava collects in a magma chamber under the volcano. Pressure on the chamber forces the lava upward through the conduit. An eruption begins when the melted rock or lava rises toward the surface. It is red hot and may have temperatures of more than 2,012 degrees Fahrenheit. The highly fluid lava flows rapidly down a volcano's slopes. The sticky lava flows more slowly as the lava cools and hardens into different formations. Volcanoes are among the most destructive natural forces on the earth. Since the 1400s, they have killed almost 200,000 persons.

Volcanoes also produce benefits. For example, many volcanic materials have important industrial and chemical uses. In ancient times, the volcanic dust was used in the building of aqueducts. Rock formed from lava is commonly used in building roads. In many volcanic regions, people use underground steam as a source of energy. It is used to produce electricity in Italy, Mexico, New Zealand, and the United States. Volcanoes serve as windows to the earth's interior. The materials they erupt help scientists learn about conditions within the earth.

We believe the Lord used the Volcano to show us the similarity of the Volcano with our soul. The volcano symbolizes our hearts and the lava symbolizes the corruption that builds up. This corruption has to come to the surface before we feel the richness of God's presence within our hearts. The lava spills over the side of the volcano. Corruption spills out of the heart and breaks up the crust around the hearts.

Deep-seated faults, rooted in our hearts, block a deep relationship with the Lord. Therefore, removing them is essential. When they come to the surface, they cause the hard crust around the heart to break up.

The different layers of the volcano can be compared to the soul. Pride, self-will, and self-love are in the deepest recesses of our heart. Old habits, fears, worries and other faults tempt us. Our feelings and emotions need healing. We know that God's love will break up the crust around our hearts.

We returned home from a trip to Europe on April 5, 1988. Our flight from New York to Albany was a memorable one. While looking out the window of the plane, we saw a beautiful sunset. This sunset looked like a volcano with lava running down the sides.

The Volcano serves as the window to the earth's interior. The material erupting from the volcano shows the scientist the conditions within the earth. The heart is the window to the soul. The conditions within the soul can be seen through the heart. The Lord had shown His love for us through the window of the volcano, the window of the heart and the window of the airplane.

August 23

I Have Drink for Those Who Thirst

"My people need food of the Spirit. Like the
tree of life, they should be fed.
The living waters are flowing for them if only they would drink of it.
I have drink for those who thirst.
They shall see My power and glory.
My light is shining for them.
Open their eyes so they may see, the Holy
Cross in the sky amongst the stars."

"A star in the night soon will be bright and then will be no more.
The cloud is forming for My chariot.
I am the light, the light that shines the Star
of David, Holy Cross in the sky.
Love the secret of My world. I hold you close. Go in Peace."

Jesus is the name above all the earth. Angels, gloriously,
adore Him. Forever, shall we be with them.

August 24

Follow Only the Reflection of Christ

At present, we see indistinctly, as in a mirror, but then face to face.
At present I know partially; then I shall know fully, as I am fully known.
(1 Corinthians 13:12)

While looking out of the bathroom widow I saw a reflection of light
along the electric wires. At first it looked like a line of car lights along
the Northway a super highway behind our house. When I looked a little
closer, I could see that it was not car lights, it was a reflection off the
wires. I knew right away that the Lord was trying to get my attention and
it had something to do with a "reflection."

I then got the words: "Make sure that the light you follow is coming
from the light of Christ and the Holy Spirit and not reflections of that

light, like in a mirror. You are to follow only the reflection of Christ. Do not follow the reflection of what may look like the reflection of Christ."

I then began to think about an image in the mirror, and the above Scripture came to mind. With these words and Scripture, I began to understand that not everyone carries the true reflection of Christ. From this point, Charles and I looked up the meaning of reflection in the dictionary and it can have different meanings.

A reflection; is that which is reflected, as an image; act of throwing back sound, light, or heat waves. 2. Reflection: thoughtful consideration ... or suggestion of discredit upon some one to blame.

Through the experience, Scripture, prayer and description of the word reflection, we understood what the Lord was telling us. He was telling us to stay out of the conflicts that are present amongst His people. Many of these conflicts are because of the problems in the world and church today. He was telling us not to play the blame game and not to follow others that carry a false "reflection" of Christ.

Others may seem to carry His image, but in reality, they are not of Him. We do not see clearly into every situation that is going on around us. We see but dimly. We may also look in the mirror and walk away not remembering what we look like. This is saying to be careful not to follow your own or someone else's image. Follow only what is His image. It will take prayer, discernment and wisdom to follow His image. Do not be misled.

Things of no value or that contribute to negative actions or responses need to be deleted from the mind. A clean slate is needed. One has to be careful of what is written upon this clean slate, so as not to contaminate the window to the mind and heart.

Our consciousness can be distracted. Praying constantly for spiritual help will free us from any contamination that slips in with this distraction. This can happen so easily by the will of others, knowingly or unknowingly. We must be on guard as the enemy prowls around like a roaring lion seeking to devour anyone he can.

August 25

Whale Watching and Footprints

Through the sea was your way, and your path through the deep waters, though your footsteps were not seen. You led your people like a flock under the care of Moses and Aaron. (Psalms 77:20–21)

While on vacation this past summer in New Hampshire, we took our grandsons whale watching. We left the Newburyport Harbor in Massachusetts where the Merrimac River empties into the Atlantic Ocean. We had a wonderful time. It ended up being very spiritually rewarding. It was interesting to learn how the whales migrate to the New England shores during the spring. Some return from the Caribbean, while others return from off the coast of Georgia or Florida where they migrate for the winter months.

We went twenty-five miles or more out on the ocean, which put us in International Waters. The children were touched by the fact that we were actually out of the USA. On the way out of the harbor, we saw a harbor seal and then as we got further out we saw Humpback, Finback and Minke whales.

We watched as the whales came up for air and then they would dive back down again leaving their footprints behind. The footprint is the very smooth spot left on top of the water. Each time that a whale would leave a footprint behind, we thought of the glory and power of God and His beautiful creation. He even gave a footprint to the whale, so others would know they had passed by. The sea is their way and their path is through the deep waters.

The Lord leads each of us to the sea and shows us the path through the deep waters of the heart. Along with Him we too, will leave our footprints behind for others to know that the presence of God has led others into these deep waters.

Rescue Boat

A violent squall came up and waves were breaking over the boat, so that it was already filling up. Jesus was in the stern, asleep on a cushion. They woke him and said to him, "Teacher, do you not care that we are perishing?" He woke up, rebuked the wind, and said to the sea, "Quiet! Be still!" The wind ceased and there was great calm. (Mark 4:37–39)

While heading out to sea on our whale-watching trip, the Captain told us that this harbor at Newburyport, Massachusetts, was the third most dangerous harbor in the USA. He then pointed out a very small boat along the shore. He said, "This little boat helps all the other boats, big or small, that might be having trouble getting into or out of this harbor. No matter what the storm or problem was this little boat would always end right side up. It would never sink because of the structure of the boat."

I felt the Lord tugging at my heart when the Captain was talking about the little rescue boat and the difficulty that a boat could have in this harbor. Insights began to unfold as Charles and I shared the things that remained in our hearts from our little ocean adventure with our grandchildren.

The Lord was telling us that no matter how hard things could or would get around us, He is there to save us. Things would come out good in the end because the little rescue boat always comes out right side up. Our son gave us another insight about the little rescue boat. He said, "When people are in the little rescue boat and are going through different situations, problems and trials, they have to row together. If they row against each other, they will go nowhere but around in circles."

In every situation, problem, lesson, instruction and difficulty, Jesus is there to calm the storm and steady the little boat. Sometimes the little rescue boat is sent out to help us and at others times it is for us to help steady and rescue others. In other words, there are times we need to be rescued and at other times, we need to be the rescue boat for others.

August 27

Tide Line

For he is our peace, he who made both one and broke down the dividing wall of enmity, through his flesh. (Ephesians 2:14)

On the way back into the harbor from our whale-watching trip out, the Captain showed us what a tide line is. It is a white line across the top of the water. This line shows where the Atlantic Ocean's salt water meets the fresh water of the Merrimac River. It was really something to see. Others do not always see this. While on another whale watching trip the following month with friends, we were unable to see the line at all.

The Captain said this section could be very treacherous at times. This is where the little rescue boat has to come to help the boats in trouble. The white tide line on the water, to us, represented the power that is present when the natural and supernatural meet. We are all living in the great ocean of God's love and eventually the soul will have to enter into this harbor.

We will come up against the natural while we try to enter into the supernatural. There is always a battle among the things of the flesh and those of the spirit. Like a boat coming into or out of the harbor, treacherous waters are being explored. The call from the Lord is to enter into these waters, drawing us into a closer relationship with Him. He is always in the rescue boat with us.

August 28

Not As I Am

"Not as I am, but what I can be," are words I received as I looked at a picture of hands. When our hands are joined with Christ's hands, they will become identical to His as they work in His service.

"May our hands be as one as you and I are one.

You need time in My knowledge and must first
live the standard you expect of others.
My grace is all you need."

Winds of Charm

Winds of Charm called us to the sea,
God's love surrounded you and me.
The day was dark and gray,
God filled us with His Holy Spirit to pray.
Walking in the sand with the winds and rain upon our face,
God gently moved us to this place.
Words of wisdom, God led us to write,
His Holy Spirit gave us new insight.
Seeing beyond the dark and gray,
God gave us the grace and blessings of the day.
The clouds did leave, you see,
Christ came over the Horizon to you and me.
We hold in our hearts the deep moments of pleasure,
As we pass through each new treasure.
God created this beautiful country for all to see,
Love, joy and peace He gave to you and me.
Time held dear, for dear it must,
Treasured in our hearts, memories never rust.
Winds of Charm placed before us comes
through God's precious creation,
Every shade of green spreads before us in jubilation.
Walls, rocks and trees surround each in just the right formation.
Rocks piled upon one another separating its locks of green,
Each field stood out quiet and serene.
Mountains, sea, lakes and streams,
Add their beauty to each scene.
Rams, sheep, cows and the like,
Walk about in sure delight.

God breathes His Holy Spirit upon you and me,
Carried upon each wind, each wave of the dark gray sea.
His graces and blessings surround us with love,
As He holds, caresses and strokes us like a gentle dove.
The breath and motion of the Holy Spirit surrounds,
He breathes His Holy Spirit into and around.
The breath and motion attracts and delights,
Making us more attentive, without fright.
The movement of the wind delights and draws us close.
The Lord is charming and drawing us to a
walk with Him in the up most.

August 30

I Love Each One of You

"My beloved child, surely you know you are My beloved child.
I love each one of you.
You are not here by chance.
I have tapped your heart.
I have forgotten no one.
I have enkindled you in a new test for love."

August 31

For Your Honor and Glory

Lord, let me use my senses for Your honor and glory.
Give me eyes to see good and Your presence in all.
Give me ears to hear only good,
Give me lips to speak and proclaim Your words.
Give me a gentle touch to reach out in Your
love, showing this love to others.

Irish Sea

'Twas by the Irish sea, you see,
We spoke with God, not one but all three.
He spoke in the breeze, salt air and water,
We were His two sons and one daughter.
Although it was windy and the sea rough,
We received many blessings and thought it was enough.
God's plans are always way above us.
We followed His prompting as though we were on a bus.
He led us through streets narrow and airy,
To His chosen Monastery.
It turned out to be the Rose of them all,
For St. Theresa's picture greeted us on the wall.
As we rested and we prayed,
A Rose in our heart was gently laid.
We saw our whole day truly blessed,
We know the hands of St. Theresa each one of us caressed.
We thank our God above,
For all of His gifts, especially His love.
We will always remember Ireland so green,
Knowing this all happened, it was not a dream.

September 2

We Choose to Reminisce

New friendships formed along the Irish Sea,
Precious mountains were reaching out to you and me.
Not knowing at the time but across the ocean blue,
New experiences were waiting, just for me, just for you.

.

In this poem written on the other side,
Our hearts continue to mature, continue to guide.

For, in these words precious and crisp,
We choose to remember, we choose to reminisce.
So back up for a moment, pray along with us,
The Lord will bring us together again in loving trust.
Look at the nearest cloud going by,
Do not look away or you will miss our wave saying, "Hi!"

September 3

Before The Cross

"The cross of freedom is for all,
With arms out-stretched, to thee I call.
Hearken to My words, little child,
Prepare to leave this world so wild."

"Adoration is to be,
Time spent alone just you and me.
No frills or worries should be there,
Only peace will be found in My loving care."

"I'll be there with you come what may,
Be it night time or be it day.
When you feel My presence true,
Know that I am there with you.
Faith, love, peace and unity co-exist with you in My love and unity."

September 4

Trusting Hands

I had a special attraction to Jesus' hands in a picture on the wall.
When meditating on this picture I received the following words:

"You don't see Me; all you see are My hands.
My hands hold you, protect you and give you blessings.
All you have to do is just ask."

"My Hands are strong, yet so gentle.

My Hands have created you and hold you close,
Not for just this moment, but for all eternity.
My hands will do and undo.
My hands are waiting to bring you to the Father, to welcome you.
My hands love and guide."

"Stay locked in My spiritual embrace. Offer
up all for My sorrowful passion.
Take Me home with you. Take the peace into your heart that
I have allowed you to experience while here these few days."

"Rejoice in My graces given to you.
The warm sun penetrates this room through the window.
Allow the warmth of My love to penetrate your heart.
Be simple, sincere and serving."

September 5

Footsteps of the Father

Listen to the footsteps of the Father
in the sounds of creation.
Hear the water
clap against the rocks, in jubilation.
A moment in God's presence, will tell what has been and what will be.
The time between each season, is where He
sits down to dine with you and me.
The young falcon cries for the guidance of the elder.
The trees sway to the breeze, the sun glistens across the water.
Glitter, Glitter, do you see?
Clatter, Clatter, do you hear them? Do you
hear the footsteps of the Father?
Frolic by the pond! Frolic by the sea!
The living waters lie across all of history.
Spring, summer, fall and winter too,
Form the reflections of My love ever so true.
Seasons in the heart are like the season of the year.

Each brings you into special times held so dear.
Be aware of the special time between each season,
Their change comes about without any reason.
Spring goes into summer, summer to fall,
fall to winter, winter into spring,
Flowing together they silently rejoice in life's new thing.
Today, is a time between summer and fall,
Coaxing the heart to answer God's call.
The Lord is dropping glitter all around,
So softly and quietly, but so profound.
The clouds cast a shadow that changes the scene,
In sudden solemnity and on low beam.
To walk on the water would be a sight,
Just keep on listening and you just might.
Clapping and clapping with joy and delight
Will bring us together in creations light.
Tall trees, small trees and bushes too,
Direct winds across the water ever so blue.
Thrown into each season is the heavenly breeze,
Carrying patches of grace ever to please.
Leaving this place is hard to do,
Leaving each season's spectacular view.
One day between the seasons in God's presence so near,
Everyone should cross over and enter here.

September 6

Breathe on Me, O Breath of God

The Lord had been speaking to our hearts all day.
Word after word flowed through us without delay.
The evening's beautiful sunset came in the same way.
Along the tips of the clouds, the light of Christ dances.
Pinks and purples caress the seams as the sun sets in the west.

Again, to rise in the east unfolding with morning's best.
With all of God's gifts and wonders, one can only shout:

"All of God's Creation dances and turns us about!"
Breathe on me, O breath of God!
Fill our hearts with Your joy.
We felt that we had stepped out of Your glory.
O Lord, through this beautiful day, You have
brought us back under Your clouds of glory.
Across the glistening pond came the gentle breeze,
Every so softly, He gave our hearts a gentle squeeze.
The breath of God blowing soft gentle breezes
stirred our hearts to listening.
He drew us near with nothing missing.
Why is it we have never looked at the sunlight and compared it to the light of Christ? Look at the heat, light and radiance of the earth's sun. Christ's light is so much more. The only way it can be compared to the earth' sun is in how it holds its position amongst the rest of creation.

Word received: "Pre-eminent" The light of Christ is superior over the earth's sun. It dominates the entire universe and is the visible image of the invisible God.

September 7

Birds of a Feather

Into the arms of trees, birds gather to rest,
Into the arms of God, we too seek our rest.
Like the birds that are happy and sing out with glee,
So we too will abide in His unity tree.
This tree of life will ever be,
A source of food for you and me.
Never more to hunger or thirst,
By its fruits be divinely nursed.
We are made, both you and me,
To be loved by the Father for all Eternity.
Thank you Spirit, Father and Son,

Through you, our redemption has been won.
We now wait this glorious day,
When angels will guide us and show us the way.
To Your kingdom up on high,
Joy awaits us never to die.
Are we alike?
Yes, birds that sticks together,
Are birds of a feather.

September 8

Patience is a Virtue

Patience is a Virtue,
Of which you need a lot.
It calls for calm and waiting,
Not demanding on the spot.
If all were given quickly,
What lesson would you learn?
Your dreams for things to come,
Your heart would not yearn.

September 9

Please Only Me

"There is good in everyone. You are just the records.
Eventually, the treasures you hold in your
heart will be shared with others.
You are to point out what is the extraordinary in the ordinary."

"Do with what you have. Follow no one but Me.
I am Your light, as you shall see.
Do not go in too many directions at once.
Please only Me. You shall rise as sure as the sun.
Appease human error.
Be as peas in a pod, fused together in Me."

When Confinement is Not Confinement

I was looking out the window when confined to bed with back problems. I could see the treetops that were shaped in steps.

Walking upon the treetops, my heart climbs towards you, O Lord.

The trees, leaves and branches reach up to the blue heavens.

In steps, I climb toward you, O Lord.

If the trees were, only strong enough I would climb upon them and run to you, O Lord. In the past two days, I have watched the leaves turn from green to red and dark brown.

What an advantage the birds have to look upon the earth from the treetops. They always have a higher view. O Lord, bring our hearts and minds to this higher view of You. I am sure the view is better from on high. The flight of the birds is free in wisdom and instinct.

Detach us from our earthly holds and let us fly as free as the birds in pursuit of pleasing You, O Lord. Somehow, confined to bed, I am as free as the birds. The heart and mind must be free in You, O Lord.

When our heart and mind is free, this body of corruption and death will bring us continually towards life, in You, O Christ. We never really die. Our physical death brings us to complete life. Therefore, we never die.

A free heart and mind while still here in this earthly life reaches heights to melt the hardest of hearts. A free heart and mind never dies. It lives on in the very center of all creation with God the Father.

Prayer: O Lord, help me to run across the treetops and climb up the colored steps to heaven. Help me hold these precious moments with You deep in my heart and mind. During this time of confinement place within my heart and mind Your thoughts and insights. Place my pen in Your hands and let words from Your Holy Spirit flow freely.

September 11

Live from the Heart

"It is by love and grace that all will come to enter My heart.
In essence, they will be entering their own heart.
We are living, God for God, when we begin to live from the heart."

"When your hearts and minds rise above all
that is worldly, all will surpass the
intellectual mind and float freely towards My
Divine Love, My Divine Heart.
Do not hold your minds and hearts in a bondage that is beyond you.
Open all doors to your heart and mind without any shadow
of the past that you hold on too, ever so tightly."

"Let your heart float freely with My love.
Let your mind float freely with
My heart and the two will become as one mind, one body.
Be of one heart and of one mind. Your hearts and
minds are one in My heart and mind."

All creation is one in the heart and mind of our Creator. When our hearts and minds become as one, unnatural perceptions can no longer hold us from the truth. The veil of untruth is split down the center. We have then become united and in harmony with our creator. Truth is, therefore what it was meant to be, when our hearts and minds are joined in what is real. We then can see our creator as we were meant to see.

September 12

Without My Love

"Without My love there can be no joy.
Without My joy, there can be no understanding.
Without My understanding, there can be no wisdom.
Without My wisdom, there can be no peace.
Without My peace, there is only death."

Are we Pharisees?

Have we not all the one Father? Has not the one God created us? Why then do we break faith with each other, violating the covenant of our fathers? (Malachi 2:10)

One Sunday at Mass, the priest spoke about the Pharisees. He said that the message that he would be giving would be a hard one to listen too. He was right!

He started by saying that we were all Pharisees, and he included himself. He asked everyone to look at their lives and see where they are Pharisees. If we want to be free in the Lord we have to be ready to ask the Lord; "what is your will for me and where am I a Pharisee?"

He said that it all starts with being honest with one another and ourselves. He said the Lord would give us the grace needed and it takes a lot of humility to stop being a Pharisee. Through the Scripture mentioned, we felt the Lord telling us that His people have been "breaking faith with one another."

Boy was this true. We just did not know at the time what to call it. We were in a situation at the time, and the sermon hit us right between the eyes. We were seeing this breaking of faith all over the place—in our own friendships and contacts with others. Confidences were being broken under the disguise of spirituality. Nothing was being held sacred and sometimes being misused in the name of faith.

The Pharisees wanted all rules and regulations adhered to, but were breaking the very laws they tried to enforce on others. In a very subtle way, the spirituality of the Pharisees has seeped into our culture, churches, and groups.

September 14

Wings of My Dove

"The wings of My dove are very tired.
My little dove looks for a nest to rest in, but few can be found.

Will you let your hearts be a nest for My Holy Spirit to rest in?
With falling ears and falling eyes, no one is
seeing or hearing My call for rest.
Those who do see and hear must lead others. Mutation needs fruition."

September 15

Drawing on the Window

All through our journey with the Lord, He has given us little reminders of a call to write. One of these was on September 22, 1991. Charles and I had just finished morning prayer when we noticed the above drawing on the window.

This drawing was on the inside of the living room window. It had very fine and silky lines and looked like a web that had been formed and drawn by a spider. We looked at it up close. We could see that it was not a spider web. We had been talking a lot about the angels that day. We began to wonder how the drawing got inside the window.

We thought the drawing looked like a rose with writing on a tablet behind it. We had to wait, like all other experiences, for the Lord and His wisdom.

We had gone on a retreat some time after this experience. When we showed this drawing to our Spiritual Director, he felt it looked like the fluttering of the Holy Spirit.

The Holy Spirit fluttering in front of the words on the tablet again was a message to us. The Lord was telling us to continue with our writing. His Holy Spirit was there to help and guide us, as we went along.

September 16

Piercing Prayer

"For the eyes of the Lord are on the righteous and his ears turned to their prayer, but the face of the Lord is against evildoers." (1 Peter 3:12)

We met Sean O. Shaughnessy in Medjugorje, Bosnia in 1990. Through our friendship with him and his wife Theresa we were introduced to his parents Noel and Irene. We became immediate friends with them when we went to Ireland for Sean and Theresa's wedding in September of 1997.

The Sunday our new friends were to arrive from Ireland for a visit with us, Charles woke up early praying. He thought to himself, our playmates Noel and Irene would soon be leaving Ireland for the USA. He then heard, "No, your prayer mates will soon be on their way. You don't seem to realize how powerfully 'piercing' in prayer your playmates are."

Right away, we knew these words had a special meaning behind them. This meaning was given to Charles through the following book.

Quotation: "Prayer, 'piercing prayer,' as Julian of Norwich, another legendary hermit called it, affects something mightily. It pierces to the heart of God, like a strong electric current coursing through the Mercy, subtly rearranging and reviving everything. Rafe was so convinced that the real work of prayer was done at this level that he used to say, only half-jokingly, that the principal job of a hermit was to "help maintain the spiritual ozone level of the planet." (6.)

As special days ahead unfolded with our friends from Ireland, we felt that our "piercing prayer" was helping us to remain in the atmosphere of God

September 17

Atmosphere of God

In His hand is the soul of every living thing, and the life breath of all mankind. (Job 12:10)

What is the Atmosphere of God and why is it important to spend time there?

The word atmosphere, taken from the Merriam-Webster Dictionary, means: a mass of air surrounding the earth; a surrounding influence: a dominant effect. Surrounding means to enclose on all sides: encircle. Influence means the act or power of producing an effect on the condition or development of something, to sway or modify.

The Lord our God, is the creator of all creation and His presence fills the very air we breathe. His presence surrounds us. Being aware of this prevailing presence can help us to enter into a completely new area of development in our spiritual walk with Him.

We need to tap into the presence, glory and power of God. We need to be "affected" by the moving power of the Holy Spirit in our lives. This will have an "effect" on our minds, life and actions. This is where we will see truth and what is good. We will recognize evil for what it is.

Spending time in praise, worship and the Glory of God brings you into the very atmosphere of God. Reading Scripture and other spiritual literature, sharing about God with others, along with prayer and quiet times with the Lord brings the atmosphere of God in and around you. We have to ask the Lord to bring us into His glory and revelation presence.

The prophets, apostles and early Christians saw the value in spending time in the "Atmosphere of God," where they received revelations from God. People like Abraham, Moses, Jacob, Samuel, David, Isaiah, Jeremiah, Mark, Luke, Matthew, and John, just to name a few, knew how to find this secret stairway.

I dropped a small piece of paper on a glass tabletop. This showed us how my little piece of paper affected the whole top. The atmosphere of evil versus the atmosphere of God and in a large or small way, we all contribute to the corruption in the world. We all add little small pieces of paper to the glass tabletop.

It is time to let the world know how the Lord is talking to His people today. We must seek out and look towards the glory and revelation of God in our everyday life. Believing that we can enter into the Atmosphere of God is especially important in our day and age.

Eleven Days in the Atmosphere of God

You will show me the path to life, fullness of joys in your presence, the delights at your hand forever. (Psalms 16:11)

We stayed eleven days in the Atmosphere of God with Noel and Irene O'Shaughnessy, our friends from Cork, Ireland. We picked up Noel and Irene at the airport one afternoon, and our eleven-day adventure in the Atmosphere of God began. During these eleven days, we ended up spending time being playmates and prayer mates.

We spent Sunday evening catching up on family news. Then we talked a little about the recent words and messages we were receiving from the Lord, especially, about being play-mates and prayer mates.

Monday morning we visited the Candle Light Shrine and the Divine Mercy Shrine in Stockbridge, Massachusetts. From there, we headed off to the Little Sisters of St. Francis in Danville, New Hampshire, for a four-day retreat.

After arriving at the Little Sisters, we joined Sr. Therese in the chapel for the Divine Mercy Chaplet. Early in evening, we went to the chapel again for adoration. After adoration, we shared the things that all of us were getting during this special time

We ended up having play, prayer and sharing time every day during the eleven days together. We had not realized at the time, but Monday was our second day of being in the Atmosphere of God. It had all started the very first evening, Sunday night, at home while we were sharing.

We stayed at the Little Sisters until Thursday and then we went on our way to the St. Rafka Retreat Center in Shelburne, Vermont. We stayed there overnight and had a great time, sharing with our friend, Fr. Anthony. The next day we visited our friend, Sr. Clare at the Sisters of Mercy Convent in Burlington, Vermont. We had another powerful afternoon of sharing. We ended this day with a pleasant boat trip that took us across Lake Champlain from the Vermont side to the New York side of the lake.

September 19

We Laughed, Prayed, Shared and Cared

We rode bikes, flew kites, wrote in the sand, enjoyed the ocean, went dancing, walking, shopping, let balloons go up, sang songs, and we laughed and laughed.

We read Scripture, prayed devotional prayers, prayed in tongues and rested in the Holy Spirit. Spending time in the presence of the Lord, we prayed and prayed.

We received words, insights, knowledge and discernment from the Lord as we shared and shared. We talked, walked and flowed in the presence of the Lord.

We ended up receiving spiritual food and physical rest and enjoyment for the whole eleven days. We thought, when we came home from our visits to the Shrines and our retreats with the Little Sisters, Fr. Anthony and Sr. Clare, we would end up entering into the regular everyday routine. None of us wanted to return home.

We were pleasantly surprised. We still had spiritual sharing and praying every day and night, right up to the last day that Irene and Noel were with us.

We had returned home from our visits and retreats on Friday and went to a Polka dance on Saturday night. While at the dance, the four of us and another couple went into the chapel that was adjacent to the dance hall. We spent a short time there in prayer and the presence of the Lord. After the dance, we went back to our house to share and pray again. During this time, the Lord had blessed us for spending time with Him that evening. We received a powerful anointing in the gift of pure holy laughter, a laughter that only the Holy Spirit could cause to happen. There were no funny jokes shared that could cause this laughter. The Holy Spirit flowing through each of us caused this to happen.

For eleven days from beginning to end, we had entered into the atmosphere of God, where the rich oils of His anointing were present to us. It was wonderful!

The Indian Chief

While on a retreat, I received these words:

"Heard most clearly in the middle
of the noise, is the soft voice in
prayer. It pierces through the darkness.
Although everything appears dark, there is still life in that darkness.
The prayers in the silence bring growth to
the life hidden in the darkness."

This same day I had a vision of an Indian Chief. The Indian had on a headdress that went all the way to the ground. The feathers were all white with blue and silver jewels on the front. He had on brown skins.

Our Spiritual Director for the week had spent many years on an Indian reservation, so I shared my vision with him. He said that the Indian Chief could represent Christ. The headdress that went to the ground represented absolute authority and obedience. White feathers represented healing. The Indians' symbol for healing is white feathers. Each feather in the headdress represented a victory. He said if we follow Christ, there would be many victories.

I had a vision of a Princess getting into a carriage. The Spiritual Director helped me understand that the carriage was the temple of the Lord. It was the tabernacle of Christ. I was getting into the carriage. I was entering the heart of Jesus. This vision also reminded me of *Cinderella* that was shared earlier.

The Indian Chief in my picture is of a statue that I had on my shelf at home. The statue, when knocked down, shattered into many pieces as it fell to the floor. The picture shows the scars of battle across the chest. The battles we fight each day will leave many scars, both physically and spiritually. That is why we need the Lord, Jesus Christ to be our Indian Chief. He is our Savior and the healer of all scars.

September 21

The Dove of Peace is Over You

"Do not fret and let your heart be heavy.
My Spirit is with you.
I see the burden you are holding on too.
The Sun will shine and the dark cloud will pass.
I see all and watch over all. Know that I am with you.
The Dove of Peace is over you."

September 22

God is With Us

The light of Christ placed on any situation, scene or season,
Exposes a completely new perspective and reason.
This light holds us together,
As we receive love and blessings as light as a feather.
When the trees are bare of the summer's growth,
The light bounces off the bark, a new reflection of both.
The evergreen stands straight and tall,
Their reflection of green creates life across all.
When the light goes behind a cloud,
The scene changes and cries aloud.
"I'm waiting for the light again to come across my bow,
Come again, come again, and come right now."
Like the trees that stand and wait,
You and I become a part of heaven's gait.
We move into the scene before us,
Knowing that the light of Christ brings life in trust.
In any situation, scene or season,
He is the way, the truth, the life and the reason.
The light of Christ shines upon us all,
Penetrating and going through any wall.
Above, below, around and under,

All that is not life is driven asunder.
His light moves over and in us, still,
Unfolding love and blessings from God's will.
There is so much to say about this light,
It would take a season, reason and foresight.
Stay in this light, as long as you can,
Let it never be known that you looked and ran.
Hold onto this light and do not flee,
Stay close and alert for you will see, you will see.
This light can be so bright,
You will have to look again to see if you got it right.
You will need sun (Son) glasses,
While revelation before you, passes.
Each beam of light,
Carries the truth and is dynamite.
Here and about in every scene,
Joy and laughter you will have to scream.
Revelation is what it is about,
"God is with us," you will shout.

September 23

Fragrance of the Rose

On the last and greatest day of the feast, Jesus stood up and exclaimed, "Let anyone who thirsts come to me and drink. Whoever believes in me, as Scripture says: 'Rivers of living water will flow from within him.'" He said this in reference to the Spirit that those who came to believe in him were to receive. (John 7:37–39)

While resting in the Spirit at a Healing Service, I felt my heart open. It opened like a flower to the morning sun. The Holy Spirit filled my heart. It was a beautiful experience. I felt I was lying under a faucet and there was no end to the riches it contained.

Something was fed into the center of the flower in my heart. It was like the in-filling of nectar to the center of the flower. It came to me to "be aware of the fragrance of the rose." I then smelt the fragrance of roses.

From the words that I had gotten, I knew the Lord was giving me a deeper meaning. The nectar of the flower is the sweetness of the flower. This sweetness gives us the beautiful fragrance. Bees use this sweet liquid, secreted by the flowers, to make honey. In this experience, the nectar is the Holy Spirit and is the simple faith, the in-filling of the Holy Spirit in our hearts.

While in prayer and interceding for others, I had asked the Lord for pure faith. My prayer was, "Let me love You, Lord, with a pure heart, mind and soul."

The Holy Spirit is the gift par excellence who dwells in us, as not only a comforter and sweet guest, but also a perpetual fount of living water.

Quotation: "So this loving Spirit, who makes us exclaim "Father!" is that Gift par excellence in which are contained all divine gifts. Hence it is that the Holy Ghost is also rightly called the Gift of God. It we but understood it well, it is certain that we would wholeheartedly desire to satiate ourselves in that fount of living water which takes away all earthly thirst and gives life eternal. "This Spirit is called living water because He satiates, refreshes, washes, purifies, renews, and give life, vigor, and robustness." (7.)

September 24

Bee Buzzing and Congestion

During a quiet time with the Lord, we heard a bee buzzing behind us. We looked around and saw a very large bee. It came to me that my mind was busy with thoughts, just like the bee. I said, "O Lord, I understand." I then tried to keep my mind from racing. The bee stopped as quickly as I said this prayer to the Lord and I did not hear it again. When we left we looked for the bee, but it was nowhere in sight.

Quotation: "The religious soul, the Mystical Bee also has his flower to which he keeps returning to pilfer the honey of pure love. This Divine flower is the host. Oh, little watcher of the sanctuary, whether so many hearts like butterflies, have come to be consumed with love!" (8.)

I began to think how a cold and congestion in the chest causes us to cough. Vapor treatments and other healing aids help to break up the congestion. The vapor treatments acting on the congestion are just like the vapors of love and grace. When we are sitting in the quiet presence of the Lord, love and grace breaks up the crust around our hearts.

Then the house up the street from us came to mind. While out for a walk one afternoon, we stopped to look at a newly built house. The ground or clay around the foundation had broken away from it. This brought to mind how the Lord works on the crust around our hearts. He breaks up the affects of sin on our heart and soul.

When the Lord places a desire for pure faith in our hearts, nothing else can replace it. It is like the bee that makes the pure honey. The desire for pure faith is making the pure honey of faith.

September 25

We Sometimes Stand in the Way

Prayer: Help us Lord to stand in the living waters and in the light and heat of the flame of Your presence. We sometimes stand in the way of Your light shining through to others.

What are the blocks that stand between us and the flame of God shining through to others? Is it our human nature? Is it self-pride? Is it feeling unworthy? Is it our shared guilt with Adam? We have to remember that Baptism freed us from the original sin of Adam. We cannot let Satan or anything in our own nature block the light and our progress in the spiritual life with our Lord, Jesus Christ.

September 26

Change in Anything Takes Time

"Will you walk into the unknown realm of My Holy Spirit?
Let the cloud of the unknown surround you.
Come into the mist of My love.
Become saturated with the dew of My grace.
Be free of all earthly things.
Let My spirit guide you. All I ask is Your
submission. Know that I am with you."

"An Honorable devotion and effort is required for change.
Change in anything takes time. These times are
for changing and undoing things that
have really set in. Sharing and understanding of
each other is very important in change."

September 27

Across the Ocean Blue

As we look across the ocean blue,
We share loving thoughts of both of you.
Miles and miles may set us apart,
However, nothing can stop what God does impart.
God's love is upon us this bright and sunny day.
His love surrounds us in a special and unique way.
Leaves are gently falling covering the ground,
With colors so majestic, one knows God is around.
Birds are singing and trees are swaying,
As a gentle breeze blows.
All are in perfect harmony,
Knowing from whom these graces flow.

September 28

As Close As the Eagles

"As close as the eagles were to you today,
I was guiding their every flight, near and far.
The flight to your mind and heart,
I caress with My love and grace.
On eagles wings I lift you up to the heights of My love.
There must be a Holy detachment, dead to self, to attain it."

September 29

And Suddenly

A precious mother and grandmother by the name of Barbara, who
reached out to others in many ways, was killed in an automobile
accident. While thinking and praying for her, these words came to me:
And Suddenly! Barbara has been lifted up into the light of Christ.
And Suddenly! The Lord took her when she was giving life to others.
And Suddenly! She has full view of all of heaven's glory.
And Suddenly! Her family, gone before, was there to greet her as she
Passed from this earthly life into her spiritual life with Jesus.
And Suddenly! Her family and friends find the
loss of her presence before them.
And Suddenly! Everything has been turned
upside down. Time and love mixing
Together will fill all hearts with Barbara's presence in a new way.
And Suddenly! All will find that the same
arms extended out to Barbara are
Holding them close together in His heart and love.
And Suddenly! All will walk forward remembering
her love for her family and friends
And their love for her.
And Suddenly! Life has a whole new meaning.

And Suddenly! Between the seasons of winter
and fall, Barbara received her call.
And Suddenly! Fall a season of harvest and winter a season of rest,
Barbara gave her answer to the Lord and it was, "Yes."
And Suddenly!

September 30

Our Son

God sent a son to you and me, as
cute and lovable as can be.
He has brought new joy and happiness into
our life, and made us closer as man and wife.
He cheers us when we are sad and blue, by
all the funny little things he will do.
He is a happy little fellow most all the while,
and always awakening with a smile.
God sure has been good to you and me, just
look at our son and you will plainly see.
A proud Mother and a Dad as there can be
because God sent a son to you and me
So Let us always give thanks to our God above,
for letting us share in His wonderful love.
May we always be guided by His way of life,
being a good Father, Son, Mother and Wife.

October 1

Autumn Leaves

One day while sitting on a log in
the woods praying, an autumn leaf fell
into Charles' hand. This autumn leaf was full of grace and blessings from
God the Father.

"This is a special time and place where faith, love, and
hope can grow in the autumn of each heart.
Be as free as the autumn leaves. They fall from
the trees and land wherever they please.
In color and splendor, they cover the earth in preparation
for the beautiful white snow of winter."

As we walked through these leaves, we felt the Lord talking to us. God's people are to walk with Christ and make a difference in the world. He made us aware of the different leaves and drew our attention to the different people that need to hear about our life with Christ.

In the rustle of the leaves, we could hear Him say, "Speak out, when walking along this path. Listen and be obedient." The colors of the leaves were clear, bright, delicate and pleasing to the eye. Through the colors, God was saying, "Be firm and gentle in trusting love." The presence of God, felt by many, is in our hearts. Faith is felt and experienced in the trust and love of God.

On another occasion, late in August, we went for a walk along a country road near our home. We became aware of the leaves on the trees as they were changing to the autumn colors. We noticed they were changing, from the outside edge, working in towards the center. There was a mixture of red and yellow colors while the center of the leaf was still very green. In the past, we would notice how the trees were turning to the autumn colors. Up until now, we never noticed which part of the leaf would start to turn first.

We knew the Lord was speaking to us, telling us that change will begin from the outside. Sometimes making drastic changes to our lifestyle, and the way we think and act. These surface changes in our life affect the changes of the heart and soul. The same as the changes of the heart and soul affecting the way we live. In all appearances we can change on the outside. The final conversion is done deep in the heart, mind and soul of each person.

When change begins in a person's life, they will notice that the direction they were taking was away from God. Seeing this, they will now reverse that direction and go towards God instead of away from Him.

October 2

The Hem of His Garment

They scurried about the surrounding country and began to bring in the sick on mats to wherever they heard he was. Whatever villages or towns or countryside he entered, they laid the sick in the marketplaces and begged him that they might touch only the tassel on his cloak; and as many as touched it were healed. (Mark 6:55)

I had a vision of the bottom of a white garment and feet that were in sandals. I felt that this was Jesus. We had understanding of this vision during a Home Retreat held at our home in 1997.

As we were resting on the floor in the Holy Spirit, the priest and two deacons walked amongst us. As their garments brushed across our faces, we thought of the above Scripture and vision. In the Scripture Jesus walked in the marketplaces where the people reached out to touch the tassel on His cloak and many were healed. We felt the hem of His garment had brushed across us leaving His garment of love, blessings and protection over us.

October 3

Alone With Me

That very same day, two of them were on their way to a village called Emmaus, seven miles from Jerusalem, and they were talking about all that had happened. Now, as they talked this over, Jesus himself came up and walked by their side; but something prevented them from recognizing him. (Luke 24:13–16, Jerusalem)

Then they said to each other, "Did not our hearts burn within us as he talked to us on the road and explained the Scriptures to us?" (Luke 24:32, Jerusalem)

We went on another retreat with our friend Sr. Clare Naramore. She lives at the Sr. of Mercy Convent in Burlington, Vermont. When we went to pick her up, we traveled north on the Adirondack Northway. We missed our exit to her place, causing us to go a different way.

As we drove along, we understood we had to go a different way to see the beautiful view. The Lord spoke to our hearts through the beautiful mountains that surrounded us. Words from the Lord filled our hearts.

"The Lord's shadow is over you.
He is showing you a new way to go that has a beautiful view.
The view is from within.
There are obstacles there to slow you down.
It will be like the unrolling of a spool of thread.
There are many crevices in the heart."

This retreat was at the St. Rafka Retreat Center about fifteen miles out of Burlington. Sister Clare had been there before, but it was the first time for us. The Spiritual Director for the retreat house was not there when we arrived, but we managed to find the key and then made ourselves at home.

The house was a large, old farmhouse and very cold. Without wasting any time, we went in search of the thermostat to turn up the heat. We knew it was going to take some time to get warm. While waiting we sat in front of the electric kitchen stove with the oven door open.

The anxiety of every day life lay heavy on our hearts and minds. It is always noticeable when one is in touch with the solitude of God. As we sat there, we thought of how we were surrounded with the beautiful Green Mountains of Vermont on one side, and the New York Adirondack Mountains on the other. We then began to settle down into the quiet atmosphere of the house. More words from the Lord settled in around us.

"You are alone with the Alone.
Not a word is spoken as love is vibrating all around.
Requiring patience and perseverance, undoing takes more than doing.
Spending time in solitude will reap great rewards."

We were still cold so we made a visit to the chapel for prayer and then went to bed. When we went into our room, Charles went over to the stand and picked up a flier that was there. This flier was all about being "Alone with Me."

October 4

Locked Gate

Saturday morning, we walked the path to the beautiful fields behind the house. We talked about the way the Lord was beginning to speak to us, already.

We walked as far out into the field as we could before we came to a gate. The locked gate prevented us from going into the next fields. The fields on the other side had both fencing and heavy brush to protect them from intruders. There was no way we could go any farther. The strong and well-constructed fencing had no openings to crawl through. We had to turn around and go back.

We had the desire to go into the field on the other side of the fence. Somehow, we knew the path went to the water. We could see a little water from the field. Disappointed, we could not walk any farther; we turned around and headed back to the retreat house. When we turned around, we saw farm machinery along side the road. We went over to the machinery, sat down and enjoyed sitting in the beautiful sun and presence of the solitude of God. We enjoyed hearing and feeling the presence of God in the quietness around us. We came back saying we wanted to walk out there again in the afternoon.

When we got back to the house, we had a little prayer meeting with Sister Clare. We sat on the porch in the wonderfully warm sun. We then fixed lunch and again stayed on the porch. After being cold the night before, we were not going to let this beautiful sun go to waste. We enjoyed the sun and each other. The rest of the weekend, we were warm in the house.

It was mid-afternoon and the two priests still had not gotten there. We began to think it was going to be just the three of us, Sr. Clare, Charles and myself. From the beautiful words, thoughts and Scripture, we were receiving; we knew that we were not alone. If we could have seen into the spiritual world, we would have seen the porch full of blessed spiritual beings from God. WOW was all we could say. Wonder of Wonders!

After our prayer meeting and lunch, Charles and I returned for our second walk down the path behind the house. We took a notebook, three small books and our camera with us. We walked out to the center of the field and sat on the farm machinery again. We did not try to go to the gate because we knew we could not get over or around it. All we could do was look at it.

We sat sharing the confirmations that the Lord was giving us of the words we had received during our prayer meeting with Sister. We got these words as we were enjoying sitting there: We are enjoying the Lord's "Majestic Melodious Mountain Music."

When we came back, we shared again with Sister. We then went to the chapel and spent some time in the presence of the Lord. We did this off and on all weekend.

Fr. Joseph, Fr. Anthony and his brother David did finally arrive. We enjoyed our supper together with them. We then sat sharing for a while and then went to bed.

October 5

The Key for the Gate

Sunday morning, Charles and I got up, washed and dressed, stripped our beds, packed what we could and went for another walk. This time we had the key for the gate to the fence. Now, we could walk into the inner field next to the woods and water. Fr. Anthony had shown us where the key was the night before.

As we walked along, Charles heard in his heart, "Grace Chastens heals." We looked up the word chastens when we got home and it means to inflict in order to reclaim. The Lord was certainly speaking to us in many different ways.

The gate to the inner field was about three quarter of a mile from the house. We unlocked the gate and walked the rest of the path to the woods. We came out upon the rocks next to the water.

We then turned from there, followed the path up the hill, and came upon the rustic chapel and hermitage. The windows boarded up for protection from the winter weather kept us from seeing into these buildings. From here, we went back to the rocks near the water. We sat soaking up the sun and cool breeze of the autumn air. The October sun was peeking over the fall trees. When we sat upon the rocks, words began to flow from the presence of the Lord.

"You will find serenity in the scenery.
There are a thousand islands in your hearts.
Come to the water, I will refresh you."

Lord, teach us how to drink of these waters.

"See how easy My ways are.
The business of the world coats over the simpler life.
In the middle of the rocks, leave a plateau for Me.
I say to these rocks, speak and they will speak.
The living waters call.
I wish to refresh you. I speak and it is.
Blessings befall when you hear My call."

October 6

Jesus is the Key

There was bamboo, or reeds, near the waters edge. How simple or basic they appeared to us. All we could think of was how Moses was found in the basket amongst the reeds. After seeing the reeds, we thought about the basket we had seen in the barn and remembered Charles calling it, "Moses' basket."

This Sunday was like Palm Sunday for us. Jesus came into our hearts in all of His Glory, just like on Palm Sunday. These thoughts made us think of the reeds again.

The Lord was speaking to us in many ways, while we sat along the water's edge. We stayed next to the water for about 45 minutes. Then, we decided we had better get back to the retreat house. We left for our walk before anyone was up. We thought they might wonder where we were.

As we walked up to the gate from the water, we began to understand the strong significance of the whole weekend. The house, the outer field, the gate, the key, the inner field, the woods and water, connected to strong spiritual meanings for us.

The house offered a spiritual, peaceful, shelter from the outside world. It was a place where we could enter a deeper relationship with God.

The outer field is the first field next to the house. It represented the walk we have to make to settle into God's presence, leaving behind the world.

The gate to us represented the obstacles that stand in the way of a deeper relationship with God. It was a line of offense drawn in the middle of the fields. It could work either for us or against us, drawing us to or away from the (inner field) deeper relationship with God.

The key is Jesus. Fr. Anthony had given us the key to open the gate. God the Father has given us His son. He is the key to our salvation. Jesus is the answer. The inner field was the solitude we experienced next to the water and rocks. Moses went up the mountains to listen to God, the same as we went to the solitude near the rocks and water.

October 7

The Gate, Our Humanness

As we closed the gate behind us, we looked back in sorrow. We did not want to leave this place and return to the world. This is where a deeper meaning of the gate and key began to unfold. We walked back to the house, talking about how we try to reach the spiritual life on our own initiative. We felt that we could only go so far in this world on our own. We then come to the gate, our humanness. Our humanness tries to cross into the deeper spiritual life that is in our hearts and minds.

The bushes around the fence were thick. The gate was the only entrance into the inner field, which led to the woods and waters. There was no other way but through this gate. Also true of the spiritual life, the only way is through the one gate, using the key that is Jesus. There were no easy short cuts, no openings in the fence. The gate was high and in good condition. There are no short cuts to the Father; all have to go to Him through His son, Jesus.

We soon find out through the power of the Holy Spirit, that this gate opens only through Jesus. He is the Key to the deeper spiritual life. Refreshing waters run deep in our hearts and minds. We can only reach these waters through Jesus and the power of the Holy Spirit. Words of confirmation of the above thoughts came from one of the books that we carried with us on our walks.

Quotation: "He has engaged to secure by the gift of the Holy Spirit a holiness in us, which could never have been obtained by our own efforts. We soon learn that sin has paralyzed all our moral motor nerves. Every person needs to withdraw into Jesus. Escape somewhere, somehow." (9.)

"The murmuring, complaining heart is one which has already commenced to disbelieve in the wise and loving lead of Christ, and is one in which unbelief will thrive." (10.)

October 8

Gleaning

'Yahweh Sabaoth says this: Glean, glean, as a vine is gleaned, what is left of Israel; like a grape picker pass your hand again over the branches!' " (Jeremiah 6:9, Jerusalem)

According to Macmillan's Modern Dictionary, the word "gleaning" means to gather stalks and ears of grain left behind by reapers ... to collect or gather with patient labor, gather whatever is left by harvesters, pick up or pick out by degrees. Collect and remove from a field, any fruits left by harvesters.

The Lord is asking us to help gather His flock and His words will be there to guide us. He wants us to be diligent and on the alert for a remnant few that have been forgotten and left behind by others. He asks us to be patient in our labor while we help to gather His people. He asks us to be attentive, non-tiring and to persevere in this task

"Let me go to the fields and glean among the ears of corn in the footsteps of some man who will look on me with favor." (Ruth 2:2, Jerusalem)

So she gleaned in the field till evening. Then she beat out what she had gleaned and it came to about an ephah of barley. (Ruth 2:17, Jerusalem)

Ruth went out to the fields and walked behind the workers, picking up the heads of grain, which they left. She knew that there was still good left in the fields of harvest. She found there was plenty left behind by the harvesters.

God wants us to be guided by His words and to help gather His people. There is still good fruit in the hearts of His forgotten people. This fruit is rich with the sweetness and breath of the Holy Spirit.

October 9

New Harvest

I had a vision in which I was walking through wheat fields. While in prayer this evening, Charles had a vision of fields plowed and turned over. Our thoughts were of a "new harvest," as we received the words:

"How deeply the Holy Spirit can settle in,
depends on who is building the nest.
Are you building the nest or is it the Lord?
When you see the birds moving about, do they look worried?"

What is the remedy for the problem of worry? How do we keep the web of worry from forming over the Holy Spirit? Prayer is the answer. Check the heart for hidden malice and impurities. Ask the Lord to separate the vile from the precious.

O Lord, bring faith, hope and love into our hearts and minds. Heal the congestion of impurities in and around us. Take the impurities and sin from our hearts and minds.

It is nice to know that the living waters are all around the Thousand

Islands in our hearts. It's nice to know that as the thread of our life is unwound from the spool of time, the Holy Spirit is there to weave it into a beautiful fabric.

A bird makes a nest to house its little ones, as it carries twigs back and forth to the newly formed nest. The little dove in our hearts makes a nest to house the presence of God. It carries love, blessings and the graces needed to heal our hearts and minds.

We were being fed the oil of renewal and were being refreshed in the Holy Spirit.

The words from a song they sang in church that following Sunday were:

"They thirst and the Lord will give them the finest wheat."

October 10

Light and Mist

Light and mist came across the autumn leaves adding to their splendor and coaxing their colors to come forth.

"Listen to your heart beat and you will hear Mine in unison with yours.
We are not far away from one another.
We are within each other.
None can come closer
As the mist of time clears, My presence can be seen.
What is mist, but a vapor in time?
What is time, but a vapor of Mine?
I am elevating your mind and hearts to an understanding
and knowledge that passes through the mist of time.
That is all that time is ... a mist
I am coaxing you to come forth just as I coax
the autumn colors into existence.
Come forth, come forth, and come forth.
Oh, child of Mine
Wipe the mist from your eyes
Time does not hold you.

I have given you a freedom that walks you through the mist.
Just reach out your arms and I will draw you
into My glory and revelation.
Reach out! Reach Out!"

"The mist is as the silence, it surrounds you.
It can be felt, for you know this to be true.
You can touch the silence.
This is true because I have given you knowledge of My presence.
Silence is golden, in so many ways."

"Look at the golden rod that grows in the wheat fields.
It rustle's not a sound as it bends back and
forth in the soft winds of My love.
The wind of My spirit blows across the brow of your
head bringing the golden glory upon you.
Come rest in My golden glory, My Golden Rod!"

October 11

Heavenly Harvest

Honor the Lord with your wealth, with first fruits of all your produce; then will your barns be filled with grain, with new wine your vats will overflow. (Proverbs 3: 9–10)

"You can't bring in the harvest if you don't have the right tools. The harvest has to be brought in at its own peak—no sooner, no later, only the right time. The tools are the fruit. This is a heavenly harvest and for heaven, the harvest has to be perfect. Give the first fruits to the Lord. The fruit (choice souls) are separated; some go to the market, some for lesser use. Tie up the broken branches and loose ends. Close off the broken and loose ends. Sometimes you cannot see the loose ends. Do not become slaves again."

What are your loose ends? What have you left unfinished? Loose ends are obstacles. They have to be revealed. The presence of Jesus in

229

your heart will help to reveal them. What blocks your growth in the spirit? The answer is the loose ends. The loose ends are things that are tied up to sin. They can also be distractions and attachments that distract us from our place in Christ.

"Fill your baskets with My first fruits and distribute them among the least of our brothers. The rays of My sun (Son) place rich fruits in your hearts, where they will be nourished in My love. Whether it is by My ocean waves or fallen leaves, the beauty you enjoy around you is only little examples of My love for you. I want to express My love in many deeper ways, but you have to open the doors to your heart, wide open, so that many bigger blessings can come in."

Prayer: O Lord, these doors are heavy. You have to help us to open them. Let us be like little children, free enough to "swing on the gates of heaven, just as a child would do." Help us to swing on the gates of heaven. Help us to be that free with not a care in our hearts.

Enter the gates with thanksgiving in your hearts with trust, love and forgiveness. You have to stay close to the quiet side of your lives. Close to the spiritual life, close to the heart of God, close to His presence amongst you.

"Try to do something each day that draws you into My presence. For each, it will be My gift just for them. Each one's gift may be different. You will know your gift because it will be placed where there is no doubt, but only love. Your hearts may be in your physical bodies, but I hold your spiritual hearts in My presence where I caress them with My love. You will know My presence because you are open to listen to My heart, My love, and My words."

"I breathe on you with the breath of My love. I hear not only your words, but also I hear your heart and at its every beat, I am present. Breathe in My presence. I heal the wounds that the world has made. He, who drinks the water from the well I give, will never thirst. He, who eats from the harvest I give, will never hunger. My Heavenly Harvest will last forever."

Touch the Hues of My Love

"Autumn is a time for harvest, full of the colors of My Glory.
Spread before you, is a blanket of My love.
All you have to do is reach up and receive
what I have placed before you.
My greens, yellows, golds and reds are richer.
All of creation is rich with My Glory.
Touch the Hues of My love."

October 13

Holy Hill

Here on this Holy Hill,
Come all who suffer or are ill.
Here three Angels are to be found,
This place for me is Holy Ground.
All are welcome, just come and see,
The joy that surrounds both you and me.
God's love and mercy are here to stay,
All for the asking, nothing to pay.
So if you are weary and all alone,
This is the place where you can atone.
Just spend some time with Him today,
Knowing your prayers, He will convey.
God knows our hearts better than we,
He is always looking inside to see.
How do we react to His loving word,
Are we true, or have we not heard?
I pray that God inside me will see,
A child like spirit, happy to be.
Lost in His love for all to see,
Together with Him for all Eternity.

231

October 14

Colors of Joy, Hope and Love

Lord Jesus, throw Your colors upon us.
Let Your red soak into our spirit.
Let Your yellow soak into our hearts.
Let Your gold soak into our mind.
Oh, colors of joy, hope and love
Bend our spirits, hearts and minds towards Your ever-gracious presence.
Let splashes of Your great gifts come upon us in all Your glory.
As we ride along life's journey, let us notice the richness around us.
Let Your colors run into each other.
Let Your joy run into hope and hope run into love.
Let Your red run into yellow, let yellow run into gold.
These colors form, shape and mold the truths
in our hearts, spirits and minds.
I see You, O Lord, holding in Your hand the
sparkling colors of joy, hope and love.
You are throwing them upon the green mixtures
in our hearts, spirits and minds.
As they mix with the trees of Autumn Season they too,
also mix with the autumn season in our hearts.
Help us, O Lord, to rest in these colors and this little place You
have brought us to enjoy, with hope and everlasting love.
Lord, touch my lips that I may speak of Your love for us.
Lord, touch my ears that I may hear of Your love for us.
Lord, touch my eyes that I may see Your love for us.
Place upon our hearts, spirits and minds the
gentle touch of Your love for us.

October 15

The Rainbow of Your Love

There are many colors in God's Rainbow of love.
Some we see and some we do not see,
Some we hear and yet do not hear.
Some we touch and yet do not feel.
His presence with us, through us and in us is melted into the
pot of Gold at the end of His rainbow in our hearts.

October 16

Make My Heart Your Heart

"Make My way your way.
Make My love your love.
Make My hopes your hopes.
Make My life your life.
Make My wounds your wounds.
Make My suffering your suffering.
Make My Joy your joy.
Make My heart your heart."

October 17

Wanting You O Lord

I want to be with You Lord, no matter where or when,
To walk where You walk, and to go where You have been.
To feel Your presence gives me peace in all I say or do.
Should misfortune come my way, I will face it all with You.
Although I cannot see You I know You are at my side.
I feel Your love surrounds me because within me You abide.
I walk along with Thee in seasons bright and gray,
Knowing You will let me see the good that comes from those who pray.

October 18

Fish Ladder

We spent an afternoon with our grandsons at the fish hatchery in Oswego, New York. This fish hatchery is a place of safety where the fish can reproduce and grow into adult fish. They spawn here and the babies are kept safe until they are large enough to go off on their own. They will return in two to five years, for they experience in their memory the taste and smell of the water where they were raised. Their sense of home leads them back to the hatchery.

The fish climb the fish ladder to get back to their home. The ladder is made of concrete and has steps that gradually end up in the hatchery. There is a small door that the fish can go through at the bottom of the step or they can go up over one step at a time. It is not easy for the fish to do this. Some do not make it.

Like the fish, we must return to our original home with the Lord. That is in a deep relationship with the Lord. This is where purification and restoration can take place.

We have to ask the Lord to take us higher and higher into the spiritual realm to live in His glory. This means going deeper and deeper into the living waters of the river of glory. This is where restoration and purification takes place.

October 19

Spiritual Ladder

Let us ask the Lord to help us climb the spiritual ladder taking us into the depths of His glory. On these stairs or ladder, we will encounter many spiritual battles and will have to fight against many forces in order to climb the ladder. Like the fish it will not be easy to do, some do not make it.

Our sense of "home" draws us toward the Lord and the different levels in the spiritual life. We must return to the living waters. Can we climb a spiritual ladder? Can we reach up into the heights of a spiritual life? This can only be done through the power of the Holy Spirit.

We have to go into the depths of a deeper relationship with the Lord in order to reach the heights. We have to give God permission in submission. This is where purification takes place and God places a desire in your heart for this relationship.

October 20

Jacobs Ladder

Then he had a dream: a stairway rested on the ground, with its top reaching to the heavens; and God's messengers were going up and down on it. And there was the Lord standing beside him and saying: "I, the Lord, am the God of your forefather Abraham and the God of Isaac; the land on which you are lying I will give to you and your descendants." (Genesis 28:12–13)

He called a child over, placed it in their midst, and said, "Amen, I say to you, unless you turn and become like children, you will not enter the kingdom of heaven. (Matthew 18:2–3)

Jesus said, "I am the way and the truth and the life. No one comes to the Father except through me." (John 14:6)

Jesus speaking to Nathanael, "You will see greater things than that," And then he added, "I tell you most solemnly, you will see heaven laid open and, above the Son of Man, the angels of God ascending and descending." (John 1:50–51)

The message from all of the above Scriptures was telling us that our expectations have not been high enough. We have settled into believing that things were going to be small. The Lord wants us to be thinking "big" in our expectations of His presence amongst us, not in numbers but in strength and power.

We believe that this is a Jacob Generation … A generation where we can expect to hear from and see the Lord … A generation of revelation.

October 21

No Chance Meetings

The Lord will guard your coming and your going, both now and forever. (Psalms 121:8)

The Lord was speaking in so many ways. Many blessings, lessons, and messages came from the words, thoughts and Scriptures that we received at home and on our Emmaus retreat.

"Keep your eyes on Jesus. You will receive refreshment.
Are you going to leave Me too? No Lord, not I."
(Every time I read this, I think of Peter and
how he denied Jesus three times.)

Prayer: Lord Jesus, cut the web of untruths that are around us. Every fiber of my heart cries for You, O Lord.

"I'm looked up to as a pauper in this world, but as a prince in the next.
Suffer with Me. I sweat blood for you. Fear
not for I am with you always.
If you would only take My hand, I will lead you."

"The Ocean may roar and the mountains may
fall. Be not afraid. I am with you.
I know Mine and Mine know Me, and no one will snatch you from Me.
Hold these words close to your mind and heart. Keep Me close to you.
The beauty I have just shown you is a foretaste of what shall be.
Peace, know that I am God. I am with you
always, but you are not always with Me.
I am calling you My children to help save souls.
Take up your cross daily and follow Me."

Go Beyond Your Expectations

"Receive My messages like a flashing
light…blue…white…blue…white.
The narrow is before you.
My abundant blessings are waiting on the other side.
Soon the door will close, do not be left out.
I await you on the other side.
When you are quiet and listening, I can speak to you.
Be prevalent, My children.
Beyond the fields of life is beyond the door.
Go beyond your expectations.
Go in peace My children."

October 23

Autumn Grace

Charles got up the morning of our thirty-fourth wedding anniversary and played our favorite song, "Moonlight and Roses." He then asked me to dance with him. When we looked in the mirror, we both began to laugh. We showed our age and looked like we had been married for thirty-four years or more. It turned out to be a very funny situation and a very special time with the Lord.

As one can see from the above picture, the tree branch is holding the winter snow above the autumn leaf. Our life is being held in the palm of God's hand where He chooses to fill our lives with autumn grace and "His Moonlight and Roses."

We have entered into the autumn's grace of our life with each other and the Lord. Graciously, the Lord was helping us to enter into our elderly years and our winter's rest. He then blessed us with special words and thoughts about the autumn time in our life and the winter's rest that follows.

Autumn's grace helps us to accept the winter's rest. With the winter's rest just around the corner, the trees are becoming bare of the autumn leaves. The beautiful colors rest upon the ground, soaking up the moisture of the falling rains. The trees look forward to the cool gentleness of the coming snow. With these thoughts in mind, sway to the music in your hearts.

We have to be in touch with the music in our hearts, the music of God's love for us. This music brings forth the colors for the artist, words for the writer, the songs for the musician.

"Bare from the autumn leaves, the trees sway in the wind,
They are playing the music of God's love for us.
God asks us to sway to the music in our hearts.
Sway, as the bare trees of autumn, sway to the gentle winds.
Let Him be the gentle wind that bends our senses in His direction.
God's presence moves in the silence in our hearts."

Prayer: O Lord, let our hearts be full of Your autumn grace. Let Your colors shine from our hearts. Bless us as You bring these beautiful colors together in Your love for others and us.

October 24

Our Heart Goes Into Seasons

Our heart goes into seasons, just like the seasons of the year.
In the spring, summer, fall and winter, seeds are planted in our hearts.
These seeds germinate and then come forth into something
beautiful, just like the seeds in a flower garden.
Find a special place to soak up the silent presence of the Lord.
Get away from the everyday clutter and clatter of the world around you.
Clutter... too much stuff in our lives.
Clatter... too much noise in our lives.
The clutter of stuff and the clatter of noise will prevent our
hearts from entering into the seasons of the heart.

It is His Blueprint

We have been given a blueprint from the Lord.

This blueprint is to follow the leading of the Holy Spirit.

We are not to use our own blueprint. We are to use His.

The seasons are His Blue Print for us all.

What happens in each season? Changes happen that are necessary for growth.

Each season is before the other and needs the other.

The fall precedes the winter; the winter precedes the spring,

The spring precedes the summer, and the summer precedes the fall.

These seasons are also seasons in the heart.

The fall brings harvest into the heart, preparing the heart to rest in winter's arms.

The winter keeps the heart in hibernation, where the Lord can coax the heart forward into spring. The spring spreads before the heart a new life, which is rich in the summer gifts of the Lord. The summer produces full growth and gets the heart ready to accept the harvest of fall.

The heart must open to the functions of the seasons on the heart. These seasons will bring changes on the heart. There are four seasons of growth with winter being in the center and deepest season with the Lord. The fall is preparing us to spend the winter in listening to the Lord. Rest in His arms this season.

Walking in the Autumn of My Heart

I have walked in the rich splendor of Your rich autumn colors.

This time You are calling me to walk in the autumn rain,

In the breezes of the evening wind and in the wet leaves upon the ground.

I hear the rain falling upon the roof and the ground.

I hear the wind blowing through the trees and the fallen leaves.

My heart wants to walk in the autumn rain and the leaves.

I want to walk in the autumn of my heart. I want to feel the rain upon me.

My heart cries to walk in this place with You, O Lord.

I want to be out in the wind, the rain and the leaves.

I want to walk in the warm breeze of the dark evening.

Everything about me cries out to walk in this place with You.

Awaken our hearts, O Lord. Let the reign of the Holy Spirit come upon us, as we listen to the rainfall upon the ground, washing and purifying as it falls. The rain is getting the fall soil ready for the winter's snow. The Holy Spirit is purifying our hearts to walk in His presence.

October 27

Along the Waters Edge

Today we took a ride to the ocean. The waves were pounding against the rocks. As we walked along the shoreline, the water splashed over the seawall getting us soaking wet. We noticed during February and October that the ocean is rougher than the summer months. It is always very refreshing to walk along the shoreline, no matter what time of the year it is.

We talked about the ocean having very strong significant meanings for us in our spiritual walk with the Lord. Then we talked about the corruption in the world pounding against us just like the rough waves that were pounding against the rock. We have to keep, foremost, in our minds the shoreline that we seek is where the living waters of the Lord splash upon our hearts and minds in healing. The Lord always gives us a message as we walk along the waters edge.

Rhythm of the Heart

Extra electrical impulses within the cells of the heart can throw the heart into arrhythmia, which is a rapid, irregular heartbeat. Charles having this condition recently brought our thoughts to the many blessings and graces that we have received from the Lord. While recently receiving care for this condition, the Lord brought our attention to how He wants our hearts to beat in rhythm with the Holy Spirit.

Medical conditions, circumstances and situations around us can throw us out of rhythm with the physical and the spiritual. Charles' heartbeat thrown out of rhythm caused breathing and other complications. The same can be true of our spiritual heartbeat. If we get to far off beat with the rhythm of God, we will also have complications. All our senses need to be in rhythm with the electrical impulses of the Holy Spirit.

The rhythm of our heart had its start in the heart and womb of God. The rhythm of our life should be in rhythm with Him. In order to hear God speaking within the heart, we have to be in rhythm with His Holy Spirit. This rhythm is with God, in God and through God. When this rhythm is off beat, going to fast or to slow, our responding to the Lord will also be off.

As our physical heart stays in rhythm carrying a natural beat within the chambers of the heart, we also have to stay in rhythm with the spiritual heart of God. Through the power of the Holy Spirit, we can stay in the chambers of the very heart of God, singing a new song in rhythm with His love for each one of us.

October 29

A Year in the Atmosphere of God

This year started on August 16, 2002, with our friends from Ireland and ended on October 30, 2003.

During this period, we made seven trips to the Little Sisters in New Hampshire, 3 trips to Sr. Clare's in Burlington, Vermont and 3 trips to see Fr. Anthony. Along with these trips, we went to Pennsylvania for a Revival Conference and the Divine Mercy Conference in Connecticut. Going to all of these places was a very important part of our year in the Atmosphere of God. It has been a very fruitful year and special time with the Lord.

We not only spent this time with the Lord, but also were able to share it with others. We brought others along with us into the Atmosphere of the Lord. All of these places were where the Lord's presence could be found, out and away from the world and the negativity that is there.

Our year in the Atmosphere of the Lord comes to a peak on this beautiful October Day. It is in the Harvest of the year with the Lord. It is not a conclusion. It is not finished. We are never finished in the Lord. We are only just beginning.

What we are seeing right now is how the negative is right there to snatch the benefits of the whole year away from us. The Atmosphere of God is being out of the atmosphere of negativity in the world. Spending time in the Atmosphere of the Lord breaks up the negativity.

October 30

Heavens Haberdashery

"Hearts united will be receptive. You cannot give outward
unless you receive inward and are receptive.
Receive, receive, and receive! Shift from the
giving gear into the receiving gear.
The giving will come forth from the receiving."

"Keep your hearts open. My gifts are on the
way that will require an open heart.
Heavens haberdashery, blessings, graces and gifts awaits you.
The very furnishings of God's love in heaven and on earth await you.
You are receiving gifts and healing from the
"looms" of heaven in ways everlasting."

October 31

Loose Leaf

They conquered him by the blood of
the Lamb and by the word of their testi-
mony; love for life did not deter them from death. (Revelation 12:11)

Under this topic of a loose leaf, the Lord is again calling us to be
free in the Holy Spirit. He is using the loose leaf in a bookbinder and the
loose leaf falling from a tree to teach us how important it is to be free
in the Holy Spirit to share our spiritual experiences along with learned
knowledge.

Sharing vs. knowledge seems to be flowing through this topic of a
loose leaf. One will really falter without the other. That is to say, knowledge of a subject will falter without the shared and lived experiences in
life. An unhealthy desire for knowledge can draw a person into the bondage of pride and control if it is not under the watchful eye of humility.
Knowledge is important, but one can be bound to the knowledge of a
subject without the needed experience within that subject.

Experience is needed along with the knowledge, and should be given
and shared with others. An example of this could be a nurse learning all
about the knowledge of nursing and never having hands on experience.
A skilled nurse may not result from just the knowledge of nursing and
not the experience needed. A person becoming a teacher in the field of
education in our school systems always has to have six weeks of student
teaching. Classroom experience with the students is required.

Another very important area where shared experiences should flow
along with knowledge is in our spiritual lives. A deeper spiritual relationship with the Lord will not develop if one stays in just the education and

knowledge about God. We have to want to know God and not just know about Him.

Quotation: "Today our eyes see further and our horizons have become wider. The means of knowledge and communication have never been greater. With the highly sophisticated technology we possess, we can explore the wonders of the infinitely small and the infinitely great. Nothing happens on the planet that cannot be communicated almost immediately. But knowing is not necessarily seeing.

"For to see, according to the message of Jesus, is to go beyond the appearances, to go beyond the surface. It is to discover what lies hidden at the heart of people and events. It is to look at the visible and see the invisible that surrounds it and sustains it." (11.)

The most important knowledge is the knowledge that comes from the Lord Himself. It is the knowledge of the possibility of having a personal relationship with Him and in that relationship experiencing His revelations to us each moment of our lives.

A freedom comes along with sharing with others about the deeper spiritual experiences one has with the Lord. Shared experiences are very important and are a testimony to our life in the Lord, Jesus. This testimony or witness will often enter into a person's heart where surface or head knowledge will be stopped at the entrance to the heart and mind. The shared experiences with others help one to enter into Jesus' presence and nearness that is deep within the heart.

Freedom to share about the Lord is like a loose leaf that falls from the tree in autumn and is then blown about in the autumn wind. It is also like a loose leaf of paper that can be taken in and out of a folder. These are examples of how free the Lord wants us to be in His Holy Spirit. He wants us to be free as the loose leaf that is blown about by the autumn wind and free as a loose leaf of paper being taken in and out of a folder.

God wants us to be free as we move in and out of circumstances and situations. He wants us to contribute to these situations and circumstances in a healthy and positive way and then be free to move on in His

Holy Spirit. A loose leaf from a notebook as well as a loose leaf blown about in the wind is free.

> "A loose leaf will fit into any folder and bring richness to the folder.
> It can be taken out and put into another folder at any time.
> Do not let others put you into the bookbinder of control.
> Stay a loose leaf.
> Little things mean a lot."

GLORY OF GOD

November 1

A New Chapter is Added

Come, let us bow down in worship; let us kneel before the Lord who made us. For he is our God, and we are the people he shepherds, the flock he guides. (Psalms 95:6–7)

We knew, as we were finishing the manuscript of *Shades of Blue*, that we would be adding a new chapter. God was telling us that there would always be a new chapter added to our lives. What we did not realize at the time was that we would be changing the whole manuscript to a daily inspirational, instead of what we had finished. This revelation carried a fresh revelation about the Glory of God.

Why we felt there would be another chapter was because Anne kept getting very strong feelings and thoughts about the Glory of God. She could actually feel the presence of these words, "The Glory of God," in her heart. When others would talk about the many things going wrong in their lives, the church, as well as the world, all she could think about was the Glory of God. She felt that everyone including herself had been forgetting about the power and Glory of God.

The Lord is calling us to become holy and to enter into intimacy with Him. The world is a constant pull on this call. Many problems in our world today are having an effect on our personal lives and families. Things have come to such a state that only the intervention and power of

God Himself can stop this movement towards corruption and destruction. It is beyond what man can do to stop this motion.

The change necessary to stop this motion has to start with each individual. Each has to seek a holy and intimate relationship with God. This will require repentance, restoration and a healing in our relationship with God and those around us. He is the only one that can cause this to happen.

When we seek a holy and intimate life with God, He draws us into His realm of glory and His presence. Here is where we give Him the permission and freedom to change our lives into holy and intimate lives. He is telling us that His hope and His love will be received when we enter into His Presence. Having this closeness with Him will help us to overcome our own problems and those in the world.

We cannot forget that our God is a mighty God. A mighty God is He!

November 2

Myrrh and Lard

I woke up one morning around 5:35 a.m. from the following dream:

I was with other people and we were waiting for two special guests to arrive. Everyone was to have a special moment with these guests. When I went up to them, they were John Paul II and Mother Theresa of Calcutta. When I touched Mother Theresa, my fingertips filled with myrrh or lard. Then John Paul II told me to share with everyone what had just happened to me. I then turned to the others and told what I had received on my hands when I touched Mother Theresa. I put my hands up to my nose, to smell the fragrance. At that point, I woke up.

It then came to me that the myrrh (lard) being on my fingertips was an anointing for the writing we were doing. After sharing with Charles for a few minutes, I got up and looked in the concordance and dictionary for the words myrrh and lard. The dictionary said that myrrh meant a bitter aromatic gum obtained from an Arabian shrub. Lard meant a clarified fat from swine, cover with lard, cover or mix with anything;

interpolate speech, writing, etc. with words, expressions, etc. for some particular effect.

From this explanation, I was drawn to the word, interpolate. Interpolate means to alter or enlarge a book for writing, by inserting new matter: to set new matter between or among what is already done.

Charles and I had been advised to take all the writings of this book, *Shades of Blue*, and make it into a daily inspirational. We were in the process of changing and inserting new and old material into the book when we began to understand the message of the dream. We had already taken the endeavor into our hearts and were working hard in making it into a daily inspirational. We thought we were just about finished with the original book, when in fact we were just beginning.

The Lord gave us another confirmation of this endeavor. I picked up a little book with a hand holding a feather pen on the back cover. A small paragraph under the drawing spoke about Mother Theresa of Calcutta and Pope John Paul II.

We felt that the Lord was encouraging us to continue in this endeavor of writing *Shades of Blue*. We found ourselves turning over another page into the realm of His Glory. Here we began to understand why we had been getting so much about the Glory of God.

November 3

Turning the Page

Six of us went to our first Revival Service on November 5, 1997 at a church in Wynnewood, Pennsylvania. It was eighteen hours of pure joy. We spent six hours traveling to the service, six hours there and six hours traveling home. We had a marvelous time with the Lord.

We had been to many Charismatic Renewal services, but this was our first Revival Service. At this service, we began to hear the call to enter into the realm of God's Glory. We were getting a much deeper meaning to the gifts of praise and worship.

We ended up going to these services for six years in a row. Ruth Ward Heflin, one of the founders of the Calvary Campgrounds in Ashland, Virginia, was a speaker at a couple of the services. The Lord working through her words and books has filled us with a deeply imbedded desire for revival and revelation to enter our hearts and minds. Ruth was very powerful in the gift of praising the Lord and spoke about praise leading us into worship and worship leading us into the glory of God. We found this to be true as it led us into experiencing the manifest presence of the Glory of God in this worship.

Quotation: "Praise until the spirit of worship comes. Worship until the glory comes. Then avoid anything that would disrupt that atmosphere of glory, and we stay there, allowing God to reveal Himself to us." (12.)

Ruth also said that we choose to praise, where in worship the Holy Spirit of worship comes and brings us into worship. Worship brings the presence of the Lord amongst His people. This is an awesome presence. Profound experiences happen between the individual and the Lord.

Praise is a very powerful weapon in spiritual warfare, and it lifts our spirits to a higher place with the Lord, where we can celebrate His presence. Praise brings down an anointing from the Lord and helps us to enter into His presence. A quiet and gentle Holy Spirit is present at this time. True worship comes from the heart, in love and adoration of the Lord. It is a time for you and the Lord. This is where He speaks to you and you speak to Him.

A person has to let go of all inhibitions, opinions and attitudes that block the spiritual walk with the Lord. Jesus' ways and thoughts are higher. He is continually calling us from the earthly realm to the heavenly, from the natural to the supernatural. He is calling us to enter into the Glory Realm, which is the supernatural realm, the mystical life of the Church. This is where we will experience the revelation and manifest presence of the Lord. It is His Glory!

Originally in the Garden of Eden

Originally, in the Garden of Eden, Adam and Eve listened for the Lord and their senses were alive in Him. That was because they were in union with Him. We are meant to walk in union with the presence of God in our heart and mind. When sin entered into creation, all the senses, along with creation, went each in its own direction, turning away from God. God was no longer the center. Self and rebellion took over.

God wants to fill our hearts and minds with His presence and to restore our original relationship with Him. He will do this through His Son Jesus, and the power of the Holy Spirit. Through the life, death and resurrection of Jesus, our life and relationship has been restored with God the Father. God is removing everything that is in conflict with His union and love for us.

Reviving His people in a new movement of the Holy Spirit, Revival Glory, God's people are moving into repentance, restoration and a deeper relationship with Him. He wants every one of our senses to be alive in Him. He wants us to be thrilled with the sound of His voice and to be deeply moved by His presence, when He comes near. After the initial excitement calms down, one realizes that they are entering into the Glory of God.

Many of the basic elements and gifts found in the Charismatic Renewal can be found in this Revival Glory. The fruits of the Holy Spirit are evident. We have experienced both and have found that this new movement of the Holy Spirit is bringing the individual to a higher and deeper relationship with God. God is sending this revival to those who will accept it. The blessings will be beyond anything we have experienced in the past.

God is calling each of us to know about and live in the heavenly realm of glory, right here on earth. He wants to give us the power that was originally given to Adam and Eve, His People of Old and the men and women on the Day of Pentecost. "... Our Father, Thy Kingdom Come on Earth as it is in heaven ... "

God is doing a new thing. Many of the manifestations of the presence of God are different from those we have experienced in the past. People have witnessed gold dust and oil on themselves and others. The fragrance of the love of God is also very often present. People have had fillings in their teeth turn to gold and some have received new teeth. People have attended revival services for the first time and have left with a powerful anointing from God along with the gifts of the Holy Spirit such as tongues, holy laughter and prophecy.

Today there is a hunger in God's people for the spiritual life. Some are entering into movements that are not of God. This is where we have to encourage them to enter into a life with the Holy Spirit, where it will bring them into the Realm of God's Glory.

November 5

Revival of the Heart

How lovely is your dwelling place, O Lord of hosts! My soul yearns and pines for the courts of the Lord. My heart and my flesh cry out for the living God. (Psalms 84:2–3)

True revival is revival of the heart, which comes with a new vision of love. It is a new vision of understanding, hope and gratitude. The heart touched by revival will seek out this vision.

We have to open the doors of the mind and heart to let the Lord bring forth revival in the heart. The riches received in this heart can only be spilled out and given to all around. This is why it is so important that it be an individual revival with the Lord first. Then and only then can it flow freely to others. His love will not wane.

The autumn time of the year is a time full of color and wonder.

The Lord wants to take us all through the autumn in the heart.

This will be a time where the eyes will seek the colors that glisten.

The ears will reach for sounds that will be magnified.

The hands will touch the gentleness of His touch.

The mouth will taste the spiritual fruits.

The nose will smell the fragrance of His love.

We have only been grasping at what revival really means. It is much more than what we have come to understand. Understanding revival will make a heart open and ready to take in all that God chooses to give. It will take strength and a commitment not to be a renegade of the heart. The Lord will draw out the things that only clutter this heart.

The Lord will walk with us into the heavenly spiritual senses. It is much, much more than the exterior physical senses. The spiritual senses are connected to the very heart of the Lord. This is where we will know how to listen and respond to the presence of the Lord in and around us.

From walking here with the Lord, "knowing" when it is truly a revival of the heart will come. Through this, we will receive a new vision of love, a new vision of understanding and a new vision of hope and gratitude. If you do not have this vision, you will not have revival.

The Lord asks us to walk with Him into the spiritual senses. Go beyond our limitations and overcome the pull of the world.

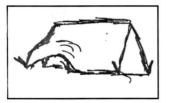

November 6

Enlarge the Space for Your Tent

Enlarge the space for your tent, spread out your tent cloths unsparingly; lengthen your ropes and make firm your stakes. (Isaiah 54:2)

Anne had a vision, within her heart, of a tent with one of its stakes flying in the breeze.

The tent post in the drawing represents a spiritual stake and the Lord was telling us to drive it into revelation Glory. This is a call in a new direction for us. Praise God! The Lord is extending our horizons, where the spiritual realm is coming clearly into view.

Quotation: "When God has said that we are at the finish line, why do we insist on going back to the start? He has declared victory. Get into the place of rest, the place of confidence, and no matter what happens tomorrow, refuse to move backward. Drive a spiritual stake based upon God's revelation to you and hold your ground." (13.)

Charles received the following words: "Dimension, Dynamics, Daily, and Duo."

This was the understanding received from these words: "You both (duo) will enter into the spiritual realm (dimension) on a (daily) basis and experience things you have never known (dynamic). There will be new directions, new ministries and new horizons."

We will be receiving daily revelations and we will have to notice and take time for them, no-matter how and when they happen. Anne had another vision of a face being stretched and actually saw the stretching of the skin or smearing of makeup on the face.

The Lord is stretching us spiritually. He used the vision of stretching the skin to show us how much He will be stretching us and taking us out of what is known and familiar to us. He is stretching us right out of the ordinary into the extraordinary.

"Your horizons are being stretched out.
You are not meant to remain in one field of ministry.
You will write. You will walk. You will talk.
You have all the ingredients."

"A big wave of the Holy Spirit is coming.
Be prepared to extend the posts of your tent.
A tsunami size wave is coming.
Be prepared to stretch out!"

Here we repeat the prayer Jabez prayed to the God of Israel: "Oh that you may truly bless me and extend my boundaries! Help me and make me free of misfortune, without pain!" And God granted his prayer. (1 Chronicles 4:10)

Anointing

We have often experienced the presence and fragrance of oil at different services and conferences. Through these experiences, we have come to understand, this is an anointing of oil and we are entering into the Glory of God and His manifest presence.

The word "anointing" means to smear with ointment or oil, or to consecrate by applying of pouring on oil. This oil is coming from the very throne of God. It is not coming from a bottle or anything made by human hands. God, Himself, is anointing us with heavenly oils. He is doing a new thing and the anointing will be new every time we receive it.

Through the power of God's love, going beyond what is normal for us, we can grow in our love for each other. We can come together in difficult areas, accepting one another and one another's gifts and ministries. Obstacles will be overcome.

Gods anointing of oil, is stronger than self and will help us to overcome self. Healing will take place in the areas that need healing. Unity and love will grow. The anointing oils will do what we cannot do and will do it in spite of how much we may get in the way. We will find ourselves giving God more control of our earthly and spiritual lives. This anointing will hold true, it is not fickle like we may be.

When oil is spilled, it will soak deep into whatever crevices that are present. The oil we are receiving is soaking into the deep crevices of our soul. It is like a double edge sword that cuts through the marrow. It is cutting away the marrow of sin. It is going to go beyond anything that we have ever experienced, for this anointing of oil is in the Glory of God.

Things are going to happen, that could only happen through this anointing. The Lord is working through this anointing of oil. His people have been anointed and will be anointed repeatedly. His Manifest Presence is inclusive, not exclusive in nature. Nothing will stand in the way of what the He is going to do with each one of us. This anointing will carry the gifts of the Holy Spirit into each heart and mind.

How is it that we still seem to be moving ahead in our walk with the

Lord? It is because of this new anointing of oil that comes directly from heaven above. The important thing is to stay in the anointing, the Glory of God. God's presence is the Glory.

Every day trials are a constant pull on this anointing. We have to desire to stay in the anointing. That desire alone will anoint us daily. It is often hard for us to realize the power of God's love that is present in this anointing.

Stay aware that the anointing is the manifest presence of God. The gold dust, oil, heaviness of Spirit, and fragrances are all part of the same anointing. Yes, there will be signs and wonders, but most important of all it is an anointing, an anointing from the Kingdom of God and is not to be taken lightly.

When this anointing happens to you, try to settle into what is really going on. Always remembering that the Lord is manifesting His presence to you. Stay with that presence. If you are active in ministry to others at that time, try to keep at least one foot on the ground. Do not be alarmed if the Lord takes over anyway and all you can do is rest in His presence. The Lord will have His way.

God is doing a new thing and when we enter into His Glory, we will experience His manifest presence.

November 8

The Hood

Two words received were *Dia cloch* (clocca) Old Latin Dia means two and Ckicca...a close fitting bell shaped hat, a hood.

We felt that the word hood stood for protection and solitude. Monks wear a hood to help them center in on the presence of God. It helps bring them into the presence of the Lord and shuts out the distractions all around.

"You are going into revelation glory, where the light
of Christ shines forth on your understanding.

Like the many facets of the crystal, or diamond, colors bounce
forth. Your understanding will go forth in revelation.
I will reveal My presence to others through you. You
have to say, "*Yes*," to the gift of revelation."

I felt fear along with the excitement of this revelation. The fear of
what the gift might mean or what the Lord may ask of us. Right after this
revelation our Spiritual Director said, "When you come you bring the
presence of the Lord with You."

November 9

Take Refuge in God

With God is my safety and my glory, he is the rock of my strength;
my refuge is in God! (Psalms 62:8)

We have had enough of what the world can do for us. It is time to
reach up into the revelation and Glory of God. Revelation Glory is in
"The Atmosphere of God" and is the only place where man can come
above the problems of the world. We must enter into the glory and
atmosphere of God. The atmosphere of the world is destroying us.

The more we speak, teach, and share about God and our spiritual
life and a life of revelation, the more we enter into the atmosphere of
God. This will help to protect us from the atmosphere of corruption that
is present and surrounds us in the world. We have to "take refuge," in all
that God has to give us.

"Stay at the door, ready to open at anytime, I am taking up residence.
My presence goes with you wherever you go, as it did with St. Francis, St.
Therese and Mother Theresa. You carry the atmosphere of this presence
to all around you. This is your vocation, today. You will begin to know
this in an unquestionable way. You are carriers of My presence needed
today. I abide in you, as you abide in Me. I have called you to something
new."

"My people will know that I abide amongst them.
I have not left them orphan.
I am still in control of My whole creation.

255

I am the refuge where each needs to abide.
Study what a refuge is.
A refuge has many sides, the same as a fort.
Giving your will to Me places the key in the
door that opens My heart of refuge.
My time is not only for the present.
You need Me more and more.
I give you Heavenly Stanchions.
I am your support in all things."

November 10

How Dark the Earth Has Become

"How dark the earth has become, from what
it was at the beginning of creation.
My beauty has been obscured and all heaven groans at this sight.
Before I can come again in Glory, all must be right.
My entry will be pleasing to the Father.
Extreme methods I will use to wake up and purify My people.
Like a woman giving birth, the pain will soon be forgotten,
Because of the joy that follows.
But in this case the joy will be eternal and never ending."

November 11

Doors Closed

"Do not box in My spirit.
I can only do what you will allow Me to do.
I want My Holy Spirit to be able to flow freely through you.
I will use you, but there is so much more I can
do through you if you will only let Me."

"There are many doors closed between My people and Me.
My love and graces are ready to burst forth upon My people.
I only need to be accepted into the heart.

Closed doors block the entrance into the glory realm.
Some do not believe they can enter here.
Others do not want to enter here."

"Intimacy with Me can only bring about My
glory upon the individual heart.
A quiet heart is a joyful heart that is resting in Me.
Seek out and desire the mystical life and intimacy with Me."

Lord I desire, Your soft gentle touches.
Hold my life, mind and spirit in Your hands.
Burn out the impurities so that Your love can flow through Me.

November 12

Golden Glory

Revival will bring us together in love. Through the power of the Holy Spirit in praise and worship, we can enter into the Glory of God. With faith and love revived, we will be making our journey in love and it will be a journey with, in and through Him. The Lord protects us in every direction as He leads us in new directions.

"The natural may spill over into the supernatural and the supernatural into the natural. My rewards are everlasting in the hearts and minds of My people. In rejection, there is direction. Submissiveness is like the strength of a loved ones arms around you. Warmth of the loved one holds your heart in theirs. The silence of love is felt, not heard. Open your hearts to the trust that can be yours."

"Spiritual insights are a matter of the heart.
The natural is caught up in the movement of the supernatural.
Every step forward in trust is a step higher in understanding.
There are no "Copy Cats" in God's truths.
There are only pure truths to behold.
A heart refreshed in God's pure love is a heart renewed in His truth.
God's truth is "true truth," not my truth, not your truth, but His truth.

This is so because His pure love mixes with
the streams of His Golden Glory."

"This golden mixture passes through our every fiber and we can only catch glimpses of it when we enter into our hearts, as they become hearts of flesh. A heart of stone cannot catch this glimpse of Glory. A heart of flesh will absorb the Golden Glory like liquid in a sponge. It is being soaked with God's truth and love. When it is squeezed, it will ooze out the riches of this heavenly gold. Truth is God's golden glory poured out. When God's truth is poured forth all matters of the heart and nature will fall into correct order and balance."

Prayer: O Lord, we ask You to purify our hearts and give us a heart of flesh. Pour Your liquid gold upon us.

November 13

Quo Vadis

One morning at the breakfast table, we were praying and talking about getting the meanings of the messages and words that we were receiving from the Lord. During this time, Charles received the words: "Quo Vadis."

This led me to look up the definition of Quo Vadis on the internet. I came across many things about the movie, Quo Vadis. These did not seem to have a message from the Lord for us.

Then, I came across a website that said ... "The one you want is the one that begins "Definition ... Read the definition and you will have a message." Wow, it was clear at this point that the Lord was leading us.

I then went to the definition of Quo Vadis and it said that it was a Latin Phrase meaning ... "Where are you going?" Around this same time, I had been talking to a friend about Ruth and Naomi in the Scriptures. Ruth said to Naomi, where you go, I will go.

From this, we knew the Lord was asking us the question: "Where are you going?"

As Ruth said to Naomi, our response was, "Where you go, O Lord, we will go."

Where are you going?
I am going to go where He is, I said
About this place, I have only read.
For it is within our reach,
Just across the ocean and down the beach.
I am taking off into spiritual flight,
Eagles spread their wings and glide upright.
You as my guide and You as my knight,
I will make this climb and make it right.
This is where I am heading, you see.
I go above all of nature to the mountaintop.
I will build a nest for you and me.
I am off to see this Kingdom on high,
I will catch my breath on my way by.
Where are you going?
I am going wherever You go O Lord.
I am going out into the fields of harvest.

November 14

Quo Vadis Continues

Around the Christmas Holidays, there were two TV shows about the life of Pope John Paul II. While we watched one of these shows, the words Quo Vadis were mentioned to Cardinal Wojtyla when he was being considered for the position of Pope. The Cardinal that spoke these words to Wojtyla mentioned how St. Peter said these words to the Lord.

This led us into a completely new search to see where the words Quo Vadis originated.

Much to our surprise, they were words that St. Peter had spoken to Jesus when He was leaving Rome on the Road to Damascus. In this search, I learned about a chapel dedicated to this experience of St. Peter meeting Jesus.

Chapel of "Domine Quo Vadis," is The Chiesa di Santa Maria in Palmis, better know, as *Chiesa del Domine Quo Vadis* (literally, the church of "Lord, Where Are You Going?") is a small church on the Appian Way in Rome.

The *Chiesa del Domine Quo Vadis* is located on the spot where tradition says Saint Peter had a vision of the risen Christ while fleeing persecution in Rome. According to the tradition, Peter asked Jesus: "Domine, quo vadis?" *Lord, where are You going?* And Jesus answered: "Eo Romam iterum crucifig!" *I go to Rome to be crucified anew.*

This convinced Peter to turn around and face martyrdom in Rome.

The two footprints on a marble slab at the center of the church (copy of a relief conserved in the near basilica of San Sebastiano) would be the miraculous sign left by Jesus. The real name of the church, very little known, indeed, is Chiesa di Santa Maria in Palmis, where *palmis* stands for the *Soles of Jesus.*

In 1983, Pope John Paul II defined the church "a place that has a special importance in the history of Rome and in the history of the Church."

(Notes taken from an article written by Holly Hayes, Sacred-Destinations.com)

November 15

The Right Hand of God

You will show me the path to life, fullness of joys in your presence, the delights at your right hand forever. (Psalms 16:11)

On July 21, I had a vision of a right hand. It was held in such a position that I could see through the side and across the palm of the hand. I knew when I saw it; I was to look through it,

"Seeing through the right hand of God,
I saw His hand upon us.
We will see revelations through the hand of God.
He will measure each portion.
We are in the preschool of revelations and He is teaching us to see.

A real blessing is to see into simplicity."

"You do not have to have it explained." Why, I asked.
"Because you can explain it and you can understand it.
Carnal man does not understand. You do
not have to try to understand."
Why, I asked again. "Because you do understand and
have received the gift of understanding analogies."

The dictionary says analogies are … a likeness in one or more ways between things, otherwise unlike … seeing what is not seen by the naked eye … the spiritual side of things.

November 16

Be People of My Glory

It is Yahweh Sabaoth who speaks—and my spirit remains among you. Do not be afraid! For Yahweh Sabaoth says this: A little while now, and I am going to shake the heavens and the earth, the sea and the dry land.

I will shake all the nations and treasures of all the nations shall flow in, and I will fill this Temple with glory, says Yahweh Sabaoth. Mine is the silver, mine the gold! It is Yahweh Sabaoth who speaks. The new glory of this Temple is going to surpass the old, says Yahweh Sabaoth, and in this place I will give peace—it is Yahweh Sabaoth who speaks.'" (Haggai 2:5–9, Jerusalem)

I was up at midnight the night before a Home Retreat in our home. I received these words:

"Be glory People! Be people of the mountaintop, no more in the valley. You can remain on the mountaintop, as long as you are in My Glory. The valley is for cleansing. The mountaintop is for receiving My eternal love. Believe! This is My gift to you in these times."

"Glory? Yes! It is possible to live in My Glory. The glory that flows from My heart to yours fills you with riches that can only come from this glory. Spend time in this glory so I can change you and teach you of its hidden riches. You know not of these riches because I have only begun to let them flow. Glory, Glory, and Glory!"

"The mountaintop is for you. You will find all that you need. You need only to come down from the mountaintop to bring another back to the top with you. You will become "sure footed" in your trips up and down. You will trust Me more and more…for that is the reward for a glory people."

"You will see what you have never seen before. You will touch and hear what you have never touched or heard before. You will believe because your experiences in My glory will be the supports that hold you in this belief. Now, My people rest in My glory. Let Me fill the temple in your hearts with My silver, My gold. It is the silver and gold of a new glory that surpasses the old. In this place I will give peace, says the Lord of hosts!"

November 17

Bring the Mountaintop to the Valley

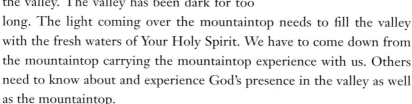

We need to bring the mountaintop to the valley. The valley has been dark for too long. The light coming over the mountaintop needs to fill the valley with the fresh waters of Your Holy Spirit. We have to come down from the mountaintop carrying the mountaintop experience with us. Others need to know about and experience God's presence in the valley as well as the mountaintop.

It is a falsehood to believe we can only experience God on the mountaintop. Every experience of God is the extraordinary in the ordinary. Every elevation or entry into God's presence does away with the valley below. Every elevation makes the valley less and less until it is even with the mountaintop.

We have entered into a new life of revelation. God's light has come over every nook and cranny in the heart. It has come over every field and desert. It has brought every mountaintop low and every valley up high.

Oh Lord, we believe that what we experience in Your presence is what the world needs. Entering into the glory and mystical life is the answer for the problems of today. We have to bring this atmosphere of God into the world. The holy and good people of today carry the atmosphere of God to other people. This, done in the Glory of God, could change the whole world.

Prayer: O Lord, wrap Your atmosphere around us. Let us be carriers of Your prevailing presence.

November 18

Inside Out and Upside Down

Today, many people do not believe in the spiritual and mystical life of the church. Revival is bringing the experience of God to His people. We need the Lord's presence in our lives today, more than we have ever needed Him before.

A deeper relationship with the Lord in the mystical life will cause a down shifting of the earthly activities and an up shifting towards the spiritual life in the depths of our hearts. It will mean shifting gears and running only on the grace and mercy of God, drawing us right into the arms and Glory of God. In many of our lives, the earthly life is dominant over the spiritual. God is going to "flip" the switch for us. He is going to turn us inside out and upside down.

"Your refuge is in the Arms of God!
I am holding you in My everlasting arms.
My arms held around you will have no openings for you to fall out.
My arms are secure, strong and firm. I will not let go of you."

"The wind of My spirit blows across the brow of your head.
It brings My golden glory upon you, rest in My golden glory!
Persevere in preserving the anointing you have received.

The light of Christ shines through the diamond in your heart.
Many will refuse the rudiments of revival."

"Docility is desired! I desire that you place your
heart and will in My love for you.
Give your will to Me. Nobolis Secured! You will find security in
your relationship with Me, when you give your will to Me.
Your place in the family of God is secured.
The light of Christ shines through the diamond in your heart.
Jesus is the child of your heart. He abides in you, as He abides in Me.
Be aware of His presence with you always. Listen to Him."

Prayer: Speak Lord, for Your servant is listening.

November 19

The River is Glory

"You are blessed with the fragrance
of God's love in the river glory. The
river is glory. Its name is glory.
Bring all, people, gifts and concerns as well as blessings to the river.
Place them in the fragrance of My love and leave them there.
If they leave the river, keep bringing them back.
You will find great peace in this and free from worry.
Healing will occur for the people you bring.
Concerns will leave and blessings will increase."

"Bring reoccurring weaknesses, sin and temptations to the river.
If you are bothered by the devil, ask him if he
wants to go to the river with you.
You will teach him how to swim in the Glory
of God. He will soon scurry off."

"The oil of anointing is upon you. It will be there when you need
it, for your own strength and for the strength and love others need. The
only way it will subside and I say subside, is if you do not draw upon the
gift. This gift will rest in your heart for all of eternity. Always draw from

the fragrance of My love. You do not need substitute oil. My oil, My anointing, remains a part of you. All you do is call My name and the oil will come. Your hearts are full of My anointing oils."

"Nothing is new … only My ways of showing it to you are new for you.

I am doing a new thing. Signs and wonders are My way of opening your hearts to My love. This is the glory of My love for you. Let Me express it; let Me show it, to others through you. Do not close any doors. I will open and close all doors, all hearts."

"Be mindful of all; don't let anyone fall through the cracks of hurts or wounds that life has made for them. Keep one hand high in praise and the other in outreach to My little ones that need to hear about and receive My love."

"Every wheel needs oil to move freely. Every dry heart needs My love to survive. The fragrance of this oil will flow and My love will remain whenever you call upon My name in complete trust and love." (I was covered with this precious oil and fragrance.)

"Bring your loved ones into the river.
This is a spiritual place and you can bring them there.
Just place them in the fragrance of My love
and the river glory will do the rest."

Prayer: Thank You, Lord for these wonderful blessings. Please keep me from wandering away from You. Keep my heart full of the fragrance of Your love.

"Call and My fragrance will surround you. You will also know when I come to you, even when you do not ask. My fragrance comes from within, yet from afar, but your sense to this has been enlightened. You will know when I am walking through the garden of fragrance to you and others."

"It comes over the horizon and across the waters, carrying signs and wonders, blessing and graces for My beloved children. I renew the face of the earth, which is all of My creation. Remember, to let Me go first. Let Me lead. You will know. I will increase the fragrance of My desires in your heart. There are different kinds of fragrance. The same fragrance can have different meanings. With this gift you have received an extra supply of discernment."

November 20

We Can Breathe Underwater

We have to live in the living waters. Everything will be there,
especially the oxygen, which is the breath of the Holy Spirit.
We can breathe under water in the living waters.
We can go deep into these waters.
We can go over our heads.
We can laugh. We can swim.
We can dance. We are free.

November 21

The Springs of Fortune

"Springs of Fortune I pour upon you.
Make your home in My temple.
Make your life in Me.
Come to the waters and drink.
My love is in great abundance.
You will be transposed, obediently and silently.
You will receive understanding and knowledge.
No man is greater than I overlooking society."

We will be receiving a great wealth from the Lord. It is not the wealth of the material world, but the deep spiritual wealth of a relationship with Him. He wants us to take up residence on His estate, in His temple in our hearts. He wants us to live our life in Him. He wants us to come to the living waters within our hearts and drink of these waters. Love will be given in great abundance. When we drink these waters, we will be transposed obediently and silently. We will receive understanding and knowledge in the great wealth of the Lord.

No man is greater than God is, as He overlooks society with a watchful eye. He has a view from a higher place. He has charge and will direct and manage to take care of us with great authority. When He passes by us, He is very indulgent. He pardons us from the penance attached to certain sins. He frees us and forgives us. His love is in great abundance. He loves us so much. We cannot begin to understand this love.

November 22

Knitting Heavenly Glory

"I am the same yesterday, today and forever.
I am doing a "new" thing, you will see.
I am using the yarn of My word and the needle of My Holy Spirit.
I am knitting My Heavenly Glory throughout your whole being."

"The revival of the past cannot compare to this that I am doing today.
The revival of the past had only to do with
the complexities of their time.
Do not go there. Center on what is happening in
your own heart. It is a "heart" thing."

"I am going to restore My people back to Myself. Some will choose to stay where they are, while others will let My words and Holy Spirit, move them into My glory realm. It is an, "inward" passage into the spiritual not an, "outward" expression that is in carnal understanding. I am already moving in the hearts of My people and they know I am speaking to them in their hearts."

"The yarn of My word is being woven throughout the tapestry of their lives. The needle of My Holy Spirit is there to carry about this task and My Son, O My Son is there to walk beside and guide them into the inner chambers of the heart. He is the "Passage," the way, the truth and the life."

"My people will understand My call and they will not be easily led into confusion. This "new" walk can only be understood spiritually. I am using the spiritual and natural gifts I have placed within My people.

Their experiences in life have been interwoven into a tapestry for this time in history."

"This tapestry already hangs on the wall in the heavenly realm. It is only waiting for their acceptance and participation. Each time the Holy Spirit puts the needle into the tapestry of their hearts, it pulls the yarn of My word through, leaving knowledge, support and wisdom to hold it together."

"I know the hearts of My people of old and I know the hearts of My people today. My same mercy was and is present to all. It is all about My mercy and My love for all that this movement of hope has come about. Again, this revival is a call to enter into the "glory" realm and power of God in this movement of the Holy Spirit today."

November 23

O Lord, Where do We Belong?

Question: Lord where do we belong?
Answer: "Take part in all of My gifts."

"You can be here and you can be there as
long as you remain in My spirit.
You are what I want you to be.
You are a free spirit.
Solid and firm in My guidance and love,
You will be here, there and everywhere."

Question: Lord do You want us to be active in revival?
Answer: "You are not to remain just in revival."

The Lord then reminded me of an important vision and words previously mentioned on November 6.

I had a vision of the skin on my face being stretched. It looked like makeup was being smeared all over my face. I then understood that the Lord is stretching even the skin on our faces—He is stretching us spiritually.

"Your horizons are being stretched out.

You are not meant to remain in one field of ministry.
You will write. You will walk. You will talk."

"You have all the ingredients.
A big wave of the Holy Spirit is coming.
Be prepared to extend the posts of your tent.
A tsunami size wave is coming.
Be prepared to stretch out.
The living waters have to first rise up within
us before they can flow to others."

November 24

Movement Toward God

I had a vision of a huge wave coming upon the shore. I then began to move into the presence of the Lord through the following words of love:

"Waves go forward in a movement toward God, always moving toward restful waters. Waves never return out to the ocean depth. They go upon the shore. They do not turn around and go back out to sea. The undertow of seawater goes back out to sea. New waves keep coming upon the shore."

"Come up! Come up! Enter in! Enter in!
The waves of the seas are clapping for the triumph that will soon be.
They will roar with laughter, they will roar with glory.
Restoration, restoration, all will come back to Me.
Clap! Clap! Splash! Splash!
O Waves of hope and glee, come back to Me, come back to Me.
New waters of restoration and glory waves of revelation will splash
upon the hearts of My people like the waves upon the shore.
They will not return void back to Me."

I kept thinking that I did not want to get wet, but said, "I will for You and me."

"Angels of glory will soon come, dancing in glee upon the sea. Fire of Unity! Fire of Unity!

Freedom is peace and peace is freedom. Heavenly fruit is Jerusalem fruit. I kiss you with the fragrance of My love. I touch your lips with My oil of gladness. You are mine and mine shall not want for anything. I hear your hearts; I hear them speak to Me. My ear is attentive to you. My heart is the bridge that connects us."

"My Garment is around you for protection, no evil can penetrate it. Crowns of glory await those who do My will. Freedom is My gift to you. My gifts cannot be stifled. They have to be used. That is where the freedom is."

"It is only for a while that I hold the reigns tight. Letting loose too soon will only bring hardship. I speak about the reign of God and the glories and revelation to come. The Father says, "Soon!" My glory shall be revealed soon."

"The Lord does not judge the way that man judges. Standing next to you will be many that you may not expect. All will see what the Father has meant to Me. When one enters into the spiritual realm, all is different and clearly understood."

November 25

Fire of Unity

Of the angels he says: "He makes his angels winds and his ministers a fiery flame;" (Hebrews 1:7)

"You have been given the gift of the Fire of Unity.
We asked the Lord what the Fire of Unity was and His reply was:
Love that burns together forms flames of unity."

Prayer: Lord let our love burn together for You. Break up the crust of disunity, both in our hearts and the hearts of those we know and love. I am running Lord, running so fast. I want to catch You, yet I am trying to run in the opposite direction.

Why, Lord? I want to be caught. I am sitting here in Your presence, yet every part of me is running away. Why, Lord?

Command me to do Your will, command me
to walk on the water, like Peter.
Command me to write, to love, to forgive, and to have discipline.
O Lord, take away the distractions.
Every part of me is crying for the ocean, for
the depths of Your mysteries.
I am crying for the waves, to come over me.
I want to taste the salt and to feel the splash of
Your presence upon my face and my heart.
O Lord, let us see Your face, face to face.
Throw Your salt water upon us, the salt of Your ocean waves.
Let Your anointing come upon us.
I am crying to You out of the wilderness.
Carry us into Your waves, the sea, and Your ocean waves.
Help us to taste the salt water of Your presence.
I know I am in Your presence.
Yet my humanness is screaming to run.
Help us to remain firm and stay in Your presence.
I know it will help us to break through the barriers of the flesh.
The controls and chains of others have been lifted.
Now, help us to work through our own controls and barriers.
Help us to get out of the boat, stay out, and trust You.
Help us to taste, smell and feel the salt of Your presence.
Fill our hearts with the cloud of Your glory.

Quotation: "When the heart is thus burning with love for its God, the soul is contemplating lamps of fire which enlighten all things from on high." (14.)

November 26

I Am Lifting You Up

We went to the Pocono Mountains in Pennsylvania for a week's vacation in August. We stopped for coffee and donuts near home before getting on the super highway heading for our trip to Pennsylvania. Just before getting on this highway, our attention was drawn to a huge hot air balloon. From that time on, no matter where we turned we would be seeing or getting something about hot air balloons.

While we were on this vacation, we made the extra hour trip from the Pocono's to Wynnewood, Pennsylvania, where we went to another revival service. While at this service, the Spiritual Director spoke out these words: "Anne, I am lifting you up!" Through these words, we understood what the messages were for us and why we were drawn to the hot air balloons. The Lord was lifting us up and calling us to come higher in Him. Shortly after this, he called us to witness about an experience that we had during the service in June.

The hot air balloon has ropes attached to it to keep it tethered to the ground. It cannot lift off the ground until the ropes are free from being tethered. The Lord does not want us tethered to the ground. He wants to lift our spirits up into the spiritual realm of His Revelation Glory. He knows that there are things that keep us from responding to His call of entering into His presence. It is hard to let go and break the ropes that keep us bound to earthly things, but God wants to cut away the things that tether us and keep us tied down.

The ropes keep the balloon restrained until there are just the right wind currents and the pilot feels it is safe for the balloon to lift. The Lord, our pilot, wants us to be free to move in just the right wind currents of His Holy Spirit, where He will lift us higher and higher into His Revelation Glory.

Hot Wire

I woke up one morning with the words "hot wire." I then began to think about an electrical wire being cut and snapping about on the ground. It is dangerous if it is not connected to the main source. We are always being warned about hot wires in an electrical storm. When wires have snapped and fallen across the ground, we have to be careful until these wires are shut down from the main source of electricity.

From these words and thoughts we began to understand that the Lord was teaching us about the power in His revelations for others and ourselves. When we step into the area of revelation, we must stay connected to the Holy Spirit. If we do not stay connected, we are like a hot wire in an electrical storm that has broken away from the main electrical source. If we break away from what the Lord is giving us through the Holy Spirit, we are throwing the revelation out into what could be dangerous. There could then be a short circuit, with a person receiving only a short cut to a longer intended message. It could become a roundabout message instead of a direct message from God.

We have to be careful not to short circuit the movement and flow of the Holy Spirit in each revelation. We could be blocking the strength and intensity that is flowing through the living waters and words coming right from the heart of God.

Our main electrical source (of revelation) is through the power lines of the Holy Spirit coming from the main source—God. If the wire is away from the main electrical source and we touch it, we could be electrocuted. If we are away from the main source of the Holy Spirit, we could surely experience death.

If we separate from the main source we will be electrocuted, if we stay with the main source we will be electrified. Staying connected to the Holy Spirit, we will be surprised, delighted and in admiration of what the Lord is doing for His people.

Revelations through the power line of the Holy Spirit will be an influence on the person's will and reasoning. It will also be an incentive for each person to respond to the movement of the Holy Spirit in their own lives.

When revelation comes from the Lord, it is full of the fire of the Holy Spirit. It will carry the gifts that are necessary to communicate the revelation to another and the understanding will come from the Lord Himself.

November 28

On Your Red Sea

Words received while on another trip to a Revival Conference in Pennsylvania were:

"It is good, you have come together.
You have tossed and turned about in your faith.
I am now doing something new.
Your faith will no longer ride the waves; it will ride in the boat,
Here I am standing to keep it from turning over.
The boat will ride the waves and I am at the bow to separate the waves.
Your boat is heading for unity and the mystical
life in the center of My heart."

"You will know the sweet heart of Jesus this week.
Your sweet tooth of desire for the Holy Spirit will be well satisfied,
Your sweet tooth is the Holy Spirit.
On your Red Sea … Go forward fearlessly,
be sure that when you come to it,
the waters will part and you will pass over to
your promised land of freedom."

November 29

Our Call is to Enter Into Revelation Glory

Revelation Glory is coming in on a tsunami size wave, right behind Revival Glory. Revival Glory will draw us into Revelation Glory. Groups will think, they are just settling into a comfortable spot with the teachings and experiences, when *splash*, right in front of them is Revelation Glory. Both of these movements, Revival Glory and Revelation Glory, are for entering into the Manifest Presence of the Lord.

Our call is to enter into Revelation Glory where the Lord reveals His presence, knowledge and truths to us. The truths revealed will help us to listen to the very heart of God. It will be beneficial to individuals, communities and the church.

This call is to go beyond the outer courts or initial experiences and enter into the deeper parts of the inner courts, where God will abide with us and us with Him. When one enters into the inner courts of the temple within our hearts, one cannot help but experience the manifest presence of the Lord.

Throughout the years, we have received many words when we did not understand their meanings. While the Lord is drawing us into Revelation Glory, we are beginning to understand more and more of these words each day. He is drawing us above our limited carnal thoughts into His glory where we will receive understanding and knowledge of Him and from Him for others and ourselves.

I remember a vision that I had years ago: I was running across a large field and different color veils of sheer silk were passing over me as I was running. I believe that this is a good explanation of what the Lord is leading us to today. When we go forward towards the Lord He is going to reveal many words, mysteries and truths to us. Veils will be lifted and we will see, hear and understand deep things of God the Father. We will come to understand whom it is that is talking to us.

"Who do you say that I am?" I say that You are the great I AM. "I AM, who I AM!"

November 30

Pastures in High Places

On every roadway they will graze, and each bare height shall be their pasture. (Isaiah 49:9, Jerusalem) See how former predictions have come true.

Fresh things I now foretell; before they appear I tell you of them. (Isaiah 42:9, Jerusalem)

"New pastures I give to you to feed on.
Pastures in high places
Mystical pastures bare height.
I call you to new heights.
Come into My Mystical pastures where I will feed and nourish you.
Mystical pastures reveal new heights.
This is where I will reveal new revelations to My prophets."

"Mystical pastures uncover new revelations to My prophets.
Through the power of My Holy Spirit, things will be disclosed.
They will become clear and simple and will go beyond doubt.
You will see them materialize."

"These revelations will be above the intellect or natural
understanding. You have the capability for this growth.
You have the natural and spiritual ability to answer this call. You are
the prophets for these days. Each bare height shall be your pasture."

"New areas will be opened for your growth. Earthly
ways will give way to spiritual understanding.
My pastures are full of wisdom that can come from only Me. This is
My invitation to you to come up and feed on the spiritual pastures.
I offer "Positive Predictions.""

December 1

Revelation of the Beginning of Creation

I rested in the Holy Spirit during the whole Mass at a revival service on June 28, 1999. During this time, I was questioning the fact that I could not get up to receive Eucharist. Charles was also questioning this when he went up to receive. Then I received the words: "You are receiving Eucharist of another kind." Charles also got the words: "She is receiving Eucharist of another kind."

After the Mass ended, the Spiritual Director started the revival service and spoke right out with the words: "Anne…I have singled you out. You are special. I am filling you with my love. Charles…Do not be afraid to step forward and accept the gifts God has for you." This happened right after I had come out of resting in the Holy Spirit.

I was in a very special spiritual place with the Lord during this time of resting in the Holy Spirit. Although physically I was very aware of what was going on around me. I understood how the Holy Spirit came over all of creation in the mist and Glory of God the Father. God had us in His mind at the beginning of creation. The thread of rebellion was placed throughout all of creation because of the sin of Adam and Eve. I then felt myself being drawn close to the heart of Jesus, while He held me in His arms with firmness and strength. Then as I felt my heart beat, it began to beat in unison with the Holy Spirit.

I then had a very clear understanding of how deeply imbedded is the presence of rebellion in our human nature. This is a rebellion against God and in one way or another, all of humankind responds to this rebellion. However, we are not to lose heart, Jesus died on the cross for each of us. He holds us close to His heart in strength and firmness while we squirm and toss about in letting go of our rebellion against God. There is security in His everlasting arms and in these arms; our hearts beat in unison with the pulsating presence of His Holy Spirit.

December 2

The Lord Opens the Understanding

Anne had a vision of walking back and forth in front of a big threshold door and received these words:

"It is time to flow in the "gift of the gifts" and not in the study of the gift. You are already at the door, why do you want to stay in the study of how you got there? It has taken studies, experiences and revelations to reach the door of My heart, now it is time to enter in."

"Up to now things have only been a preview of what is to come.

A fuller view is coming into focus. It is a no nonsense time. There is no more "hanging" around the outside. It is time to "enter in" in full confidence and trust. All the gifts will blend, mix and match. My love is unfurling over each one of you."

"Be spontaneous in your hearts and minds. If you flow in My Holy Spirit, you will be at ease in your thoughts, deeds, and words. I will place My words in your heart and on your tongue. Trust, do not fret or worry about what you will need. Trust in My Holy Spirit."

"When I lift you up into My revelation glory, you will have all you need in wisdom, discernment and understanding, all which is needed for the love of My heart. Love the heart of the other person and you love My heart."

Through the revealing power of the Holy Spirit, the Lord opens the understanding of the heart of the other person. We are only the "earthen vessels."

December 3

Dressed Up for My Pleasure

Words received the night before going to another Revival Conference in Pennsylvania were: "Melancholy melanoma" and "dejection depression."

Melancholy is a feeling of great dullness or being low in spirit. Melanoma is a serious form of cancer. Dejection is to be cast down and depression is to be pressed down or dejected. We felt that the Lord was asking us to pray for those that have fallen into a dullness of spirit. He was saying that this dullness could become like a cancer, binding them to a spirit of depression.

We then received these words:

"Days are coming when you will be used in
ways you will dream not possible.
My words will come forth.
Soon there will be no more faltering.

The uneven will be evened.
I am removing clouds of hesitation.
You cannot be held guilty for what another person does.
That person stands in his or her own judgment with Me.
I am calling you. Come follow Me."

Vision received: Buster Brown collars with white bows.

"You are little children being dressed up for My pleasure.
I am teaching you. Just go this week and receive.
I have much for you to receive.
Don't let the past or present block your reception."

Vision: white feathers with black tips.

"Many areas you have given to Me. However, the finishing
tips, the patterns of life, need to be purified.
The finishing tips are becoming the finishing touches. You alone
if need be to receive, can separate yourself when necessary.
You can do this with thousands around
because your center rests in Me."

Vision: hand with a branch. It was an olive branch, the branch of peace.

"Take and Receive. I give My peace, just accept it."

December 4

Your Heart is My Castle

"Let My words be your food and drink.
See Me and hear Me in everything.
Be My light for others.
Show My love and hope.
Abide in My abode. Joy is My wish. Peace is My gift.
You have all you need right at hand.
Your heart is your storage of My graces.

Your eyes and ears are My windows.
My people need your help and love.
Make your way My way.
Make your life My life.
Make your love My love.
Your heart is My castle.
Your love is My branch. You are My light at every corner."

"Make those around you aware of My presence.
This will be done through your example and My words.
Take up your post and let Me be your life.
Handle My life as your life.
Make no mistake; I am your life, your hope and your love.
Be at peace in love with Me always.
Your shoes are to walk the earth with My footsteps for your stride.
Your heart is to carry My luggage (burdens).
Pass no one that you cannot see Me, for I am there, in each.
Look up to the heavens to know that I am always
within you with the fullest of the full.
Hope is your walk. Faith is your ride and love is your home.
Obedience is your guide.
Pay no one with false words or false hope."

"Be for Me what I am for you.
Do not have empathy as your guide, but have Me for your book.
(I think this is telling me not to let my feelings be
my guide, but only go by the Word of God.)
Give Me all your hopes and dreams for you are My child.
Walk with your face to the sun (Son) and your back
to the world for you are a chosen one.
The world can not close the door I have
opened and what I say is the word."

Time Out

We know that all things work for good for those who love God, who are called according to his purpose. (Romans 8:28)

Throughout the years of writing and putting this inspirational together, the Lord would place my husband or me in a "time out" situation, where we were confined at home and put to bed. It was always very beneficial. It placed us in a situation where we had to stay put and listen to the Lord. We had no other choice.

This is true, again—while putting the final additions together on this inspirational, my husband and I have been very busy trying to change the original manuscript. We have been advised to change the whole manuscript into a daily inspirational. This is an all-new endeavor for us to take on.

Much to our surprise the Lord had another "time out" tucked in His pocket for us. While rushing to get ready for a class on prophecy, I tripped over the bedspread. Snap, crackle, pop! You probably guessed it. I broke my foot

When I had shared this with a friend, she told the story of how the shepherd will break the leg of the sheep to keep it from wandering away from him or the herd. Breaking the leg was done to teach the sheep to remain close to His side. Wolves would eventually destroy the sheep if it keeps wandering away from the shepherd.

This reminded me of a picture I had seen in another friend's home. Her picture portrayed Jesus as the good shepherd. He was carrying a little lamb on His shoulders after getting it out of the briers. Like the little lamb, I was rushing around and not paying attention to where I was walking and sure enough, the good shepherd came to the rescue. God is certainly using this time to get my attention.

We do wander away from His side and are stuck in the briers, wondering why. We better stay close to His side, and let Him love and teach us. He has a lot to tell us. One of the first things He is telling us is that He is giving us extra time to spend in solitude with Him. The second thing is that resting in the atmosphere of solitude will help bring this inspirational together. All we have to do is let Him love us and carry us on His shoulders.

This is already becoming a special time to be tucked away in His pocket. We are getting the full meaning of Thanksgiving and Christmas without being exposed to the worldly atmosphere of corruption, greed and commercialism.

While being confined for the next two months with my foot in a cast, Scriptures, prayers, insights and words came together to support this daily inspirational … the new is being inserted into the old, adding some extra wonder. All we can say is "wonder of wonders."

December 6

This is Heart Time

What would I have been doing with this time, if I had not broken my foot?

The truth—deep in my heart I am enjoying the time set apart from the everyday activity. I probably would not have been enjoying the beautiful morning sun shinning on the trees or the white snow falling to the ground.

"It appears to be foot time when in truth it is all about the heart. The branches on the trees stand still when there is no breeze or wind to move them about. The Lord wants us standing still so we can receive the wind of the Holy Spirit. He wants us in the breeze that brushes across our hearts with His love and understanding. We not only catch the breeze, but we catch the very breath of God that fills our senses with His presence."

December 7

My Alabaster Jar has been Broken

When He was in Bethany reclining at table in the house of Simon the leper, a woman came with an alabaster jar, of perfumed oil, costly genuine spikenard. She broke the alabaster jar and poured it on his head. (Mark 14:3)

One morning during the two months of confinement and quiet time with the Lord I woke up and heard the words: "There is more than a broken foot in this cast." Shortly after this, the Lord brought my attention to the Alabaster Jar and how my Alabaster Jar had been broken, just like the foot.

This time out with the broken foot was contributing to the time we needed for healing. Like any injury to our physical or spiritual health, we need support and a time for healing to come about. The cast represented the support I needed for the broken foot and the support of the extra quiet time with the Lord for spiritual healing.

Through this experience, we have come to believe that there are situations and wounds in our lives that are tucked away in our own special Alabaster Jar. In this jar, we keep many of the good experiences and treasures as well as the wounds of the heart. Many of us have "heart hurts" that only Jesus can touch and heal.

The potter Himself must strike the first blow to break our Alabaster Jar. He will let us struggle just so long, and then He places situations in our lives when we are forced to make a different choice.

The Lord removed us from a situation that we did not seem to have the courage, strength or will power to remove ourselves. We could not quite get the whole thing together enough to see the need for healing in hidden areas of our lives and hearts. Our own weaknesses and wounded-ness stood in the way. Then one day, *pow*, the blow came, and our Alabaster Jar was broken.

We believe that there are all kinds of healing, but when it comes to the Alabaster Jar, you are getting into more intricate and deep seeded weaknesses. You are now entering into the treasures of the heart. God is the only one who can hold the Alabaster Jar upright in His hands while He brings it to a point of breaking. He balances everything in His grace and love while deep healing takes place.

The penitent woman had many treasures and expensive fragrant oils in her Alabaster Jar. She took her Alabaster Jar broke it and poured the special fragrant oils over Jesus.

Jesus is asking us to break our Alabaster Jar and pour over Him all the special and not so special treasures that we try to keep hidden. The fragrance of His love and healing oils will continue to flow over us even after the jar has been broken. We would be giving the deepest treasures of our hearts to Him in trust, which is a sweet, sweet fragrance to Him. He died on the cross for us and He will take our deepest treasures to the center of His heart of love and mercy.

December 8

Coming to the End of Ourselves

We went to the Calvary Pentecostal Campgrounds in Ashland, Virginia, in the summer of 2004. While there, I received the words, "Coming to the End of Ourselves."

Off and on since then the Lord has been giving us the meaning of these words. The first understanding was how we had to come out of our preconceived ideas, opinions, motives, intentions, attitudes and ways of thinking. These things along with wounds of the heart have become treasures of the heart.

Our participation in the movement of the Holy Spirit should be full time and permanent. It should not be a part time participation. The full time participation brings us into humility and a spiritual maturity. When we live more in this fullness, we come to realize that we are drawing from another source more powerful than we are. Staying open to the Holy Spirit will open the rivers to the "Living waters" in the center of our hearts. Then in turn, what flows into the heart will flow out to others.

Even though physical structures will always be around us in our programs, we have to seek the inward spiritual freedom. Flowing in this inner freedom will keep our hearts open to how the Lord is moving in our lives. When we "come to the end of ourselves," self will begin to take a back seat and we will allow the free movement of the Holy Spirit. Becoming more aware, what the Lord is doing in and around us, will help us to "come to the end of ourselves."

Just six months from getting the words, "Coming to the End of

Ourselves," I have come to realize that they have a large part to do with letting the prophetic word come forth from God to others and ourselves. Ruth Ward Heflin mentions in Revelation Glory how we have to come out of ourselves.

Quotation: "It is time to say to the Lord, "Lord, help us to push aside everything that hinders us. Make us ready to receive whatever You want to reveal to us. Bring us into a realm of knowing. "Lift us out of ourselves" and into Your glory. Lift us into a place of seeing. Anoint our eyes to see and to know those realms of glory that You have prepared for us." (15.)

This quote confirms that we have to let go of all that hinders us from receiving what the Lord wants to reveal. As mentioned above, some of these stumbling blocks can be our own ideas, opinions, motives, and attitudes.

Ruth shared an experience in her book where the Lord taught her that she did not have to worry about anyone understanding her because He is the one that opens the heart of the other person to understanding and receiving Him. This is a big step out of ourselves, where we carry a burden we do not have to carry. We are only the instruments to be used, the "earthen vessels."

Coming to the end of ourselves will open the treasures of the heart, letting them flow freely in the healing graces of the Lord, Jesus. Jesus is the only one that can guide us on this narrow path.

December 9

What is that tree to me?

My first glimpse of the Beautiful Blue Spruce Tree
Was of it growing in the fields for all to see
Standing straight and tall in glee
I heard my heart say, "What is that tree to me?"
"What is that tree to me?"
From the beauty of this tree I could not be led
For God had planted the seed of glory, instead

Among so many others its beauty stood out
Branches reaching up and ready to shout
"It's Glory to God that I'm all about."
I left these fields with joy in my heart
Blessings and graces never to part,
I had been in the presence of God this day
What can I say, what can I say
I had not really left this tree behind
Its joy remained in my heart, to find
Trees and sections marked the lot
I knew I would have to return to this spot
Yes, return we did to take this tree
In its spot among many, it will not be
Now, it stands in our home so tall
Waiting to be decorated with love by all
It still stands in glory, you see
This is what that tree is to me
The Glory of God is placed in our hearts
Here to stay and never to depart
I find great comfort in it standing there,
Straight and tall with much to share
"I have stood among many
In the field of nature's beauty and plenty."
"I have stood reaching for the sky
Shouting, "All Glory and Honor upon high."
Now, ready and waiting, I stand right here
Giving the glory to God, my dear, my dear."
Twelve foot high, this tree, you see
Lend out its branches to you and me
A good eight foot expands across
Space in the living room, was at a loss
"That can not be, the tree said in demand
"There is not a loss in where I stand."
"My branches reach up and I am ready to shout,
"It is Glory to God that I am all about."

December 10

Treasures of the Heart

"Do not store up treasures for yourselves on earth, where moth and decay destroy, and thieves break in and steal. But store up treasures in heaven, where neither moth nor decay destroys, nor thieves break in and steal. For where your treasure is, there also will your heart be. (Matthew 6:19–21)

What treasures do we hold in our hearts? Through prayer, fasting and a closer walk with Jesus, we began to understand that the path to the river of living waters is very narrow. We have to be ready for what may be asked of us as we go deeper along this narrow path.

As the path becomes narrower, some may become claustrophobic. They dread what is around the next bend and all they want to do is run in another direction to get away from giving up any of the treasures that are tucked away in the heart. Even if they do not run, they will juggle the treasures around to compensate. As I have mentioned in a previous day's inspiration, once on this path, there is no turning back.

Some treasures are "heart hurts" or hidden wounds, along with our pre-conceived ideas, motives, intentions, attitudes and ways of thinking. We protect the treasures of the heart. Our strong will is one of these treasures. We will have to leave these treasures checked at the door of our hearts. Jesus is the only one who can reach into these treasures and replace them with His treasures.

The free flowing presence of the Holy Spirit will carry the currents directly from God Himself. We hope that the Holy Spirit will carry our treasures to a place of healing.

A very large part of us is active all the time, in whatever we are doing or planning on doing. We have to ask the Lord to bless us with His wisdom and knowledge and help us to see the dividing line between what is of self and what truly flows in His Holy Spirit.

What really matters in a situation and in our lives? Are we flowing in the Holy Spirit or in some of our old treasures? Always remembering that God has everything under control will help to answer these questions.

Rivers of God's fragrant oils will flow from the center of a free heart as the treasures of the heart are given to Him. He wants to be the only treasure in our heart.

December 11

He is with Us

He is with us when we walk along the ocean shore. The waves roll in upon the sands erasing the marks that the previous wave has left behind. The seagulls bask in His presence, as they face the setting sun (Son) for they know the glory of where they bask.

He is with us as we look upon the autumn foliage. He has mixed the colors in the palm of His hand and thrown them upon the landscape for His glory to be seen. My heart wants to paint these beautiful colors upon the canvas of my soul, expressing the love and joy of God's presence that is placed there.

He is with us when we walk among the beautiful blue spruce trees. Looking for the tallest and fullest tree is the Christmas tree we seek. When we go in and out amongst these trees, our spirit is held captive among them for we know each tree represents a Child of God that has hands held high in adoration.

December 12

Joy Will Triumph

"Let Me into your midst. I am the way, the only way to happiness. My cross will lead you. The clouds will lift and the light will shine.
My Mother is the light. She is protection against the wicked. Roses, sweet roses, adorn her feet. A Crown of love lies at her feet."

Prayer: O Sweet Mother, heavy is your heart because of what must be done.

Pray for us to your Son.
He will listen, as His Father will listen to Him

Forsake us not as the light grows dim.
Answer: "My Son will guide you through bad times.
Have faith, pray and you will come out the victor."

"Love Me as I love you. Love her as she loves you.
The hour draws close. Cries grow loud.
The earth shall mourn, but joy will triumph.
Music and song will ring out, loudly.
Always give praise.
The Lord is merciful to those who adore Him.
Fear not, for I am there with you always.
Go My Child in peace. The Dew will fall as the cloud will rise!"

Jesus, sweet Jesus, all glory is ever Yours.

December 13

Echoes of the Heart

"Soothing echoes for God's servants
My presence echoes across the chambers of the heart
Hear me! Hear me!
My sound echoes in the heart"

"I love you, I love you can be heard
If you do not hear it in the words spoken, listen for it is in the echoes
Repeat it; repeat it, "Echoes of the Heart""

"It is time for you to listen and write what you hear.
If you do not get it the first time, you will get it in the echoes
Your heart will ring with My wisdom
I will be heard and I will ring so loud it will be heard"

"Nothing can or will replace My words to you
There is no end to the echoes and sound of
My voice in the heart and soul
My echoes, spoken across the chambers in the
heart, will carry to the ends of the earth"

"I have not given up on My people

They will hear Me call and I will respond. I
will hear them and answer them
Their sounds of joy and praise echoed through the heavens
Joy and peace comes forth, peace and love echoes back"

"You will hear the sounds of My footsteps
Even the fish hear My call
Come home! Come home!
It is time to respond to the call"

"My voice echoes in the chambers of your heart
You will hear Me and be drawn from the natural to the supernatural
Climb the ladder. Close the gap between us
Respond! Oh, My people respond"

December 14

One Size Fits All

Walk in His footsteps, not behind them, but in them. His footsteps are only one size and that is "one size fits all." His footsteps are always visible and not covered by the dirt and dust of worldly trials. They are always visible for us to see.

Follow one-step at a time. Each time we put our foot into His footprint, we know He has gone before us to make the way safe for us. Put yourself in His footsteps as well as in His hands.

No matter what our burden, our depth in His footprints remains the same. None are deeper than another is. Our walk is the same with Him, in Him and for Him. We never walk alone. He is always with us in our journey here on earth.

Some of us have only a short walk, while others a long one while we are here on earth. In the end, we all reach the same goal, following Christ's example to everlasting reward and peace.

God's words are the footprints of life for us. We have only to walk in them by reading them and living them.

Our footsteps may be invisible to others when following Christ's, but they are always visible to Him. The gift of unity and footsteps go together. One step at a time is all He asks of us. After all, we are babies and just learning to walk in the spiritual footsteps of life and love. There can be many, there can be few, it is all up to you.

Our redeemer's footsteps lead us to paradise. Follow them and you will never walk alone. You will be, "sure footed in God's way!"

December 15

Spiritual Feet

Lord we are waiting to hear from You
With open hearts and sincerity too
Give us a vision that we may see
The plans for us that come from Thee
Let us be happy in what we do
Knowing it is done for the love of You
Take all obstacles that stand in our way
From listening to all You have to say
We know we are heading for Revelation Glory
With You as our guide, boy what a story
We will share it with all the people we meet
Hoping to encourage some Spiritual feet
To follow the road leading to You
Where love reigns forever and is true
Your Glory will shine on all who are there
With no more fears or crosses to bear
They have entered into the Glory You foretold.
No matter how young no matter how old
Paradise again will be restored as it was in the
beginning and will be forever more.

December 16

Blanket of White

The snow falls, softly, upon the ground
Weaving a white blanket, without a sound
Wrapped in this blanket of white
Our hearts fill with His delight
Each snowflake carries blessings, graces and love
Our Lord and Savor, sends these from heaven above
Quietly, quietly, ever so quietly it falls
To a life of grace, each calls
Melting into the blossoms of spring
is the direction it will take
Drawing us to the decisions, we must make
Which way will we choose to go
To the left, or to the right, one does not know
His hiding place, He will reveal
In the center of the soul, He will place His seal
Only God can lead us there
To this place, where the soul will share
Quietly, quietly, God's Spirit will touch
Areas that need His love, so much
Wounded hearts, minds and emotions
He will heal with His Divine devotions
In faithfulness, His love will weave
A blanket of joy, never to leave
Around us, you will see His light
Holding us together, in unity and might
Quietly, quietly, it touches the ground
For all around, to all abound
Softly, softly, with a hush it is there
The blanket of white, for all to share

December 17

Trust in God's Will

"Detach yourself from the past.
I came into the world as love trusting in My Father.
My discomfort became your comfort.
I lay upon the straw of your labor, as the oxen
in burden, gave Me warmth."

"Come what may, is the Father's will.
His faithfulness and love is always there.
Jesus Christ wore the garment of purity.
Flames of pure love lie on the bed of straw.
Comforts of Jesus and peace came forth.
Our merciful savior sent endless mercy to all creation.
Come what may, trust in God's Will."

December 18

Listen, You Can Hear Them

While sitting next to the window, during a heavy and beautiful snowstorm, I received the following words.

"God's grace falls softly and quietly upon you,
White snow falls gently upon the ground.
Ever so gently do they fall, not even noticed are they.
Listen! You cannot hear them, but they are there.
It is the silence, be aware."

"You sit in the silence and if you do not look out
the window you still know it is snowing.
You do not hear the snow fall, but you know
it is falling upon the ground.
My graces are the same. You do not hear them
fall, but they are falling upon you."

"The snowflakes fall upon one another and build up many inches.

My graces fall upon you and build up many virtues.
Listen, you can hear them!"

December 19

How Do You Love God?

God led me to ask and answer the following question:
"How do you love God?"
My answer was:
"I love Him in the dying man, where I began to know His compassion.

I love Him in the prisoner, where hearts can be set free.

I love Him in my family and friends, where love begins and extends.

I love Him in the nature around us, where He teaches me with His truths and riches.

I love Him in each new day, where His grace fills my every hour."

Prayer: Jesus, I reach my arms out of my self-will and ask You to embrace me in Your Divine will. Help me to embrace the Father's will.

December 20

Mystical Mirror

Beloved, we are God's children now; what we shall be has not yet been revealed. We do know that when it is revealed we shall be like him, for we shall see him as he is. (1 John 3:2)

"Enter into My mystical mirror.
My images surpass the normal view of the naked eye.
This view is transparent.
You will see, you will see.
Do not give up on the vision I have planted in your hearts.

The light that directs you is the light of Christ.
Stay in this light.
Energy and power come from this light."

"Can you drive a car without wheels?
Can you fly an airplane without wings?
Can you row a boat without oars?"

"Like the car, that needs the wheels,
Like the airplane, that needs the wings,
Like the boat, that needs the oars,
You need the strength and power that comes from
being in the light and power of My Holy Spirit.
Nothing can be done outside of this light."

"The car without the wheels cannot move forward on the road.
The airplane without the wings cannot even get off the ground.
The boat without the oars cannot move across the water.
Like all of these means of transportation, a functioning part is needed."

"Growth in the Holy Spirit is to function in the Holy Spirit. On every road, you can move forward in new directions. Blessings and graces of love are carried to you from the heavens above. The living waters from the very heart of God flow in the deepest recesses within your own heart. For you to move forward in a deep relationship with God, You have to let the Holy Spirit function in your life."

"Let the Holy Spirit move you forward down the road in new directions. You will be high and lifted up to float in the mist over the sea from above. This mist will bring you into the mystical mirror that only reflects God's image and love. Let the Lord carry you on the wings of the Holy Spirit, bringing you in for landings, where only He knows the mystery behind the mirrored images."

December 21

Rippling Waters

The Lord gave us the meaning for the following words:

> "Abruptly independent of all
> Special periods of methodically
> Abundantly bereaved
> Looking up and was sad
> Into the night the words go
> Rippling waters undoing justice
> The veils of light into the night"

"The rippling of My living waters flows over the soul, forming music that soothes the soul. My living waters have to first rise up within you before they can flow to others. Rippling waters flow across the rough rocks in a brook or stream. They flow freely and are bold in direction."

"The waters move forward suddenly, unnoticed and without ceremony. They are not subject to control or influenced by obstacles ahead. They flow in special periods of order and unity along with the rest of the surroundings in the stream."

"My living words flow freely across the soul like the rippling waters flowing across the rocks in a brook or stream. They come suddenly, unnoticed and without ceremony. They are free, bold and separate indeed. They come in special periods of order and unity as part of My plans. Sometimes they will be for the whole body and sometimes for the individual. They will be plentiful and ample for what you will need. Not listening to these words a person becomes fully hindered from possessing or enjoying My presence in My words. They will then look up and are sad."

Into the night's darkness the words can go without notice if we are not careful to listen. Alternatively, they can go into the darkness to bring light into that darkness. The rippling waters filling the heart can undo punishments. These living waters carry veils of light into the darkness of the night.

December 22

O How Precious is My Word

"The Word, the word, O how precious is My Word.
You will know My word for it lives within you.
You are the food I will give to others.
You make My plan complete
The angel of the Lord keeps a watch over you and your loved ones.
Give Him your fears and doubts and He will
carry them off with the winds.
Make no mistake; this is real for the real exists in not
what you can see, but in what you do not see."

"Your life I hold in My hand with all My many saints.
Love, love, love, let every part of your being; sing … love, love, love.
Sing … Jesus, Jesus, Jesus.
Take time to rest, time to play, time for love and time to pray.
Time is what it is all about. Love … Jesus … Amen!"

December 23

If We Only Take the Time

If we listen to the wind in the trees and watch
the different colors of their leaves—
We can hear and see—if we only take the time.
If we listen to the animals in the woods and watch
them prepare their winter goods—
We can hear and see—if we only take the time.
If we listen to the roar of the sea and watch
the waves come upon the shore—
We can hear and see—if we only take the time.

If we listen to the ripple of the brook and
watch the smoothness that it took—
We can hear and see—if we only take the time.
If we listen to the ice fall from the eaves and
watch the snow fall, as you please—
We can hear and see—if we only take the time.
If we listen in our daily chores and watch the hours tick away—
We can hear and see—if we only take the time.
If we listen to the years gone by and watch the years ahead—
We can hear and see—if we only take the time.
If we listen in the quiet of our prayer and watch the hand of the Lord—
We can hear and see—if we only take the time.
If we listen and watch life, Dear Lord as You bring—
We can hear and see You in everything—If we only take the time!

December 24

Christmas Night

The scene is set for Christmas night,
The snow has fallen and all is white.
Songs of joy will be sung this day,
The newborn Savior is on His way.
He will light up the world with His love and peace,
Filling our hearts with joy never to cease.
We pray this day will be for you,
Full of gifts holy and true.
And may this season of Holiday cheer,
Guide you through the coming year.
May Christ be in your hearts and say,
"I'll guide you to an everlasting Christmas Day."

December 25

The Snow Storm on Christmas Day

He does great things beyond our knowing; For he says to the snow, "Fall to the earth;" likewise to his heavy, drenching rain. He shuts up all mankind indoors; the wild beasts take to cover and remain quietly in their dens. (Job 37:5–7)

God forced all creation to spend Christmas day in a day of rest. No one could go anywhere because of the bad roads and travel. Plans were changed and all had to adapt to the snowfall. Creation was being cleansed in a blanket of white.

The light of Christ glistens off the snow capped trees and icicles on the roof. Many were put to the plows and shovels while others to the household celebrations. This storm could have been on a workday or school day, but it was not. It was on a day where all could celebrate Christ right at home.

God placed us all in an atmosphere of Himself. Even though the storm came, the light of Christ was still shining through. When the storm subsided, the sunlight (Son-light) glistened on the snowcaps and icicles.

Within hours into the next day, mobility was back. Nevertheless, God had His moment with His People. He gave us a gift and that gift was of a refreshing snowfall, full of His love for us. Each crystal of snow that fell upon the earth had its own shape that fit into God's plan of Glory. Sure, it would melt into the spring refreshment for the earth's needs. In the meantime, it rests on the ground for us to enjoy both in physical and spiritual refreshment.

God stands with His creation in full view. He projects His love, mercy and grace into this view. Therefore, how can we lose? His richness is the support for His creation. Thank You Dear Lord, for letting us be part of Your plans for all mankind.

As the earth turns, all creation turns. One thing to remember we are in full view of the creator, almighty God, Father, Son and Holy Spirit. So creation, move as you will! God, Himself has us in full view!

December 26

Jesus, Be Born in Us Today

"The mercy of Jesus is in the midst of our struggles.
His love becomes our structure, overshadowing our faults.
Everything we are striving for is where He was born, in a stable.
Jesus is born in us, today.
We are striving for Him to be born in us."

"As a solid wall of brass, you need consistent polishing.
Be persistent, working day by day, moment to moment.
Be on guard doing the things you ought to do with Me in mind.
Your serenity is doing the will of My Father.
The fluidity of the Holy Spirit is keeping you in perfect harmony."

December 27

Black Diamond

The sin of Judah is written with an iron stylus, Engraved with a diamond point upon the tablets of their hearts. (Jeremiah 17:1)

I had a dream where I kept getting the words "black diamond," and my grandson, Nicky, said that it was in Maccabees. Along with others, we were listening to a speaker that began to talk about the gifts of the Holy Spirit. He spoke about a fragrance coming from the mouth. After he said this, I turned around to a person behind me and said, "This is the oil fragrance that we kept getting in our mouth and all over us during our experiences in revival." This person was annoyed with me and said, "Won't you ever let go of those experiences?" I said, "I hope I never would forget them. I then woke up.

The first thing I did when I got up was to glance through Maccabees. I went too 2 Maccabees 2:24–32, which was the Scripture I received when we first began to answer the call to write *Shades of Blue*.

After I read this Scripture, I looked up the word diamond in the concordance. This led me to Jeremiah 17:1 (quoted above) and to Job.

"That with an iron chisel and with lead they were cut in the rock for-ever!" (Job 19:24)

I then looked up black diamond in the encyclopedia...a black diamond is of lesser quality and used for industrial use and can cut through any hard rock.

I knew from the words black diamond and the above Scriptures the Lord was saying that we were not meant to forget our experiences with Him. When the black diamond strikes the heart, the cut remains forever. They were deeply engraved, etched and chiseled into our hearts. The cut was a diamond cut. They were meant to be shared with others.

The important diamond is the diamond in the heart. The lesser diamond, the black diamond, will cut through our hearts of stone and uncover the purest diamond within the heart.

The day before I had the dream, I got the words: "He is restoring. He is revealing. Remember, remember His promises!"

December 28

Blues of Growth and Greens of Intimacy

"The shades of blue of growth, bring you into the shades of green of intimacy. There are different levels of spirituality in each. You will be in different ones at different times. The different combinations will bring you into the mysteries of a spiritual walk with Me. This is a special place where the revelations of My mysteries become part of My love within your heart."

"Stay close to the blues of growth and the greens of intimacy. Both the intellect and spiritual are My gifts to you. Knowing is the secret of when to be in one or the other, or both together."

"My gifts for some are to be under the boundaries of the intellect for a while with the spiritual boundaries nearby. While for others, they are to be under the boundaries of the spiritual with the intellect at hand. One can be stronger than the other can, but with My grace and love, you will slide from one to the other when needed."

"The mystery or revelation is to be simple both in your mind and in

your heart and you will be healthy in both within My will for you.
Let My vision be your vision.
Let My listening be your listening.
Let My words be your words.
Let My fragrance be your fragrance.
Let My touch be your touch.
Let My thoughts be your thoughts.
Let My heart be your heart.
Let My love be your love.
Let My will be your will.
Let My blues of growth be your blues of growth.
Let My greens of intimacy be your greens of intimacy.
The intellect and spiritual will be all encompassed
under the bounds of faith, hope and love."

December 29

Walk With New Life

"Walk with new life, through the pages of
life. Close the book of the old.
Do not leave the love, blessings, graces, lessons
and experiences received behind.
Carry them with you.
Carry them in a leather briefcase made up of My strengths.
Carry them full of surprises and wishes for others to receive.
Carry them in the right hand of righteousness.
Carry them full of the rich colors of My grace and love.
Carry them into the new life, empty of old.
Carry them and walk with new life, through the pages of life.
Carry them!"

Little Stone Shoes

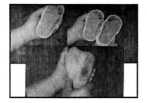

We moved into our new home on July 1, 1977. We loved our home right from the first time we walked into it and love it even more after living in it for 29 years. We have had many blessings and graces given to us while living here.

The only problem we had with our home was that it had a shallow well; therefore, the water supply could be dirty and low at times. We put up with the bad water problems for many years. We tried to have the public water system brought to our home, but did not have any luck. Our neighbors had been trying for years to get this done. It turned out, that we had to have a driven well put in. This well supplied us with good water for a few more years, but it was always a concern how long it would last.

After many prayers and different experiences, the long wait for the public water system was over. We hooked our home up to this system on November 14, 1995. The men hooking the lines up to the house had to deal with a lot of rain and soft ground. It was so late in the season that we had to wait until spring before we could work on the small mounds of mud that were left behind. This is where our concluding experience unfolds.

Late spring, early summer the following year, we finally started to rake and shovel the small mounds of dirt left from November's project. Charles and I took turns at this task. One day as Charles was raking the dirt, he came upon a rock that looked like a child's shoe (first picture). When he first saw it, he thought it was a real child's shoe. He brought it into the house to show me.

He went back outside and about fifteen minutes later, he found another rock (second picture). This was about twenty feet away from where he found the first one. He brought the second rock into the house. We looked at them both together. They looked like a pair of children's shoe (third picture), with a left and right shoe. Much to our delight, they fit perfectly together forming a human heart.

We guessed, along with others, as to what the stones stood for. We knew it was something special. We thought it might have something to do with the abortion issue. We found them around the same time that the partial birth abortion bill was vetoed. These stones could easily fit this issue. The little shoes could represent all the little babies destroyed through abortion. The shoes held together formed a heart, a heart of stone. Have our hearts grown so cold? We stand on the words that the Lord said in Scripture that He would turn our hearts of stones into hearts of flesh.

December 31

Perpetual Reminders

One morning during prayer, Charles and I thought about the little shoes of stone. We asked the Lord about our original understanding of the stones. We then began to get a completely new understanding of the little stone shoes. We do believe that each person who sees them will have their own thoughts about the shoes.

Through the Scripture of Joshua 4: 5–7, the Lord gave us a completely new understanding of the little stone shoes.

Joshua said to them: "Go to the bed of the Jordan in front of the ark of the Lord, your God; lift to your shoulders one stone apiece, so that they will equal in number the tribes of the Israelites. In the future, these are to be a sign among you. When your children ask you what these stones mean to you, you shall answer them, "The waters of the Jordan ceased to flow before the Ark of the Covenant of the Lord when it crossed the Jordan. Thus, these stones are to serve as a perpetual memorial to the Israelites." (Joshua 4: 5–7)

Like these stones, our stones are to serve as a perpetual reminder to us, of the many blessings, graces and mercy of God. After great difficulty, we did get the new water lines into the area and our house. This, we are sure was through divine intervention. These difficulties, along with many others, contributed to the many blessings that we received throughout our lives.

Charles and I both walked in the childhood shoes of faith, with lives formed from the start by faithful parents. Little did we know at the time that the faith of our parents would be given to us. It is up to us now to pass the "shoes of faith," to our children and grandchildren. We give to them, the faith that was given to us. We ask the Lord for this blessing to be upon them and you and your loved ones

All the experiences shared in *Shades of Blue*, are remembered and etched into our hearts and minds. Etched into stone, they will have a lasting effect on our spiritual journey.

The words of Scripture, the dreams, visions, insights, and inspired words and prayers shared are "Perpetual Reminders" in *Shades of Blue*.

Conclusion

Pillar of Light

In the daytime the cloud of the Lord was seen over the Dwelling; whereas at night, fire was seen in the cloud by the whole house of Israel in all the stages of their journey. (Leviticus 40:38)

The Little Sailboat can be found sailing in and out of many hidden experiences with the Lord within *Shades of Blue*. We are the little sailboat, and every stage in our journey is being guided along the shore line of the Glory of God.

How this picture came together: I took a picture of the Adriatic Sea in Croatia, formerly Yugoslavia, and put it behind the little sailboat figurine on my scanner. The little sailboat did not have a rainbow across the sail, but when it came out of the scanner it had two rainbows. One is along the side of the dove and other is across the sail. When I was trying to lighten the picture, I put the ocean scene across the little sailboat, not attaching it to the scanner cover. When I did this the ocean scene wrapped down around the sailboat. This is where the rainbow came down from the center of the picture (which looks like a pillar coming down from heaven) joining at the tip of the little sailboat.

The rainbows of color reflect off the little sailboat, as the reflecting light of Christ reflects off the experiences contained in *Shades of Blue*.

Your Pillar of Light is wrapped in a rainbow.
From heaven above—it does flow.
You lead us by day wherever we go.
As Your fire of love protects us at night, we know.
All around us You spread Your affection
With graces and blessings coming from every direction
Colors of the rainbow bounce off our sail,
As Your Holy Spirit's guidance will not fail.
The tip of this pillar touches our hearts,
As deep as can be—to the depth of all parts.
Help us to float in this sea of grace,

As You bring us closer to Your secret place.
O Pillar of Light, ever so bright
Fill our hearts with Your guiding light.

A Leap of Faith, A Test of Faith

Faith is the realization of what is hoped for and evidence of things not seen. (Hebrews 11:1)

We came across the Tate Publishing Company as we were searching on the Internet for a Christian Publisher to publish *Shades of Blue*. We were drawn to Tate Publishing because of their Statement of Faith. Through this statement we were encouraged to send some of our material to them. They responded in a very encouraging manner and expressed an interest in publishing *Shades of Blue*.

They are not a self-publishing company and are very open to checking the manuscripts of new authors. They require the author to invest in their own projects. Therefore, an author's investment fee is required. (As we worked along with them on this project we found this requirement to be very beneficial.) We knew from the very beginning that we did not have the author's investment fee and it would take a miracle for this to come about. The miracle begins to unfold after a day long visit with our niece.

Charles had a dream a couple of weeks before the Christmas of 2006. When he shared this dream he was told that he would receive many blessings. The Thursday before Christmas we went to our niece's home to see her new home and have lunch with her. We only expected to spend a short time, but ended up spending the whole day.

We spent the whole time sharing about our experiences with Gold Dust. Gold Dust is one of the manifestations of the Presence of the Lord amongst His people today. At one point in our sharing about the Gold Dust, I stood up from the chair I was sitting in and it was covered with Gold Dust.

As we entered our niece's home, I set my pocketbook and gloves on the steps near the door. When we were leaving to go home, I picked up my pocketbook and gloves and they were covered with Gold Dust. The next morning it was on a red tablecloth that was folded and setting on the table. For three to four weeks from this moment on we kept getting the Gold Dust. Every time I opened my pocketbook, the Gold Dust was on my wallet and checkbook. We began to believe that it meant financial blessings.

When we were at our niece's we asked her who she used to rent her home during the racing season. We told her we wanted to rent this year if we could. She gave us the realtor's name and we proceeded to list our home for the track season.

When the young Jewish realtor came to our home, practically the first thing he said to us was, "Trying to rent your home is a leap of faith." We began to get very excited at this point. All the time we were thinking of renting the house, we were planning to use some of the rental income for the author investment fee required for the publication of *Shades of Blue*.

We had to keep giving the project over and over again to the Lord because it looked like we would not be renting the house. Then the door opened and the house was rented the night before the track season started. This was not only a leap of faith, but it was a test of faith. Would we take the leap and rent the house? Would we believe that the Lord would give us the financial blessings needed? Would we lose faith, or would we trust in the Lord to bring this all about?

We have had many Christian functions at our home in the past, and should not be surprised that the Lord had used our home for us to receive the finances to publish *Shades of Blue*. We have a prayer, which hangs on the side of the fireplace, stating that we told the Lord our house was His house and in the prayer He reminds us that we did give the house to Him

Before we left, we wished the couple renting our home success at the race track. The next morning after their first day in our home, they stopped to our son's house to ask a couple of questions, as we were still there for a couple of days. As we stood there in the driveway talking, I noticed Gold Dust on the woman's face under her eyes. As we wished her success at the track, she proceeded to tell us that she won $600 the first day and was all set for the rest of the season. When talking to her at the end of the track season, she proceeded to tell us of the many blessings she continued to receive. For us, the Gold Dust represented the financial miracle that we had received through the rental of our property. *Shades of Blue* could now be published.

Faith Held High is Faith Held Out

"They conquered him by the blood of the Lamb and by the word of their testimony;" (Revelation 12:11)

Faith held high is faith that is witnessed too,
It is held out, given and shared with others, anew.
Here comes Faith, walking about,
It is given out quietly or with a shout.
Carried in the heart that is full of trust,
It is ready to be shared, ready to thrust.
No doubt about it, it is contagious.
When the heart is soft, it can seem a little outrageous.
Faith carries extra hope for the hopeless and support for the weak.
Not left out, is the rest for the restless and security for the meek.
Life's journey is a little more at ease,
As Faith is held out, it will appease.
God's plan for all to see is the faith that He has given to you and me.
"Caring and sharing your faith is what it is all about," says He.

Hidden Mysteries

I will give you treasures out of the darkness, and riches that have been hidden away, That you may know that I am the Lord, the God of Israel, who calls you by name. (Isaiah 43:5)

There are many spiritual mysteries hidden in the cover of *Shades of Blue*. The Lord brings peace, joy and many spiritual insights into the hearts of His people as they stay open and listen to His voice hidden within even the cover of a book. Under close observation and with a sensitive and tender spirit, one can see the wings of the Holy Spirit and the swirling colors of the ocean blue.

We showed a copy of the cover design to our friend, Cecelia Monaco, who is an artist both in the artistry of painting and in the use of the gifts of the Holy Spirit. Her reply when seeing the cover, "This cover has *moving vapors* that are still moving and will continue to move." This ended up being very true. At 5:30 a.m. the next morning, I sat at my computer where the Holy Spirit moved into my spirit with moving vapors of insight and understanding about the cover design.

The cover design is a good example of the DNA of our spiritual and natural life. The chromosomes of the spiritual and natural life run side by side and mix, forming our whole existence in life's journey towards the Lord. Arteries within the wounded human heart carry direct physical and spiritual nourishment as the heart beats in unison with the very heart of God, Our Savior and Creator. *Our life line connects directly to the Aorta of God.* We are intravenously fed by His Holy Spirit. Each person will reach their own depth and the depth of God as every twist and every turn in their spiritual and natural life seeks out a personal and spiritual relationship with the Lord.

We went on a retreat where the subject of the retreat was about the painting of Icons. Icons are symbols of God, and the more a person learns about Icons and prays with them, the more they can see into the mysteries behind the symbols. Icons have colors that are considered earthly and others that are spiritual. These show how the natural and spiritual life blend together forming a masterpiece. The color of blue represents the heavenly and spiritual realms. In the *Shades of Blue* cover, the colors swirl about in the spiritual realm dropping insights and mysteries of God into our spirit. The Lord wants us to be *His living Icons.*

The Lord promises that the seal around our human understanding will be broken. Only His seal of love and grace will prevail, as He forms mysteries in multiple colors. As the cover is opened the first time and every time after, new understanding and insights will come forth.

The word *blue* on the cover is in the deepest color of blue. On our ocean voyage towards the Lord, we start out our journey in this deep blue. This blue in the book represents the distance that our hearts and minds are from the Lord. This is where we are riding on the edge of worldly desires, with the spiritual quest only in the distance. We have to be brought to the basement of our humanness in order to rise to new heights. The ordinary has to run to the very edge of our humanness, so it can be brought to the heights of the extraordinary.

The green color of intimacy can be found in the cover design. As we move closer to the Lord in spiritual growth, we move into the different shades of blue, ending up on the shores of the Glory of God, which is in the light green of intimacy. We mention in the book how this is equally as important as the different shades of blue.

I had an experience one night as I was walking down the hall to our bedroom. I was surrounded by a light green color and substance that looked like whipped cream. I could not move because of the strong presence of the Lord. We understood this to be a spiritual color and substance where God's love and presence was being poured into our lives. We wondered how this color could be brought out in the book, and much to our delight it has come out in the cover design. We could not match or find this color on any natural paint charts.

As the reader opens the cover of *Shades of Blue*, they will be opening the ordinary into the mystical. The word *blue* coming right up to the edge of the cover can represent coming to the edge of the ordinary as it spills and runs over into the extraordinary. This is what the book is all about, and if one looks real close, their own sailboat can be found bobbing up and down in the mystical waters of *Shades of Blue*.

Endnotes

Photo Guide

Adding pictures to *Shades of Blue* came later and quite by accident. Originally, we did not intend to have pictures. We were in Croatia in 1997 and had taken some pictures of the beautiful Adriatic coastline. I added one of these pictures to one of the daily inspirations and found it enhanced the beauty and meaning of the words already done. We then began to feel that pictures would bring many spiritual graces into the spirituality of the reader. Therefore, we now have the following pictures listed telling where they originated.

Photo Date	Title	Where Picture Originated
January 1	The Bow of the Ship	Mother's gift for Charles
January 3	God's Call to Write *Shades of Blue*	Statue of angel at home
January 9	Extraordinary in the Ordinary	Our Wedding Day 11-5-61
January 10	Union of Love	25th Wedding Anniversary
January 11	Settle Your Hearts and Minds	Winter scene at home
January 18	Gathering a Holy People	Bosnia former Yugoslavia
January 19	First Promptings of the Holy Spirit	Chips and juice at home
January 20	The Best Teacher	Grandchildren with horses
January 27	Deeper Waters and Security Blankets	At home
February 1	Cinderella	Christmas gift at home

May 1	Trinity Tree	Shelburne Pond Vermont
May 5	Dew Drops Refresh the Roses	At home
May 8	Taste and See the Goodness of the Lord covers us.	Atlantic Ocean Wave
May 14	Come Into the Clearing	Chapel of the "La Pieta" Vatican City Rome, Italy
May 20	Porthole of the Heart	Figurine at home
May 26	The Onion	Charles at home
May 27	Reminders of His Presence	Transposed picture on computer at home
June 1	The Clouds	Sky above our home
June 6	He Kissed Me	Charles at home
June 10	Little Sailboat	Figurine at home
June 15	Walk Out of the Forest	St. Rafka Retreat Center Shelburne, Vermont
June 20	Breaker, Breaker	Hampton Beach, New Hampshire
June 26	The Dove in the Web	Trees at home
July 1	Little Seed in My Heart	Valentine gift
July 7	Return to Solitude	Lake Champlain Vermont
July 10	A Call to a Early Christian Solitude	Laurie Glogowski's picture Glen Lake, New York
July 14	The Wadi Cherith	Statue of Elijah in Bosnia, Former Yugoslavia
July 19	Chapel	Little Sisters of St. Francis Danville, New Hampshire
July 24	The Tree Alone	State Park near home
July 27	Holly Tree	Egg Harbor, New Jersey
August 1	Seeking Only God	Rams-Tipperary, Ireland

1. *Catechism of Council of Trent* by John McHugh, O.P. and Charles Callan, O.P. pages 142 and 143, Tan Publisher, Inc. Rockford, Illinois

2. *Self-Abandonment to Divine Providence* by Father J.P. deCaussade, S.J., Tan Publisher, Inc. Rockford, Illinois

3. *The Word Among Us*, 9639 Doctor Perry Rd. #126 Ijamsville, Maryland 2175-Article on "Prayer Journal."1996.

4. *Self-Abandonment* by Father J.P. de Caussade, S.J. page 32., Tan Publisher, Inc. Rockford, Illinois

5. Unknown Author

6. *Mystical Hope* by Cynthia Bougeault, page 84, Cowley Publications Boston, Massachusetts

7. *Mystical Evolution* by Fr. John G. Arintero, O.P., pages 175 and 176. Tan Publisher, Inc. Rockford, Illinois

8. *The Way into the Holiest* by F.B. Meyer, CLC Publications P.O. Box 1449 Fort Washington, Pennsylvania 19094

9. *The Way into the Holiest* by F.B. Meyer, CLC Publications P.O. Box 1449 Fort Washington, Pennsylvania 19094

10. *The Interior Life* by Louis Colin C.S.s.R. page 80–81, Newman Press Westminster, Maryland

11. *Revelation Glory* by Ruth Ward Heflin, McDougal Publishing, Hagerstown, Maryland

12. *Springs of Living Waters* by John Lochern, page 19, The Columba Press Blackrock, Co. Dublin, Ireland

13. *Revelation Glory* by Ruth Ward Heflin, page 295, McDougal Publishing, Hagerstown, Maryland

14. *The Three Ways of a Spiritual Life* by P'ere Garrigou LaGrange O.P. page 99 Tan Publisher, Inc. Rockford, Illinois

15. *Revelation Glory* by Ruth Ward Heflin, McDougal Publishing, Hagerstown, Maryland